Management Control and
Organizational Behaviour

Dr Phil Johnson is a senior lecturer in organization behaviour at Sheffield Business School. **Dr John Gill** is a reader in management at Sheffield Business School. They are joint authors of *Research Methods for Managers* (1991), also published by Paul Chapman Publishing.

MANAGEMENT CONTROL AND ORGANIZATIONAL BEHAVIOUR

Phil Johnson and John Gill

SHEFFIELD HALLAM UNIVERSITY

P·C·P
Paul Chapman
Publishing Ltd

Copyright © Phil Johnson and John Gill 1993

Illustrations © as credited

Paul Chapman Publishing Ltd
144 Liverpool Road
London
N1 1LA

British Library Cataloguing in Publication Data

Johnson, Phil
  Management Control and Organizational
  Behaviour
  I. Title II. Gill, John
  658.3

  ISBN 1 85396 163 9

Typeset by Inforum, Rowlands Castle, Hants
Printed and bound by Athenæum Press Ltd., Newcastle-upon-Tyne

A B C D E F G H   9 8 7 6 5 4 3

Contents

Preface

Alistair Mant (1976) suggests that the term 'management' should be used to describe three related phenomena: an activity, an occupational group and the values or ideology of that group. As this book is primarily concerned with 'management control', it deals with a particular aspect of management that, according to Mant, comes from the word's mixed French and Italian roots, which give it an almost hermaphrodite character in that it means both to cope and to control. Mant argues that the term 'manage' derives from the Italian word, *maneggiare*, which means handling things (especially horses). This is a masculine concept that implies taking charge or directing, especially in the context of war. Mant suggests that it also comes from the French word, *ménager*, which means using something carefully and a word that has more gentle, almost feminine connotations.

Although there are several empirically based models of managerial work (e.g. Mintzberg, 1973; Stewart, 1967, 1976; Sayles, 1979), there is little consensus about what managers' everyday activities actually are. This uncertainty is made worse because management is not an undifferentiated, homogeneous occupational group. This is not to imply, however, that there is no consensus about the purposes of these everyday activities. As Mant says, writers at different times and for different audiences seem to agree that management's main purpose is the exercise of control over human and inanimate resources in various organizational contexts (e.g. Burnham, 1941; Humble, 1970; Poulantzas, 1972; Braverman, 1974; Wright *et al.*, 1982; Storey, 1983; Goldsmith and Clutterbuck, 1984). So while it is important *not* to treat management as a monolithic whole, and while management's work requires a variety of skills (Stewart and Stewart, 1981), there appears to be a unity of purpose in managerial hierarchies and in different organizational contexts: that is, management's role is, to a large extent, that of controlling.

Storey (1983, p. 96) argues that, despite contrasting approaches, a manager's 'quintessential role', especially when dealing with labour, is that of control: 'the incessant though tactical rather than "strategic" day-to-day campaign to render labour tractable'. Control means making potential labour power real, and it also entails controlling and manipulating the non-human factors that make this power possible. If managerial work is concerned with controlling human resources, then all managers will have to cope with the vagaries of organizational behaviour and with their subordinates. Therefore, all managers must be able to understand and predict how humans behave in organizations.

This book does not intend to provide managers with a series of recipes to aid them in their endeavours to control; rather, by focusing on 'management control' it introduces the reader to organizational behaviour and makes accessible some recent developments in the literature. It also tries to help the reader develop a more critical understanding of what management control involves, of the ways control might be attempted and of the complexities of behaviour that can affect any outcomes. We try to avoid a functionalist approach that would follow Parsons' (1960, p. 23) view of managers as providing a purely integrative function in organizations: 'a generalized capacity to secure the performance of binding obligations by units in a system of collective organization when the obligations are legitimized with reference to their bearing on collective goals.' In such an approach, management's legitimacy is taken for granted, and management control becomes a narrow concept, being simply the most efficient technical means of integrating an organization's human resources with management's goals. These goals are considered to be 'collective' where, often, consensus does not exist. We thus avoid an approach that regards management control as being unproblematic and based on management's assumed needs in the exercise of its legitimate custodial functions. Many influential management-control texts that adopt such a perspective rarely mention such issues as power, resistance and conflict, which is not particularly helpful to managers who are trying to understand these organizational problems.

The study of management control in modern times was originally very narrow, being regarded primarily as something technical, synonymous with financial control, and thus within the realm of management accounting, which was, in turn, usually studied in isolation from behavioural matters. At Harvard Business School, for instance, Anthony and his colleagues (1965, 1976, 1984) considered management control to be an aspect of management accountancy – an approach that became highly influential. This approach viewed management control as a routine activity concerned with monitoring activities and ensuring that resources were used effectively to accomplish the organization's strategic objectives. Management control was seen as something that mediates between what Anthony and his colleagues call 'strategic planning' (senior managers and specialists setting objectives for an organization) and 'operational control' (the apparent concern of line managers and supervisors and relating to carrying out specific tasks on a day-to-day basis). Defining management control in such a way allowed the focus to be fixed almost exclusively on accountancy-based organizational controls aimed primarily at controlling the managers' behaviour itself (Puxty, 1989). As Puxty goes on to argue, it is wrong to assume that such accounting-derived controls are the only or main means of management control: Anthony and colleagues' model is too simple, and it assumes away too many problems in two important ways. First, strategic planning cannot be divorced from control since effective control must involve developing and changing plans and objectives. Second, operational control cannot be divorced from management control because, ultimately, control over an organization's activities comes down to controlling the organizational behaviour of individual members, who have been assigned specific tasks and responsibilities through vertical and horizontal differentiations. By ignoring the important links noted by Puxty, Anthony and his colleagues failed to describe control in organizations adequately, and what resulted was an emphasis on the technical elegance of accounting controls at the expense of understanding other kinds of control in organizations. This had a strong ideological bias in favour of those in powerful positions that seek to find more effective ways of controlling others; all this was at the expense of considering the behavioural processes and contexts that impinge on control processes, and it was compounded by a much too narrow concern with intra-managerial and shareholder–management relations. This view of management control ignores the broader concerns of this book – the exercise of control by any organizational superordinate over any other subordinate, managerial or otherwise.

One aim of this book is to introduce the reader to these broader behavioural concerns and, in so doing, the authors recognize that they are pursuing an approach that will bring in ideas from a very disparate body of work – work that has, in some instances, tried to broaden management control's scope to include behavioural issues and that, in other instances, has adopted a critical stance to these concerns.

A broader concept of management control can be traced back to Argyris (1954), who applied organizational psychology to his study of the effects of budgetary controls on managers' and supervisors' behaviour. At the same time, such sociologists as Gouldner (1954), Selznick (1953) and Merton (1957) were researching both the anticipated and unanticipated consequences of control systems on members' organizational behaviour. This work suggested that the unanticipated effects of such formal administrative controls were not only a result of subordinate resistance but also a result of failure to be accepted informally at a collective or individual level – something that was necessary if they were to influence members' everyday organizational behaviour (Hopwood, 1974).

An influential approach that is critical of such a managerialist view is illustrated by the work of Clegg and Dunkerley (1980a), Lowe and Machin (1984) and Chua, Lowe and Puxty (1989). This view, which varies in its approach, argues that, as control in organizations involves the control of some people by others, its investigation cannot be restricted to a consideration bound within the technical perspectives of conventional accountancy or physical engineering. Its investigation, therefore, must be extended to include the operation's social and behavioural processes – processes through which such controls are constructed and reproduced. Moreover, this analysis must include all manner of control systems and processes that are often excluded by an overly technical perspective: the recruitment and selection of members, the deliberate manipulation of members' cultures and the impact of socialization processes.

However, what makes a critical perspective most distinctive is that, instead of assuming that managers exercise a legitimate prerogative in the collective interest of the whole organization, organizations are seen as being composed of a multiplicity of groups whose interests vary and often conflict. This approach avoids what Roberts (1989) has called an 'asymmetrical approach to power and control'. This, Roberts argues, is not only manipulative but is also likely to be counterproductive for managers who will never be able to achieve complete control over subordinates.

This book, therefore, deals with a fundamental aspect of organizations – namely, the processes by which an organization's members determine what things get done and how they are done. These processes have attracted the attention of a number of specialists, such as accountants, engineers, sociologists, psychologists and economists, each of whom tends to examine the processes from their own specialist point of view. Obviously, the authors of this book have their own discipline-based perspective, which has influenced the content of the book; however, we have tried to adopt a broad approach and have drawn on a wide range of sources in an attempt to make clearer what has often proved to be a very confusing field. Moreover, as has already been said, the idea of control developed in this book tries to provide a unifying framework for understanding a variety of organizational concerns: organizational design, leadership, culture, communication, motivation, power, co-operation and conflict. Control is thus seen as a general, underlying principle that allows an integrated consideration of a variety of topics, which are so often treated as if they were discrete single phenomena.

Chapter 1 considers the context of management control – that is, how vertical and horizontal differentiation raises the 'problem' of control. In doing so, the chapter looks at a series of interacting elements, which include organizational structure; the various cultures to which members refer and defer in making sense of their 'worlds' and in constructing meaningful action; and the social, economic and political environments in which organizations exist. Chapter 2 considers the variety of control influences on members' organization behaviour. Taking Hopwood's (1974) model as a starting point, it reviews how administrative controls are constructed socially, and how their impact on members' organization behaviour is socially mediated; the chapter also raises questions concerned with different kinds of self-control. Chapter 3 discusses motivation theory: human needs, motives and goals, and how these influence the direction and maintenance of intentional individual behaviour. This chapter then goes on to review the various assumptions that have been made about the moral and ethical significance of work.

Chapter 4 tries to avoid the universal, psychological approach to motivation discussed in Chapter 3 by suggesting a model that takes into account the cultural diversity and complexity deriving from members' subjectivity. This model is then used to analyse the components, design and operation of output-based administrative control systems.

Chapter 5 explores the vexed issue of organizational culture further. It examines managerial attempts to control members' organization behaviour by deliberately manipulating the organization's culture to influence the value premises of such behaviour. In so doing, the chapter examines whether or not it is possible for management to change or develop a homogenized organizational culture that accords with management's aims and objectives – as current thinking suggests.

Chapter 6 to some extent continues the exploration of areas discussed in Chapter 5 in its consideration of self-control, self-management and leadership. Chapter 7 investigates power in organizations with specific reference to management control. An important aspect of this is a consideration of what have been termed the 'hidden faces' of power, which, in turn, support the managerial prerogative. Finally, Chapter 8 tries to outline the nature of current and future trends in the management control of human resources in work organizations. In this, it reviews aspects of the recent debates about organizational flexibility, human resource management and post-modern organizational forms.

The ideas presented in this book have been discussed with many people over many years – sometimes only inferentially, sometimes controversially, but always in a manner that has been stimulating. We would like to thank our colleagues at Sheffield Hallam University (formerly Sheffield City Polytechnic) and elsewhere, as well as our students, past and present, who have consciously or inadvertently contributed to our understanding of management control and organization behaviour. We would particularly like to thank Peter Ashworth, Tony Berry, Alan Coad, Steve Cooke, John Cullen, Steve Farrar, June Fletcher, David Golding, Keith Harrison, Chris Hutchinson, Tom Lupton, John McAuley, Nick Rahtz, John Shipton, Ian Tanner, Sue Whittle, Hugh Wilmott and Tony Wood. We would also like to thank Peter Cooke, Dave Hawley and Ken Smith who were kind enough to read earlier drafts of the book and provide incisive feedback.

We also gratefully acknowledge the help of Janet Green and Martin Cooper, who rescued us from the intricacies of Word Perfect 5.1 on so many fraught occasions. Thanks, too, to all the librarians at Totley for their help on so many occasions. We would also like to thank Marianne Lagrange and her colleagues at Paul Chapman Publishing for their support and encouragement. Last, but by no means least, thanks to Brenda and Carole's forbearance for so many months.

1

The Organizational Context of Control

Introduction

In this chapter we set out what we consider to be the important aspects of the context in which control issues arise in organizations. In doing so, we argue that this context is made up of a series of interrelated and interacting variables, which include

- the organization's structure;
- the various cultures to which members of an organization refer and defer in making sense of their 'worlds' and in constructing meaningful action; and
- the social, economic and political environments in which the organization exists.

These variables have ambiguous and complex relationships with the control processes and mechanisms in organizations. For instance, although an organization's structure and cultures are crucial aspects of that context, they also directly influence members' behaviour and are hence often seen as important forms of control in their own right. While we will try to clarify these variables to some degree, we will also make reference to the implications of environmental issues. However, we do not deal with the environment specifically as a contextual variable – rather, 'its' implications are considered, where appropriate, in subsequent chapters, where we elaborate on the all-pervasive influence of culture on members' organizational behaviour, as well as exploring the relationship between organization structure and control.

In this chapter we provide an initial overview of the relationship between control in organizations and certain contextual variables, a relationship that has been the subject of much theoretical and empirical research. We build on this starting point in later chapters.

Understanding the Organizational Context of Control

In attempting to understand the organizational context of control, it is useful to begin by trying to imagine the situation that confronts members of 'small and simple' organizations as they begin to expand in terms of the tasks done as well as in the number of people involved in doing those tasks (see also Gill, 1985). A person known to us has recently started a small business, which developed out of his hobby of growing a wide variety of heathers in his own garden. Through trial and error, he has found that it is relatively easy to propagate most varieties of heather, provided suitable cuttings are taken at the correct times of year and so long as they are rooted in the appropriate medium and are provided with a sufficient amount of humidity and warmth. At first, these activities extended merely to increasing his own stock of heathers for his garden and to giving away young plants to friends and relatives. However he discovered, by chance, that there was a thriving market for his heathers. This discovery coincided with and, to an extent, encouraged his decision to take early retirement.

A small business thus developed out of a gardening pastime. This business involved the purchase of two new greenhouses, which he erected at the bottom of his garden next to the one he was already using, and his investment in further varieties of heather to increase his stocks. At the time of writing his business is doing very well financially, but it remains a 'one-man-band', since all the activities essential to his business are undertaken by him, the owner-manager. He decides on, and plans, his activities by referring to the seasonal fluctuations in the gardening calendar, which influence the best time to take cuttings, as well as customer demand. He selects and buys all the necessary materials and new stocks of heather while maintaining the maturer stock from which he regularly takes thousands of cuttings for propagation. These he cares for until they are ready for sale through a variety of outlets, one of which recently has become mail order. He maintains all his own equipment and even keeps his own accounts and so on.

Thus, under his direct involvement in every aspect of propagating and selling heathers, this man's original hobby has developed into an apparently thriving small business. He is now tempted to expand and diversify by including in his range such plants as pelargoniums, fuchsia and lobelia. By propagating and growing new plants he hopes to enter the highly lucrative hanging-basket market. However, such an expansion and diversification will create problems. He knows, for instance, that expansion will require the purchase of land and the erection of at least one large greenhouse connected to electricity and water supplies. However, his main worry is that it will not be possible for him physically to do all the additional work created by these developments. In sum, he is faced with the prospect of either forgoing the proposed expansion and diversification or employing people to work for him. Although he wants to develop his business he is fearful about employing people. As he says, 'I know what needs to be done, how, when and where . . . But can I trust people to do things as I want them to be done?'

It is important to note that, up to this point in his business's life, our acquaintance has relied completely on what has been called 'entrepreneurial control' (Pollard, 1965; Hopper and Berry, 1984). This is where the entrepreneur retains the authority to take (and copes personally with) most of the major decisions in an organization and, thereby, maintains simple and direct control over the activities of that organization (see Edwards, 1979).

In many early factories, such attempts at maintaining entrepreneurial control resulted in the employer having a very wide range of responsibilities both inside and outside the factory. In some cases, the employer would patrol the shopfloor, 'belabouring his men with his own walking stick' (Pollard, 1965, p. 232). In this way they 'exercised power personally, intervening in the labor process often to exhort workers . . . and generally acting as despots, benevolent or otherwise' (Edwards, 1979, pp. 18–19).

In the case of our horticulturalist, perhaps the limited growth he plans would not require a significant move away from a control strategy based on the centralized and personal supervision of the entrepreneur. However, this kind of control – through centralized decision-making – is only effective in small and simple organizations because, as organizations become larger and more complex, such a strategy becomes increasingly difficult as the demands on the entrepreneur's capacity to make decisions increase (Ouchi, 1977; 1978). To expand this further, Offe's historical analysis (1976), which uses the concept of 'task-continuity', is useful. Offe argues that, in the small, simple companies typical of the early stages of the Industrial Revolution, organizations tended to resemble the state of affairs that predated industrialization – task-continuity, where the organization's status hierarchy and knowledge hierarchy coincide. In task-continuity, the entrepreneur has detailed knowledge of the production processes in use, and could indeed control them by personal supervision and by the application of personal knowledge of what the tasks involve. This type of organization was characterized by the 'unity of simple, direct and personal surveillance, ownership and control, premised on an intimate mastery of all the tasks at hand' (Clegg, 1990, p. 88). However, with the increasing size and complexity of organizations brought about by the concentration of capital into larger units, and the bringing together of different types of production process, the unity of status and knowledge hierarchies became disrupted (Offe, 1976). In these conditions of 'task-discontinuity' it was 'increasingly unlikely that any one person would have sufficient knowledge of all their processes to be able to control them in an adequate manner' (Clegg, 1990, p. 10).

Delegation

One result of increasing organizational size and complexity is that it becomes necessary for the entrepreneur to delegate decision-making to subordinates in some way. This means that certain decisions are 'passed downwards and outwards' to different subordinates (Child, 1984, p. 146). By following Carlisle (1974), Child (1984, pp. 146–53) proceeds to consider the advantages of centralized and delegated approaches to decision-making in organizations. The advantages associated with centralization may be as follows. Concentrating decision-making among a relatively small number of individuals, who should have a strategic grasp of what needs to be done, makes it easier to co-ordinate organizational activities. Such centralization avoids the proliferation of managerial hierarchies and activities. It economizes on managerial overheads and puts power into relatively few hands, thereby allowing the opportunity for strong leadership.

The advantages of delegation are that, by relieving the burden on senior management or the entrepreneur, delegation gives subordinates greater discretion and immediate control over their work (Child, 1984). This can have important motivational implications, as it fosters job satisfaction and commitment. Delegation also allows the person who is directly involved with a problem to handle that problem in the most appropriate ways. This permits greater flexibility in an organization, since it allows the person who is 'on the spot' and who should have 'local knowledge' to deal with things immediately without seeking the approval of relatively remote superiors – thereby improving their control over domains of responsibility.

Which is most suitable, centralization or decentralization? A series of circumstances will determine which option is the most appropriate (*ibid.*). The most important are summarized as follows.

Size
As we saw earlier, when an organization grows, greater and greater demands are placed on the entrepreneur's decision-making capacity. It becomes impossible for the entrepreneur to continue to be involved in all aspects of the organization's activities. Although many may resist the need to delegate, organizational growth clearly demands delegation in order to cope with the danger of work overload.

Geographical dispersion
As an organization grows its operations may become increasingly scattered geographically. This puts further pressure on the entrepreneur's ability to cope, since it is impossible 'to be everywhere at once'. The centralized approach of entrepreneurial control means that problems and decisions have to be relayed back to the centre for solving and consideration. This can create considerable delays, as well as overwhelming the capacities of the entrepreneur or the senior management. People at the centre may not have the local knowledge necessary for dealing with the issues passed on to them. The wrong people may be making decisions, about things they do not fully understand and much too late in the day. Hence, the greater the geographical dispersion of an organization's activities, the greater the need for delegation (*ibid.*).

Technological complexity
The difficulties created by growth and geographical dispersion, which put so much pressure on the entrepreneur's decision-making capacities, are made worse by increasing technological complexity. In general, as the organization's technological complexity increases, so does the demand for people with different kinds of specialist knowledge and skill. It is highly unlikely that entrepreneurs and senior management possess such a wide variety of attributes and, therefore, it is inappropriate for them to attempt to maintain control in the personal and direct ways that are possible in small and technologically simple organizations. Their lack of knowledge should make them delegate decisions to those members who actually possess the appropriate skills and abilities.

Environmental stability

The pressures on the entrepreneur's decision-making capacity noted above are increased when an organization is operating in a highly unstable environment. Where the environment is very stable it is possible to predict what the conditions are likely to be at some future date, and thus to plan accordingly. This may allow decision-making to be centralized in the 'hands' of the entrepreneur or senior management team. However, if an environment is, or becomes, unstable (e.g. due to volatility of customer tastes and demands), it is impossible to predict with any certainty what things will be like in the future. This means that the organization must be capable of flexibility in the form of rapid change and adaptation to new and unpredictable circumstances. In large and complex organizations, the ability to cope with such changes is facilitated by delegation, since delegation allows the people with access to the relevant information to make the appropriate adaptations without constantly having to refer up an extensive hierarchy for permission or ratification. By contrast, in small, simple organizations, such instability may be best handled by a concentration of decision-making at the 'top', which allows for adaptation to external change through strong leadership and incisive decision-making (Child, 1984).

In the example with which we began this chapter, it is evident that our gardener's decision to expand and diversify his business's activities would, to some extent, require him to delegate to his employees particular tasks and responsibilities that had previously been his alone. Obviously, the scale on which this happens depends largely on the organization's eventual size, complexity and geographical dispersion, as well as the nature of the environment in which it operates. For instance, he may need to employ people to maintain his current mature heather stocks, to take and propagate cuttings, to look after and develop his new ranges of plants, to maintain equipment and buildings, to sell his products and to keep accounting records. If his business continues to grow, employees may have to begin to specialize in particular tasks (e.g. marketing, production, maintenance and clerical work), which may be located on different sites. These processes, by which the various tasks and decisions that make up the business are delegated to various members of the organization, can be said to result in horizontal differentiation and vertical differentiation.

Horizontal Differentiation

As organizations become larger, technologically complex and more dispersed geographically, they rely increasingly on horizontal differentiation – that is, an organization becomes divided into different segments, each with tasks that differ in various ways from the tasks of other segments. The result is that different people within each segment only deal with a very small part of the whole organization's activities. From the entrepreneur's point of view, such specialization through a division of labour can confer many benefits – particularly, it is assumed, in improving efficiency and productivity by developing competency through focus and repetition. Indeed, some writers consider that such a division of labour resulting in specialization is a characteristic of the process of industrialization and the development of large-scale organizations (see Kerr *et al.*, 1964).

Vertical Differentiation

However, horizontal differentiation creates a need for some means of co-ordinating the resulting disparate and specialized activities; hence occurs what we can call vertical differentiation – the 'unbundling' and distribution of power and authority in an organization. Vertical differentiation results in the creation of a hierarchy of responsibility, with different individuals being apportioned different amounts of power and authority to influence different sets of organizational activities created by the division of labour. For example, we could imagine how our horticultural example might appear in a few years, assuming that growth and complexity have resulted in the combination of horizontal and vertical differentiations as shown in Figure 1.1. This organization chart is a representation of the organization's 'basic structure' (Lorsch, 1970). It shows how various tasks and responsibilities have been divided up formally and assigned to different groups and individuals to accomplish them. In this way the structure specifies not just what members' jobs are supposed to be but it also represents the various levels in the organization's hierarchy. It also indicates different people's spans of control and the various reporting relationships that express the patterns of responsibility formally established through vertical and horizontal differentiation. Clearly, the socially created set of roles and relationships represented by the chart is only one possible set of 'strategic choices . . . exercised by decision makers' (Child, 1972, p. 2). Obviously, there exists a whole range of possible alternatives, and these alternatives have led to much speculation, theorizing and empirical research about the design of organization structures.

Organization Structure: Contingency v. Classical Theory

Early work in organization structure attempted to form a set of general prescriptions about effective managerial practice, usually derived from the

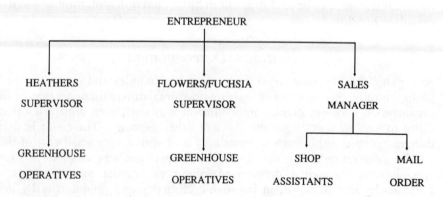

Figure 1.1   Horizontal and vertical differentiation

authors' practical experiences. For example, starting from Fayol's (1914) work, such writers as Gulick (1937) and Urwick (1943) attempted to draw lessons from their own experiences as managers or military officers, out of which they distilled a body of principles or rules – Fayol's (1914) 'acknowledged truths regarded as proven' – which would be universally applicable to any work organization irrespective of its context or purposes. This group of writers are usually called the 'classical' school, since their prescriptions usually 'followed architectural and literary styles which emphasised formality, symmetry and rigidity' (Buchanan and Huczynski, 1985, p. 337). These principles included the scalar concept, the principle of unity of command and the span of control concept (Lussato, 1972). Combined together, these principles prescribe a hierarchy in which all members are placed in a single pyramidal structure of relationships, with authority descending from the apex to the base, so that no subordinate receives instructions from more than one hierarchical superior who, in turn, has no more subordinates than he or she can effectively oversee (Mooney and Reiley, 1939). Although Urwick (1943) does give a formula for determining the size of this span of control there was no precise agreement regarding how large it should be. Other principles proposed by the classical school included such things as the division of labour by specialization, and the delegation of routine tasks to subordinates under the direction of hierarchical superiors (Figure 1.2).

As Fayol's (1914) various pronouncements regarding *esprit de corps* illustrate, the human element is not completely ignored but, generally, these theorists assumed that people were primarily motivated by economic reward. This rationalistic assumption, together with an overall lack of attention to behavioural issues, has led commentators (with some justification) to describe

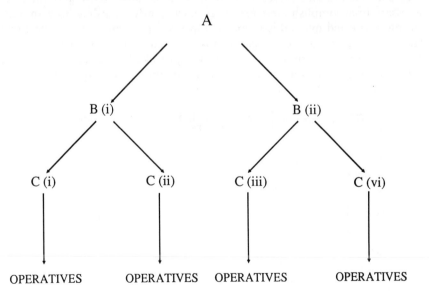

Figure 1.2   The 'classical' organization structure

classical theory as applying a 'machine metaphor' (Morgan, 1986), since it treats the members of organization like 'cogs in a well-oiled machine' (Kast and Rosenzweig, 1979), which, in effect, creates a concept of organizations 'without people' (Bennis, 1966).

Although the popularity of the classical school must not be under-estimated (see Hunt, 1979), its generalizations about 'effective organisation' are insufficiently supported by empirical evidence. Indeed, Simon (1957, pp. 21–36), having examined most of their prescriptions, characterized them as vague, fundamentally ambiguous and 'essentially useless' proverbs.

Contingency Theory

Subsequent empirical research, however, suggests that the prescriptions advocated by the classical school were not so much incorrect as limited in their appropriateness and applicability (Woodward, 1965; Burns and Stalker, 1961; Lawrence and Lorsch, 1967; Pugh *et al.*, 1968). As Burns and Stalker (1961, p. 125) comment, 'The beginning of administrative wisdom is the knowledge that there is no optimum type of management system.' To varying degrees most of these writers approached their subject by implicitly and explicitly bringing to bear an 'open-systems' orientation (Von Bertalanffy, 1967) grounded in an 'organismic' analogy or metaphor (Morgan, 1986). This led to a focus on the interaction between the organization and its wider environment as the organization is seen to import 'energy' and resources from the environment and to convert these into various goods, services and by-products, which are then exported to the organization's environment, thus changing the environmental circumstances in which the organization operates (Figure 1.3).

This idea led to much research into the various 'subsystems' and 'interfaces' necessary to accomplish these processes, particularly regarding how an organization is affected by, and is in many respects dependent on, its environment. There was a focus on how organizations needed to adapt to the demands of their environment (if they were to survive), just like biological organisms. For our purposes, one of the most important outcomes of this approach is that it

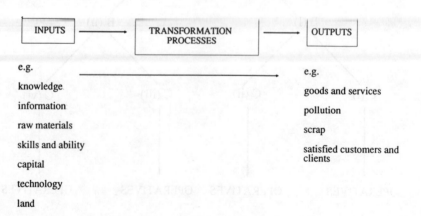

Figure 1.3   The organization as a system

led to a clear break with the universal prescriptions of the classical theorists by creating what is known as 'contingency theory'.

The first research to use the term contingency theory explicitly was that of Lawrence and Lorsch (1967), who attempted to reproduce an earlier study by Burns and Stalker (1961). Burns and Stalker had found that the 'suitability' of different forms of organization ('mechanistic' v. 'organic') were dependent (contingent) on particular environmental imperatives ('stability' v. 'dynamism'). For instance, mechanistic organizations were defined as being characterized by situations where

> the problems and tasks facing the concern as a whole are broken down into specialisms. Each individual pursues his task as something distinct from the real tasks of the concern as a whole, as if it were the subject of a subcontract. 'Somebody at the top' is responsible for seeing to its relevance. The technical methods, duties, and powers attached to each functional role are precisely designed. Interaction within management tends to be vertical.
>
> (*Ibid.* p. 5)

In relatively stable environments, especially when the organization uses an unchanging technology and working methods, such mechanistic structures were found to be appropriate. Readers will have noted the similarity between the 'anatomy' of Burns and Stalker's 'mechanistic' organization and many of the prescriptions of classical theory. Contingency theory does not suggest that classical theory is wrong; rather it is appropriate or inappropriate depending on the organization's particular circumstances.

In contrast, where an organization must cope with high degrees of uncertainty that were caused by unpredictable new tasks created by the demands of a rapidly changing environment (for instance, because of fickle customer tastes), an organic organization structure was found to be more appropriate:

> Organic systems are adapted to unstable conditions, when problems and requirements for action arise which cannot be broken down and distributed among specialist roles within a clearly defined hierarchy. Individuals have to perform their specialist tasks in the light of their knowledge of the tasks of the firm as a whole. Jobs lose much of their formal definition in terms of methods, duties and powers, which have to be redefined continually by interaction with others participating in a task. Interaction runs laterally as much as vertically. Communication between people of different rank tends to resemble lateral consultation rather than vertical command.
>
> (*Ibid.* pp. 5–6)

Matrix Organization

An example of this type of organization is the matrix (Figure 1.4). While the horizontal lines in the figure show the functional specialisms from which team members come, the vertical lines represent the teams in which the specialists combine to undertake tasks or projects. Hence, formal communication and authority channels are simultaneously both lateral and vertical, breaking classical theorists' prescriptions regarding hierarchy and unity of command. The figure also shows the varying combinations of members into non-permanent multi-functional teams, to deal with current projects and problems. Thus a

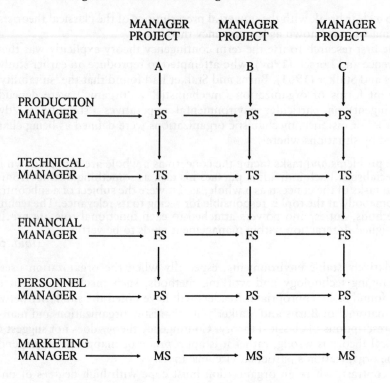

MS/PS/FS etc indicate different types of specialist

Figure 1.4   A matrix structure

matrix allows for a great deal of flexibility in the ways these teams are constituted, disbanded and reconstituted as different issues and tasks arise and are
responded to.

There are problems with matrix organizations. They can create role conflict
and ambiguity for the members of the various teams – particularly since they
have to cope with situations where dual authority exists. Moreover, the matrix
requires people and technical resources to be readily available as new projects
arise. Where people and resources are scarce or not easily redeployable, this
can lead to internal conflict over which projects should be supported. On the
other hand, apart from enabling enhanced flexibility, a matrix structure can
lead to higher technical standards as teams of specialists interact with members
of their functional specialism and other areas of knowledge and expertise –
each member of which may further their personal development by enhancing
their experience (Knight, 1977). The various advantages and disadvantages of
matrix organizations mean that it is vital to identify the circumstances where
such 'organic' structures are most suitable (Davis and Lawrence, 1977). In this
the work of Lawrence and Lorsch (1967) is initially useful.

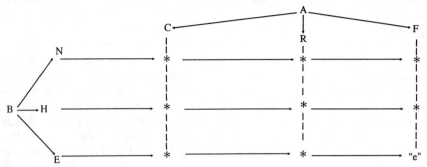

Figure 1.5 A company matrix structure

Exercise

In an organization at the forefront of space exploration there are three project managers, each of whom is responsible for one of the following projects: nose cones (manager C), rockets (manager R) and fuels (manager F). All three managers report to director A, who is responsible to the board for all project work. There are also three functional departments – nucleonics, hydraulics and electronics – each of which is under the control of managers N, H and E, all of whom report to director B. These relationships are shown in Figure 1.5.

As illustrated in the diagram, e is a very junior but highly specialized and vital member of F's project team, as well as being a member of E's electronics department. Indeed, e is so highly specialized that E has only a vague idea of her competencies. She is also often called in to help out with particular, highly specialized problems, which the teams of C and R intermittently confront and which only she can deal with effectively. The problem is that e wants three weeks holiday. Who decides when she may take this holiday, which is due to her under her conditions of service?

Interplay with the Environment

Lawrence and Lorsch (1967) elaborated on Burns and Stalker's (1961) findings by highlighting the complexities that arise from this interaction between organizational elements and the environmental 'contextual factors', which are the imperatives and constraints on the appropriateness of different structural designs. Lawrence and Lorsch pointed particularly to how different parts of an organization interact with different kinds of environment, and that they should thus be structured in different ways in order to be able to cope with those varying demands. For example, in some organizations the research and development department may interface with a highly uncertain and rapidly changing environment, compared to that faced by the production department. They will therefore need different types of structure to cope with these different demands. An organization's overall structure may therefore involve some combination of, and a balance between, different forms of mechanistic and organic structure (see also Knight, 1977).

Although these prescriptions for a 'best fit' have since been refined and developed (as illustrated in our discussion of the appropriateness of centralization and delegation, given different circumstances – see p. 4–5) the thrust of this approach remains generally unchanged (Lawrence, 1981). A particularly persistent theme has been that certain organizational arrangements are more effective than others in coping with 'uncertainty'. The degree of uncertainty experienced can be seen as a function of the disparity between the amount of information needed for task performance and the amount available for processing (Galbraith, 1973). The contextual factors considered to increase such uncertainty include environmental dynamism and complexity, which make it difficult to predict and therefore to plan for events in the environment (Burns and Stalker, 1961; Thompson, 1967; Duncan, 1972), as well as task and technological complexity, which make it difficult to specify in advance what should be done, by whom, how, where and when (Woodward, 1965; Perrow, 1967).

It appears that organic structures allow for better performance in certain circumstances. Not only do they give an organization greater flexibility and therefore allow for quick adaptation to unforeseeable demands but they also create a greater information-processing capacity since they enable the development of lateral links within an organization (as advocated by Galbraith, 1973) as a means of coping with uncertainty and complexity. But the whole issue is further complicated by the existence of other contextual factors that also impose particular demands on the choices of organizational arrangement. Factors that seem particularly important include the organization's size (Child, 1975), how diverse its activities are (Stopford and Wells, 1972) and the presence or absence of employee norms and expectations regarding self-regulation and autonomy (Lorsch and Morse, 1974).

Some of these demands are best accommodated by the flexibility given by an organic structure. This is particularly so because such a structure is thought to encourage creativity, risk-taking and innovation (Klatt, 1978), as well as being more conducive to intrinsically rewarding work (Lawler and Rhode, 1976). However, other contextual demands, such as large size, environmental stability and predictability may be handled best through the characteristics created by a more mechanistic structure.

The contingency approach to organizational design is a clear divergence from the universalism of classical theory. It assumes there are no universally valid rules for organizational design except that 'it all depends'. The contingency approach puts an emphasis on decision-makers' diagnostic abilities to design structures that best fit the contingencies they are able to identify.

Control

But whatever the particular arrangement, it does not, by itself, provide a solution to the concerns expressed by our horticultural friend. There remains the problem of ensuring that members of an organization actually do what they are supposed to do in an efficient and effective manner. That problem may become more apparent as an organization grows, and the number of levels in the hierarchy increase, along with the complexity of the division of labour. As organizations move away from entrepreneurial control, because of differentiation, the problem arises of how to integrate these diverse activities.

This, basically, is the issue of control in organizations – how can members be motivated to expend effort in attaining the wishes of hierarchical superiors? In small, simple organizations characterized by task-continuity, it is possible for the entrepreneur or senior management to observe, monitor and control subordinates' activities personally and systematically. In large organizations, however, with complex divisions of labour, task-discontinuity and hierarchies of responsibility, it is not physically or cognitively possible (or appropriate) to have such a simple approach to control. In such hierarchical organizations,

> policies and objectives are typically set or at least ratified by occupants of higher-level positions and are then communicated to lower participants who are then charged with the responsibility to carry out the necessary actions. It is up to the higher-level managers to determine whether or not the objectives have been met and, if not, to take the appropriate steps. This is the process of control.
>
> (Ouchi, 1978, p. 173)

Without some attempt to control what people do in organizations there is a danger of 'centrifugal' tendencies developing – that is, people begin, intentionally or unintentionally (Evans, 1975), to do 'their own thing' by working towards their personal goals and perceived self-interests. To counteract the tendencies created by the processes of differentiation and to ensure what is sometimes called 'goal congruence', there is a need to create 'centripetal' forces in an organization, which will control and integrate members' diverse activities.

This could, theoretically, be accomplished through the design and implementation of control systems and processes. These are developed with reference to the organization's goals (established by the 'dominant coalition') and are 'operating mechanisms' (see Lorsch, 1970). Thus this formal and intentional type of control in organizations refers primarily to the ways in which certain members attempt to ensure other members of the organization behave in ways that are considered most likely to result in the attainment of the objectives the former perceive as desirable. However, this does not deal with several issues, particularly the following:

1. What are these systems and processes of control that make up the operating mechanism?
2. How do they achieve their intended results?
3. What are the factors that influence their efficacy?
4. How do different types of control interact with each other?

Although we expand on these questions in subsequent chapters, it is important to emphasize that there are no simple answers to these questions. For some readers, fearful of a *1984* scenario, this may come as a relief, since an easy answer to such questions may appear to have dire consequences for human freedom and liberty. For others, this situation constitutes a 'problem' that needs to be resolved in order to improve the efficiency and effectiveness of modern organizations.

Either standpoint entails the projection of particular beliefs, values and moral codes that lead us to view social and organizational life in particular ways (Burrell and Morgan, 1979) and through particular belief and value-laden perceptual 'filters' (Berger and Luckmann, 1967; Spinelli, 1989). However, the questions listed above are problematic largely because of two interrelated issues that are, ironically, in turn related to how different people perceive organizations according to their own beliefs, values and moral codes.

First, in any large, complex organization there will be a large number of different control mechanisms and processes, which have varying degrees of influence on members' behaviour. Some of these will derive from the conscious and purposeful attempts of hierarchical superiors to influence the behaviour of subordinates. Others arise spontaneously out of mundane, everyday social interaction between members, during which informal rules or norms arise that can also begin to regulate behaviour. While each may promote regularities in members' behaviour, often, in any organizational situation, the kinds of behaviour created by one set of influences may be in conflict with the patterns of behaviour created by other influences operating simultaneously in the same context (Roy, 1952; Lupton, 1963). For instance, the behavioural norms promoted by consciously designed control mechanisms may well be at odds with those that have arisen through members' everyday social interaction. The outcome of such conflict will depend upon a variety of factors, which relate largely to the spontaneous processes noted previously.

As Emmanuel and Otley (1985, p. 10) point out, attempts to control the behaviour of an organization's members 'is a complex and ill understood activity precisely because it involves an attempt to control a complex network of self-controlling human beings'. In this they are implicitly drawing attention to the role of human subjectivity in producing human behaviour or, more accurately, human action, and thereby avoiding what is known as determinism.

Determinism

A deterministic approach to predicting and explaining human behaviour in organizations treats human subjects as if they were unthinking, inanimate entities (such as molecules of water) at the mercy of external stimuli. People at the receiving end of the 'operating mechanism' are treated as if they were an amorphous and homogeneous mass of passive recipients, responding automatically to the prescriptions and injunctions encoded into those mechanisms – just as a kettle of water responds automatically to the action of heat so that it boils at 100°C. This is, of course, a distorted view of human beings in any context – organizational or otherwise – who are, in fact, free agents capable of making choices based on their subjective interpretations of the situation that confronts them, with reference to their own perceived needs, interests and goals (Silverman, 1970, Shotter, 1975).

Voluntaristic

A contrasting view of 'human nature' is the voluntaristic approach to human action in organizational contexts (Burrell and Morgan, 1979). This standpoint suggests that human action is meaningful because it arises from the meanings people attach to what is going on around them. The voluntaristic view comes

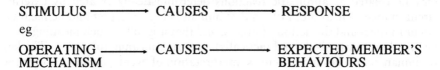

Figure 1.6   Mead's reflexive arc

from the work of George Herbert Mead (1934), who considered that the critical distinction between animals and human beings is that human beings possess subjective powers – 'the mind' – which has freed people from what he called the 'reflexive arc' (Figure 1.6).

A stimulus–response model may well be satisfactory for understanding, explaining and predicting the behaviour of non-sentient phenomena, such as billiard balls, in terms of the responses appropriate to particular sets of stimuli in certain conditions. Mead, however, argued that, rather than simply responding to external stimuli in a puppet-like fashion, people actively attach meaning to and interpret the events that surround them, and it is out of such subjective processes that people construct planned and considered action. While a billiard ball's behaviour might be explained and, indeed, predicted in terms of the responses necessary to particular external stimuli, the actions of any billiards-player can only be explained adequately with reference to the player's subjective motives and intentions; and these come from the player's interpretation of the situation and his or her knowledge and understanding of the rules of the game (Figure 1.7).

In similar fashion, Blumer (1969) also attacked the view that human action

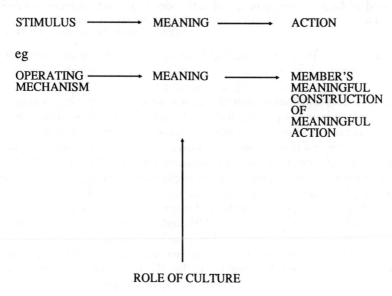

Figure 1.7   Mead's freedom from the reflexive arc

may be treated as automatic reactions deterministically created by external circumstances. He argues instead that human beings interpret and define their circumstances and the action of others, and that it is out of such meanings that people then (purposively and tactically) construct meaningful action. The key to human action lies in the actor's interpretation of events; meanings form the basis of the actor's selection of particular courses of action, which are subsequently initiated and their effects monitored. As Blumer (*ibid.* p. 64) says,

> In order to act the individual has to identify what he wants, establish an objective or goal, map out a prospective line of behavior, note and interpret the actions of others, size up his situation, check himself at this or that point, figure out what to do at other points, and frequently spur himself on.

This surely lends force to Emmanuel and Otley's (1985) observation about self-control (see above).

Culture

If the 'operating mechanism's' impact and, indeed, 'basic structure's' impact is determined by members' active interpretation of the situation, their subsequent behaviour may be unpredictable; therefore, the efficacy and predictability of attempts to control a member's behaviour may be open to doubt. It follows from this that understanding the processes by which people come to make sense of their 'worlds' must be integral to any study of control in organizations. This brings us to the role of culture as an influence on how members behave. The concept of culture refers to

> the unique configuration of norms, values, beliefs, ways of behaving and so on that characterise the manner in which groups and individuals combine to get things done. The distinctiveness of a particular organisation is . . . manifested in the folkways, mores and in the ideology to which members defer, as well as the strategic choices made by the organisation as a whole.
>
> (Eldridge and Crombie, 1974, p. 89)

As we show in later chapters, fundamental to a concept of culture is that culture consists of shared meanings and understandings, which influence members' perceptions of events (organizational or otherwise), and it is out of that 'filtered' perception that meaningful action arises. Culture plays a crucial role in influencing how people respond to attempts at controlling their behaviour. Culture is also an influence on how operating mechanisms and structures are designed in the first place, since variations in such values, norms and beliefs are reflected in different 'structures and systems' (Handy, 1982, p. 176).

While many commentators seem to imply that, although culture varies between organizations, culture is in many respects monolithic in organizations; that is, there is a single constellation of norms, beliefs and values that is shared by all members (e.g. Handy, 1982). Although hierarchically senior members of organizations may well want to achieve such an homogenized or unitary end-state, usually 'a distinction must be drawn between the organisational sub-cultures of groups and departments within the organisation – which may, to varying degrees, be antithetical to the activities and priorities of the organisation's elite' (Salaman, 1979, p. 184).

Any large, complex organization may be composed of a variety of different collectivities of people with different cultures or subcultures (Schein, 1984b). Although the degree and substance of difference may vary, the likelihood of there being a plurality of cultures in any organization adds a further layer of complexity to control. This can be illustrated by reference to Tannenbaum's concept of the 'cycle of control' (Figure 1.8). In the figure, Tannenbaum shows control as a cycle, where person A is attempting to control the behaviour of person B. This control process begins with A deciding what he or she would like B to do. Obviously, A may have little real choice in these matters, since the decision may be largely determined by the strategic choices and requirements deriving from A's hierarchical superiors. Having made sense of those injunctions, A must decide how he or she can influence B to carry out the desired activities in an appropriate fashion. This must involve the selection of the various rewards and punishments A considers necessary for ensuring B's compliance. Those decisions having been made, A must then decide how all this information is to be communicated to B – and then transmit this information.

In undertaking all these activities, A is inevitably bringing to bear all kinds of assumptions influenced by the culture to which he or she refers in making sense of the world. For instance, decisions about the battery of rewards and punishments to be put on offer to B may be greatly influenced by A's assumptions about what it is that 'makes people tick' i.e. human motivation. Someone who believes people are inherently lazy and will work harder only when they are certain that financial rewards are available for that extra effort will have a very different strategy from someone who believes that people will apply themselves best when work is in itself interesting and rewarding. Such 'common-sense' assumptions about, and conceptions of, 'human nature' may well be applied without adequate reflection or testing. They embody preferences and

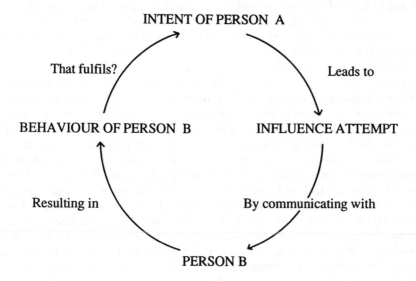

Figure 1.8   Tannenbaum's cycle of control

understandings justified through some combination of moral adjudication, pragmatism, experience and/or aesthetic judgement. As such, those assumptions are intimately bound up with the processes by which individuals or groups comprehend and evaluate 'what is?', as well as make judgements about 'what ought to be?' – which in turn influence their selection of appropriate actions.

To return to Tannenbaum's model, having decided on the content and means of communication, A then transmits it to B. B's reception of this communication is *not* a passive or automatic process. Rather, B will actively attempt to make sense of what it is that A wants, and evaluate what is being put on offer. This interpretative and calculative 'web' is extremely complex since it entails B bringing to bear all kinds of beliefs, understandings, values, attitudes and expectations. For instance, B's decision on what action to take in response to A's communication may be decided partially by his or her evaluation of the attractiveness or desirability of what it is that is being offered for compliance, and his or her beliefs about whether or not those rewards will actually be forthcoming. In addition, B will consider, perhaps in a very calculating manner, his or her understanding of what A might do if he or she is ignored. Culture is again at the heart of these interpretative and calculative processes.

B's resulting actions and behaviour and their subsequent scrutinization by A complete Tannenbaum's control cycle. This largely concerns A's perception and interpretation of what it is that B has actually done in comparison to what A had originally intended. This in itself can be an inherently difficult process, particularly if B is undertaking a complex task. Assuming that A's surveillance is effective, and say he or she discovers that B has done something different from what was intended, this leaves A with the problem of deciding what to do in order to correct an apparent deviation. It also raises the problem of how to handle any potential conflict. The issue of power also emerges, since, just as 'being in control' implies the successful exercise of power by a controller over someone or something, so a 'breakdown in control' can imply, conversely, a lack of power on the part of the controller and/or resistance to his or her machinations through other members' exercise of power.

As Tannenbaum points out (*ibid.* p. 7), if the cycle breaks down at any point (e.g. because A is unclear in his or her transmissions about what is desired – that is, bad design of the cycle's infrastructure – or because of successful resistance by B) control is lost, which can lead to a 'breakdown in the organization itself'. Moreover, Figure 1.8 shows just one control cycle out of many that bear on both A and B. Some of these control cycles may well be designed formally by someone in order to influence their behaviour while others may arise spontaneously among peers during everyday social interaction. Clearly, these various control cycles will not always be congruent with, or supportive of, what A intended in the example given. This may particularly be true of informal cycles, which operate at the informal level in organizations, as group norms develop around what members perceive to be important issues – such as production levels. So no matter how well A might attend to ensuring that their particular cycle does not break down, a breakdown may occur because of the existence of other control cycles, both formal and informal, which are in conflict with A's transmitted intentions.

Conclusion

We have introduced a variety of ideas that have some bearing on control in organizations. These include the following:

1. The variety of controls in organizations and their interaction.
2. The conscious design of the infrastructure of an organization's operating mechanism.
3. Human motivation.
4. Culture and its impact on the various parties involved in control relationships.
5. Power and conflict in organizations.

In order to understand control in organizations, it is important to be aware of these basic issues and how they are related to, and affect, one another. Although we have so far made only oblique reference to environmental considerations, we include an analysis of the impact of these 'external' social, political and economic issues, where relevant, in the following chapters.

Exercise
With reference to any organization with which you are familiar, consider the following:

1. How are various tasks and responsibilities formally divided up and assigned to different groups and individuals (i.e. describe the mode(s) of vertical and horizontal differentiation)?
2. What type of 'basic structure' is created by the above form(s) of differentiation?
3. Using Child's taxonomy of contingent variables, analyse the appropriateness of this 'basic structure'.
4. In what ways does this 'basic structure' influence what organization members actually do?

Further Reading

From their empirical research in Scottish and English organizations, Burns and Stalker (1961) identify two different types of organization and analyse the implications of these. An excellent account of the development of matrix structures in the US aerospace industry is given by Kingdon (1973), and an analysis of some of the problems and ambiguities matrix structures can create is described by Davis and Lawrence (1977). A more recent and very useful overview of contingency theory is provided by Donaldson (1985). Mintzberg (1979a) presents a sophisticated and comprehensive contingency model of organizations based upon a review of over 200 articles and books. Although Mintzberg identifies structural hybrids, his model specifies five 'ideal-type' organizational structures and considers the impact of contingent variables, such as organizational size, age and environment, on 'best fit'.

For a helpful consideration of the debate regarding the relationship between organizational control and organizational structure, see Ouchi (1977). Silverman (1970) provides an important critique of systems theory, which leads him to construct an alternative approach (action theory) to understanding the people's behaviour in organizations that emphasizes the role of human subjectivity.

2

The Variety of Control Influences in Organizations

Introduction

Such writers as Hopwood (1974), Dalton (1971) and, to an extent, Mintzberg (1979a) have developed conceptual schemes that identify the different types of control influence in organizations, and they consider how those influences relate to and interact with one another. Hopwood and Dalton especially provide useful starting-points for our consideration of the variety of control influences in organizations, since they provide similar classifications of the types of control that exist and interact in any organization.

Although his terminology is rather different, Hopwood, like Dalton, begins by identifying three categories of control whose interaction has a significant bearing on the 'control situation' in an enterprise (see Figure 2.1). Hopwood's categories of administrative, social and self control more or less correspond with Dalton's notions of organizational, informal and individual controls. We consider each type of control as distinguished by Hopwood (and, by implication, by Dalton) and, in doing so, attempt to reveal some of the complexities that arise from their interaction with each other. As Hopwood says, these three types of control can never be considered and fully understood as independent phenomena.

As we try to show in this chapter, formally designed administrative controls are socially constructed in the sense that they have various assumptions, beliefs and values encoded into their design and mode of operation. They are applied in a social context that mediates their functioning, particularly in the sense that they confront the spontaneously arising social controls groups have informally developed to regulate members' behaviour. Finally, social and administrative controls are implemented ultimately through the agency of self-controlling individuals. The result is that the control situation in any enterprise can only be understood and explained fully in terms of the interaction of these three variables. Because it is likely that there will be a variety of possible interrelation-

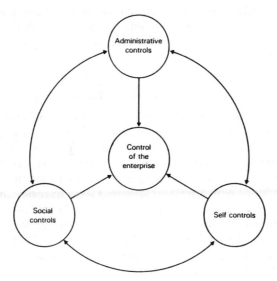

Figure 2.1 Hopwood's three types of control (adapted from Hopwood, 1974, p. 2)

ships between these different types of control, people who design, maintain and operate administrative controls in organizations need to have an approach to the analysis of the control context that reflects all three types of control – administrative, social and self – and their interaction.

Unfortunately, there is a tendency to consider the elements identified in Hopwood's model in isolation (see Ansari, 1977). For example, it could be argued that many accountants have been guilty of concentrating on the technical ease of accounting-derived administrative controls at the expense of their social and behavioural contexts, and without reference to non-accounting forms of administrative control. Given the current spread of accounting controls into new decision-making areas and substantive decision-making areas (such as the NHS) it is worth emphasizing Emmanuel and Otley's comment (1985, p. 82) that 'the ultimate criteria by which any accounting control system should be assessed is behavioural – that is, how does it affect what managers and their subordinates actually do and how do such activities fit into overall plans, etc.?

Administrative Controls

This category of control refers to those mechanisms, techniques and processes that have been consciously and purposefully designed in order to try to control the organizational behaviour(s) of other individuals, groups and organizations. They are ostensibly aimed at creating a situation in which people are more likely to behave in ways that 'lead to the attainment of organisational objectives' (Flamholtz, Das and Tsui, 1985, p. 38), which presumably have been decided upon by particular coalitions of members or have been set for the organization by powerful, interested parties. In this sense, Mintzberg's (1979a) model of what he calls 'co-ordinating mechanisms' may be seen as a taxonomy of different types of administrative control; and, although this is helpful, it tends to ignore those things brought about by the impact of social controls and self-control.

Rules and Procedures

Perhaps the most pervasive form of administrative control is the use of formal rules and procedures, which Mintzberg (1979a) categorizes as an attempt to standardize work processes. Most large organizations use such normative means to regulate members' behaviour (Hopwood, 1974). Creating a body of rules and procedures, backed up by various means of monitoring members' subsequent behaviour with attendant sanctions so as to ensure members' compliance, serves to pre-specify what members should and should not do in particular situations. In this way the rules constrain the range of members' behaviour, increase the predictability of their actions and increase the probability that perceived organizational requirements dominate that behaviour.

To Max Weber (1947), such a framework of intentionally established and impersonal rules to govern performance was one of the most salient and distinctive features of bureaucratic administrative systems. For Weber, this process of bureaucratization meant increasingly subordinating people to the precise calculation of the means by which specific ends might be achieved (formal rationality), which imprisoned people in an 'iron cage'. As we saw in Chapter 1, such bureaucratic systems may be regarded as being effective only in certain sets of circumstances; the same may be said about one of their hallmarks – establishing and utilizing rules and procedures to control members' behaviour.

It is important to note first that bureaucracy can lead to unforeseen dysfunctions, in the sense that the strict observation of rules can become an end in itself, thereby often subverting the original objectives the rules were intended to enable (Merton, 1957). Second, it is also clear that, as a result of some of the basic characteristics of the work being done, it is not always possible to predict or calculate the means by which ends may be achieved or to pre-programme, by creating rules and procedures, what members should do, how, where and when. As Perrow (1967) argues in his analysis of the impact of technology on organizations, there are two important aspects to the tasks being undertaken that influence the extent to which those tasks may be pre-programmed. The first is the number of 'exceptional cases' – new events, situations and problems – encountered in work and perceived as unfamiliar. The second is the nature of the 'search process' undertaken by job-holders when those exceptions occur. This search may be analysable in that problems are resolved in a fashion that involves logical, analytical steps. But, if the problems are vague and 'poorly conceptualized', the search process is virtually unanalysable, and the problems can be resolved only by drawing on a 'residue of unanalysable experience or intuition' (*ibid.* p. 195). From these observations, Perrow constructed the model illustrated in Figure 2.2.

Along the horizontal axis tasks are classified according to whether there are few or many exceptions – thus indicating how variable the tasks are. Although

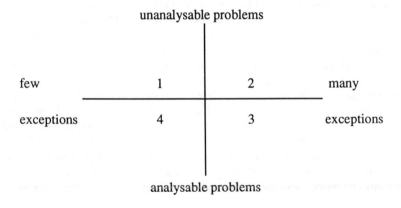

Figure 2.2 Analysable and unanalysable problems (adapted from Perrow, 1967, p. 196)

an organization may attempt to minimize situations where there are many exceptions, if this is not possible it becomes very difficult to develop rules and procedures to govern the performance of the tasks. The vertical axis shows the types of search procedures possible when organization members encounter exceptions. Where a problem is analysable, it is possible for members to search existing databases, etc., to find viable solutions. But where a problem is unanalysable, it is inherently more difficult to resolve since it is vague and ambiguous. In such circumstances, any recourse to existing procedures and data is unlikely to be productive, so members must rely on their skill, experience and intuition to cope with such complex exceptions.

The combination of these axes creates Perrow's fourfold typology (Figure 2.2). In cell 4 we have the situation where work is extremely routine, repetitive, well structured and predictable, and it is possible to create a body of rules and procedures to control the performance of these 'programmed' tasks (Simon, 1977), which in effect reduces their discretionary elements. If we contrast this with the situation in cell 2, where tasks are largely non-routine and unpredictable, with few tried and tested analytical techniques to draw on, it is evident these tasks cannot be pre-programmed through a prior elaboration of rules, etc., and they can be coped with only by members' use of problem-centred, adaptive, creative and intuitive discretion. Such tasks demand controls that allow flexibility, to enable members to use their knowledge, skill and discretion in dealing with unforeseeable and difficult-to-understand problems (Perrow, 1967, p. 197–8).

In cell 1, where exceptions are few but unanalysable, and in cell 3, where exceptions are many and analysable, a mixture of controls allowing both higher and lower degrees of discretion are necessary. It is possible to bureaucratize many – but by no means all – of the tasks members perform through the development of rules and procedures that pre-programme how they perform those tasks and cope with analysable problems. But how may control be established in circumstances where the establishment of rules and procedures to govern task performance is not only inappropriate but, indeed, also impossible, because of the unpredictability of those tasks (i.e. in cell 2)? In order to establish rules and procedures, 'proper' desirable behaviour must be identifiable in advance. Rules then facilitate the monitoring and evaluation of members' actual behaviour, with reference to what is considered appropriate. But, as we have seen above, appropriate behaviour may be unknown or un-knowable. In such circumstances 'the observations of actual behaviour are of no use for control purposes' (Ouchi, 1978, p. 175). This situation leads us into Hopwood's second form of administrative control – output control. This type of control entails the standardization of work outputs as opposed to the stand-ardization of work processes (Mintzberg, 1979a).

Output Control

Where tasks are complex and unpredictable, it is impossible to create predeter-mined rules to regulate members' behaviour. Indeed, for many activities under-taken in organizations, it may be crucial to allow members to exercise their own discretion. Output controls, since they focus on the 'after-effects' (Ouchi, 1978) of behaviour rather than the actual behaviour itself, can ensure control while leaving the everyday accomplishment of tasks to members' judgement and discretion. Where output controls are used, it must be possible to measure the consequences of behaviour – i.e. what has been achieved in task performance.

As Figure 2.3 shows, any output-based administrative control can leave the means of task accomplishment to the job-holder's discretion, through the application of certain mechanisms and processes. First, objectives (or stand-ards) must be decided on that state the required outcomes of members' task performance. Second, there must be some means by which the actual task performance achieved may be observed and measured, in relation to those objectives, so that it is possible to compare actual performance with the target. It is not necessary to know how tasks are done in order to control (as in the case of rules, etc.), but accurate and reliable measurements of the desired outputs must be available for inspection. There must also be some way for deviations in attainment from the original objectives to be analysed and ex-plained so that, if necessary, appropriate actions can be taken to correct task performance. Where the desired objective has been attained, there should be some kind of reward strategy, aimed at reinforcing and encouraging the job-holder's behaviour.

Many types of administrative control common in modern organizations (e.g. budgets, management by objectives and some forms of wage payment system) rely largely on these processes and mechanisms of output control. Here, we have merely introduced the notion of output control by describing the basic elements of this form of control. In subsequent chapters we explore some of the complexities inherent in the problematical processes of objective setting, measurement, comparison, analysis, feedback and reward, in their behavioural and organizational contexts.

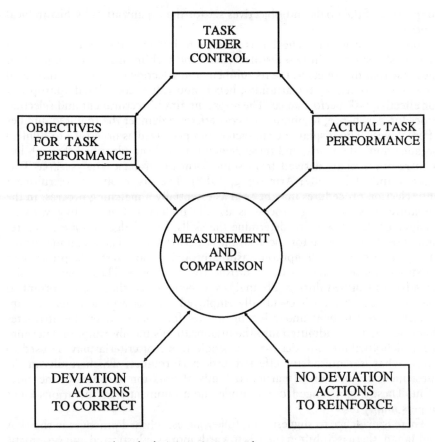

Figure 2.3   Output-based administrative control

Internalized Objectives

The development of rules, procedures and the various types of output control described above may be seen as purposeful attempts at ensuring that subordinates' behaviour at work is dominated by the objectives and priorities of hierarchical superiors. This is often called 'goal congruence'. However, such overt forms of administrative control cannot achieve completely the aim of regulating subordinates' behaviour to attain goal congruence (Hopwood, 1974, pp. 24–5). Moreover, where outputs are unmeasurable in any meaningful sense, and where tasks are unpredictable, either form of administrative control will be inappropriate (Ouchi, 1977; 1979). Therefore they are often reinforced by or, indeed, replaced with, a series of equally important but less obtrusive forms of administrative control. Instead of focusing on members' actual behaviour or the outcomes of that behaviour, these hidden forms of administrative control focus on the basic value premises that surround members' behaviour and decision-making; that is, they attempt to ensure subordinates internalize or have internalized the values, beliefs and attitudes supportive of the goals and objectives set for the organization by hierarchical superiors.

Some commentators believe it is possible to influence the value premises of members' behaviour in two distinct ways. One such means is 'pre-emptive' in the sense that this refers to the recruitment and selection of new organizational members who display the attitudes, beliefs and values considered appropriate for effective task performance. The apparent aim of recruitment and selection procedures is, hence, to obtain in a cost-effective manner the required number of employees who display the characteristics perceived as necessary to fulfil an organization's demands, and these demands have been identified through human resource plans derived from some form of strategic analysis (see Torrington and Hall, 1987; Armstrong, 1988). The organization's recruitment and selection procedures may be seen as essentially a matching process. In the literature, this matching process is usually understood as starting with an analysis of the vacancy to determine the skills, knowledge, abilities, etc., required of the employee for successful task performance. The remainder of the process is largely an attempt to measure, through various tests, the presence or absence of those characteristics in prospective employees. These characteristics have been identified during job analysis as being those that are important so that the 'right' person is eventually employed. In this way, a systematic approach to recruitment and selection allows for control over the attributes possessed by those admitted into the organization's membership. In determining which attributes are desirable, a whole range of criteria may be used to assess what is required for effective task performance, which results in the subsequent application of particular kinds of tests for purposes of measurement. These might range from aptitude and attainment tests to various kinds of personality test.

There is evidence to suggest that, following established practices in the USA and Japan, there is a shift in the UK towards more sophisticated and systematic procedures for recruitment and selection in order to shape pre-emptively the attitudinal and behavioural characteristics of organizational members (Townley, 1989). These developments include an increasing use of personality and psychometric tests, personal history inventories (biodata) and indices of loyalty and appropriate attitudes. Townley argues (*ibid.* p. 101) that this changing 'locus of control' is a movement towards developing more flexible and adaptive organizations. Such developments, it is argued, require new forms of control processes, which allow for members' exercise of discretion during task performance. As Townley (*ibid.* p. 103) points out, 'Discretion . . . obviates the exercise of bureaucratic procedures . . . Discretion requires the internalisation of the organisation's "goals" or "norms" to ensure that the individual interprets the area of discretion correctly from the organisation's point of view'. Clearly, the intentional selection of new members who already display such propensities and predilections can be seen as a pre-emptive attempt at 'insidious control' (see Blau and Schoenherr, 1971) through the maintenance and reinforcement of particular value premises of behaviour, so that the 'application of authority and power is no longer necessary in the achievement of the organisation's goals, because the goals have been internalised by those who are to pursue them' (Anthony, 1977, p. 258).

Recruitment and selection procedures are not the only means by which such control may be established. Research has noted the malleability of people in the early stages of their organizational membership (Katz, 1967; Brim, 1968). Similarly, with specific reference to new managers, writers have stressed the critical importance of the first year of organizational membership (Berlew and Hall, 1965), for it is during this 'initiation stage' (Schein, 1965) that these new members are sent on management training and development programmes. These programmes, together with recruitment and selection procedures, have been identified as an important strategy for establishing control by ensuring the transmission of 'appropriate' attitudes and values (Hellriegel and Slocum, 1978). This is made easier by the newcomer's primary concern to 'seek safety' (Hall and Nougain, 1968), by demonstrating their worthiness and organizational competence through learning about, and adjusting to, the demands of a new and uncertain social setting.

Instead of the pre-emptive approach, potentially available through recruitment and selection procedures, management may attempt to influence the value premises of members' behaviour by trying to restructure their attitudes and beliefs so that they are more in tune with what is thought to be appropriate for more effective task performance (Wood, 1986). It is possible that either approach could form the elements of a control strategy aimed at establishing 'responsible autonomy'. This

> attempts to harness the adaptability of labour power by giving workers leeway and by encouraging them to adapt to changing situations in a manner beneficial to the firm. To do this, top managers give them status, autonomy, *and try to win their loyalty to the firm's ideals (the competitive struggle) ideologically.*
>
> (Friedman, 1977, p. 5, emphasis added)

Although we consider such attempts at 'culture management' in more detail in subsequent chapters, it is useful here to discuss a type of administrative control that may be seen as a vehicle for restructuring attitudes and beliefs – information disclosure.

Information Disclosure

Douglas (1971) demonstrates how the ability to make apparently authoritative statements can endow someone with significant powers of control. In organizations, the information disseminated by such experts can purvey a powerful version of reality, by giving a particular course of action the appearance of being the result of an irresistible logic and rationality.

An example of 'expert knowledge' is provided by accountancy information. The disclosure of accountancy information to employees and their representatives has been seen in such legislation as the Employment Act, 1982 (and see also Commission on Industrial Relations, 1972, p. 21; ACAS, 1977) as a panacea for industrial relations 'problems'. Much research also suggests this. For example, Foley and Maunders (1973, 1977), Palmer (1977) and Pope and Peel (1981a, 1981b) all argue that, out of self-interest, management should disclose accounting information for collective-bargaining purposes. There are several arguments in favour of such disclosure. While claiming that increased disclosure is consistent with industrial-relations legislation, they argue that disclosure could also lead to a readier resolution of conflicts of interest through more efficient 'distributive bargaining' (Walton and McKersie, 1965). Presumably this occurs because it is considered that accounting data enables neutral arbitration of the organizational financial reality confronting the various interested parties – something, incidentally, that is contested by many accounting scholars (e.g. Tinker, 1985; Hines, 1988). Moreover, by encouraging 'deeper trust and confidence' (Foley and Maunders, 1973, p. 121) between parties, it is more likely that 'integrative bargaining' – problem-solving based upon an identification of common interests (Walton and McKersie, 1965) – would occur, particularly as causes of conflict deriving from 'differential information sets' (Pope and Peel, 1981b, p. 143) are removed.

Craft (1981, p. 98) disputes these claims by proposing a contingency view of disclosure derived from his initial premise that 'more consideration needs to be given to the organisational and behavioural factors that can influence the desirability of and approach to financial disclosure to unions . . . [Management] must assess the potential impact on resource allocation, coalition stability, and management's own objectives'. Craft goes on to discuss the actual strategies available to management about how much information they should share with trade unions. Although its specifics do not directly concern us here, Craft's analysis culminates in producing a list of strategies about the degree and kind of disclosure management ought to employ in particular organizational situations. In reply to Craft, Foley and Maunders (1984, pp. 104–5) claim that, while his contingency view is appropriate, it needs reformulating, since it lacks a 'dynamic view of the effects of disclosure. For this we have to turn to the potential use of voluntary information disclosure as an attitudinal restructuring tool which, if effective, can lead to shifts in the labour–management relationship . . . and so can lead to positive managerial pay offs'.

Clearly the participants in this debate see the disclosure of accounting information as a means of projecting particular images of organizational reality and as a way of engendering within members attitudes that are congruent with managerial perspectives and purposes. Behind this 'front' (Douglas, 1976) designed 'to paint a specific image of itself' (Cicourel, 1958, p. 55) data are brought together 'on the basis of characteristics that presumably are relevant to the purposes of the people constructing the information' (Douglas, 1971, p. 53). In other words, accounting information disclosure, contingent or otherwise, may be an attempt at 'ideological recruitment' (Brannen *et al.*, 1976) on the basis of 'attitudinal restructuring'. This may create a new basis for control, since

> management can utilise the disclosure of information as a means of emphasising the technical nature of the problems confronting the organisation and the role of management as technical experts seeking technical solutions. Within such a framework the conflict inherent in collective bargaining may be dissolved into a search for mutually satisfying outcomes in which the only salient imperatives are those of efficiency, technology and the market . . . Thus accounting information may be used as a means of socialising trade unions into endorsing the primacy of market criteria for management decision-making.

> (Ogden and Bougen, 1985, p. 221)

Empirical support for Ogden and Bougen's contentions is provided by Jackson-Cox *et al.* (1984). They found that management's systematic and selective disclosure of information to trade unions was associated with management's concern to engender in employees and their representatives an identification with the company, or some segment of the enterprise or part of its activities (*ibid.* p. 257). Such identification was considered important by management because it provided a way of transcending sectional interests and created an alternative to identification with the trade-union movement. Hence, through such disclosure management aimed to 'fix employees' consciousness on the nature of the enterprise, so that they are more aware of the vicissitudes of the business situation, and consequently will adopt a more "co-operative" and "responsible" attitude' (*ibid.* p. 271).

However, as we show in later chapters, the outcome of this and other strategies aimed at shaping members' preferences and cognitions is not always straightforward. Much depends on the meanings members attach to the disclosed information. It is wrong to assume that, through the disclosure of information, recipients will automatically become 'better influenced and more controlled' (*ibid.* p. 91).

So far we have reviewed three types of administrative control that may be distinguished from one another in terms of those aspects of members' task performance they are intended to constrain and influence. This is illustrated in Figure 2.4. Although we have treated these types of administrative control separately, in practice, attempts to control members' behaviour will involve more than one type of administrative control – indeed, as we show in later chapters, some 'control packages' (such as 'scientific management') can entail all three types of control.

Social Controls

When looking at administrative controls consciously designed to influence members' preferences and cognitions, we are in effect reviewing the ways particular cultures are passed on intentionally to members, be they neophytes or otherwise. This type of administrative control may be of greatest importance where bureaucratic controls are inappropriate because the controllers lack sufficient knowledge about what employees' tasks involve, and where, because it is difficult to measure output, output-based controls are not viable. These unobtrusive forms of administrative control have many of the subtleties associated with what Hopwood (1974, pp. 26–7) terms 'social controls'. In considering the impact and nature of these social controls we return to 'cultural plurality' in organizations, noted in Chapter 1.

In Chapter 1 we saw how 'culture' directed attention to the customary ways of doing things, which are an expression of the networks of shared meanings members refer and defer to when making sense of their 'organizational worlds'. However, we also emphasized that organizations are usually composed of various 'subcultures', which may be mutually antagonistic; these subcultures thus compete overtly and covertly as different groups of organizational members seek to establish or impose their distinctive meaning systems and definitions of reality.

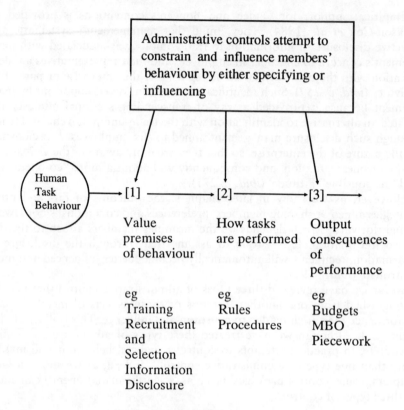

Figure 2.4   Three types of administrative control

Smircich (1983), Schein (1984b) and Louis (1985) all emphasize how there may be various sites or 'loci' of culture embedded in the various groups that make up an organization. Therefore, the 'likelihood that there are multiple organisational subcultures or even counter cultures' (Smircich, 1983, p 346) must not be neglected. Turner (1972) defines a subculture as a distinctive set of meanings shared by a group of people that underpins their behaviour in that group within the organization. In other words, there are habitual ways of acting and thinking members as a group consider natural and legitimate.

It is possible, therefore, to imagine the difference between administrative controls that attempt to transmit particular subcultures purposively, and social control. Both concern socialization in organizations whereby the individual learns a group's culture and adopts the patterns of social behaviour approved by that group. Where management attempts to disseminate a culture through consciously designed, planned strategies to regulate and inculcate particular systems of belief and meaning in subordinates, we are referring essentially to the formal area of administrative controls. By contrast, where socialization is not the result of planned strategy but, instead, arises spontaneously out of the everyday social interaction among members, we are referring essentially to the informal area of social control. Perhaps it is best to visualize this as the extremes on a continuum rather than as a clear dichotomy, since in practice it is often difficult to distinguish between consciously designed processes and the spontaneous.

When considering social controls it is best to begin by distinguishing the processes that establish them and their subsequent effects.

Informal Socialization

Social controls in the main involve the informal socialization processes by which members induct one another into membership of particular cultures (van Maanen, 1976). Important to understanding the notion of socialization is the idea that, as a person moves from one organizational context or status to another, his or her 'self-image' – the 'set of values, beliefs and opinions held by the person about himself . . . embedded in [a] set of social relationships that give it stability and continuity' (Faunce, 1968, p. 93) – may change as the group of 'significant others' (whose perspectives and standards he or she shares) also changes. This idea was first suggested by Mead (1934), who claimed that, if people are to anticipate and plan their actions and activities and reflect upon and learn from their past conduct, they must be able to look upon themselves in the same way as they look upon any other object they might encounter. According to Mead (*ibid.* p. 138), this human capacity for self-consciousness depends on the individual's ability to absorb and internalize the attitudes other people have towards him or her – that is, 'the individual experiences himself as such, not directly, but only indirectly, from the particular standpoints of other individual members of the same social group, or from the generalized standpoint of the social group as a whole to which he belongs'.

Our understanding of ourselves is, to Mead, a reflection of other people's standpoints: other people who are significant, or important, in our lives. Particularly important 'significant others' may be the 'reference group' or audience for whom the actor renders a performance. Shibutani (1962, p. 132) defines a reference group as 'that group whose presumed perspective is used by an actor as the frame of reference for his perceptual field'.

A reference group therefore has a role as a source of (or reference to) ways of thinking, feeling, perceiving and evaluating – and as an audience that may be physically present or absent in any interaction but towards whom an actor orientates his or her conduct. A member's subjective world may be heavily influenced by social interaction with certain people, who become a reference group to which the member becomes increasingly orientated and which the member utilizes for personal assessment. Van Maanen (1976) demonstrates the importance of these social networks in socialization, and notes the link between an individual's acceptance of a particular subculture and his or her involvement in social networks. However, an individual's direct involvement with a particular social network does not mean that that network automatically becomes a reference group for that person. Newcomb (1966), in his study of the influence of reference groups on the attitudes of students at Bennington College, found that, while the success or failure of socialization procedures was largely dependent on the extent to which the student group displaced an individual's family as a reference group, the individual's evaluation of possible reference groups was an important factor influencing his or her acceptance or rejection of such groups. So, 'in a membership group in which certain attitudes are approved, individuals acquire approved attitudes to the extent that the membership group (particularly as symbolised by leaders and dominant sub-groups) serves as a positive point of reference' (*ibid.* p. 262).

However, it is important to emphasize that reference groups will not necessarily transmit norms and values that agree with those of the particular culture(s) adhered to by hierarchically superior coalitions of members. Indeed, research into the behaviour of groups of shopfloor workers provides many examples of employee values and norms that are reflected in everyday practices (e.g. restriction of output) that conflict directly with the aims and expectations of management (Roy, 1960; Lupton, 1963; Turner, 1972). Even within the managerial hierarchies of one organization there is much evidence to suggest a diversity of cultures, some of which may be antagonistic to others. Dalton (1959) observed a tendency for cliques to develop around perceived sectional interests that were often antipathetic to senior management. Burns (1955) found that cliques with norms and values contrary to those of senior management could develop among older managers who lacked promotion prospects and felt a need to act defensively. Burns contrasts these coalitions to the 'cabals' that develop among younger managers, whose perceived individual interests are served by compliance with senior management's culture.

Thus by establishing social relationships with colleagues (who may be hierarchical peers or superiors or, indeed, subordinates), and by beginning to value and enjoy them, individuals may become socialized into accepting the particular norms and values dominant within that social network. Maintaining these relationships not only depends on the individual displaying knowledge and acceptance of the social network or group's prevailing culture, thus demonstrating that he or she is a competent member, such relationships also transmit them.

This brings us to another important point: the 'significant others' an actor may adopt and identify with subjectively as a reference group may not necessarily come from a group with which the actor shares overt membership. This is because people 'frequently orientate themselves to a group other than their own in shaping their behaviour and evaluations' (Merton, 1957, p. 234).

Since 'beauty is in the eye of the beholder', it is conceivable that, despite the various informal social pressures groups exert on members to conform to their norms, beliefs and practices, individuals deviate from their group's culture by identifying with alternative or 'aspirant' reference groups with which they do not share overt membership. Thus social control through the informal transmission of particular values, beliefs, attitudes and expectations is not just exercised 'horizontally' between hierarchical peers – it can also occur 'vertically' between hierarchical superiors and subordinates.

It is in this 'vertical' dimension that it becomes difficult to distinguish between the less obtrusive forms of administrative control described earlier (aimed at influencing the value premises of members' behaviour) and the social controls described here. Some commentators (e.g. Ouchi and Price, 1978; Ouchi, 1980) have noted how large Japanese corporations, which have employment policies founded on a presumption of long-term employment, can provide the basis for unobtrusive social control (the 'industrial clan') based on the dispersion and acceptance of norms and values that generate sustained solidarity with the organization. Employees come to believe their personal interests are subordinate to, and/or are embodied in, their commitment to the 'needs' of the organization – presumably as defined by hierarchical superiors. Deal and Kennedy (1982) and Peters and Waterman (1982) note how such 'strong cultures' provide sources of belief, meaning and interpretation that percolate through an organization. They emphasize particularly how such cultures may be inculcated and reinforced by a variety of rituals and slogans that allow for public displays of commitment to the 'organization'. These displays are symbolized by the near deification of corporate heroes, the significant others who personify corporate ideals and goals. While it is evident that aforementioned writers wish to enable organizations to purposively develop such 'strong cultures' it remains unclear whether or not the organizations Deal and Kennedy and Peters and Waterman have observed have developed in the way they have through chance and spontaneity (i.e. social control) or through conscious intent (i.e. administrative control, albeit unobtrusive). This emphasises our earlier observation that, in practice, social and unobtrusive administrative controls merge and may be difficult to distinguish.

In the previous section we tried to show how social controls emerge from the mundane everyday interactions of organizational members. As such they are made up of the shared values, norms and beliefs adhered to by group members, whether they are the denizens of the executive suites or shopfloor blue-collar employees. In this way, they 'form a kind of backdrop for action' (Smircich, 1985, p. 58). It is therefore important to emphasize at this point that not only can these social elements affect the operation of any administrative control but they also can have a direct influence on how administrative controls are designed in the first place.

Hopwood (1974, pp. 27–9) shows how administrative structures designed and applied by hierarchical superiors in order to control subordinates' behaviour vary according to the beliefs and values of those superiors. Of critical importance in this are the beliefs and values about 'human nature' projected onto subordinates by their hierarchical superiors. While rarely acknowledged, such assumptions about what causes human behaviour are implicit in the design of any administrative control (Argyris, 1957). Although in later chapters we look at this in much greater detail, it is worth emphasizing here that managers' culturally derived assumptions about people, by filtering their understanding of the events they might experience in organizations, influence how they manage; and by implication how they might design and operate various administrative controls.

So, as we have attempted to show, the complexities at the social or cultural 'level' in organizations influence not only how administrative controls are designed and applied but also how they are perceived and responded to by members. Although we take up the implications of this more fully later, Hopwood (1974, p. 27) makes an interesting point that is worth quoting here:

Control, in whatever direction, is not only achieved by formal means but also by pressures exerted by individuals over one another. For in any situation, the controllers and the potentially controlled have a social relationship with one another. The motivations, expectations and personal relationships of all the members of the enterprise therefore exert a significant effect on the outcome of the control process.

Self-Controls

For social and administrative controls to be effective influences on members' organizational behaviour, they must be expressed through the actions and attitudes of individual managers and employees (Hopwood, 1974, p. 31). They must operate as 'self-controls' – the controls people exert over their own behaviour. In order for this to happen, the norms embodied in administrative or social controls must be 'either directly or indirectly . . . internalised by the members of the enterprise and operate as personal controls over attitudes and behaviour' (*ibid.* p. 31). Hopwood goes on to point out that for this to happen, the administrative and social controls in question must convey rewards the individual values and desires. This complex situation may be best explained by way of the example in Figure 2.5. The figure represents an organizational setting where the three types of control considered in this chapter are operating. Here the individual is confronted by a wage-payment system that management has consciously designed to maximize productivity. For example, each extra unit of output achieved by the individual over a certain amount and in a specific period of time, such as a working day, could be rewarded financially. However, as with any administrative control, this incentive scheme does not operate in a social vacuum. Particularly important here are the norms that have developed around the levels of productivity deemed appropriate by the group. These norms restrict output to a level below what is actually possible to produce in a working day. Just as the payment system promises rewards for conformity, the social controls are enforced by sanctions that include friendship and social acceptance for conformity to the prescribed output norms, as well as the threat of ostracism and social disapproval for deviance. How will an individual respond to these different controls, which are working counter to one another? While conformity to the payment system may increase the individual's economic rewards, it may do so at the expense of various social costs.

Conversely, conformity to the group and interpersonal pressures from peers may gain many social rewards, but at the expense of financial rewards above those defined by the group output norm. Hopwood considers the answer to this question lies in the individual's personal motives and desires regarding what they want or need out of work.

However, Hopwood fails to point out that 'internalization' is only one possible type of conforming response to external influences deriving from social and administrative control processes. Kelman (1961) proposes that internalization is only one of three possible forms of conformity, the others being 'compliance' and 'identification'. To Kelman, compliance is the mode of conforming behaviour adopted by a person who is motivated by a desire to gain a reward or avoid a punishment. Such behaviour lasts only as long as the promise or threat of sanction exists. On the other hand, identification is a conforming response to social influence brought about by a desire to be like the people

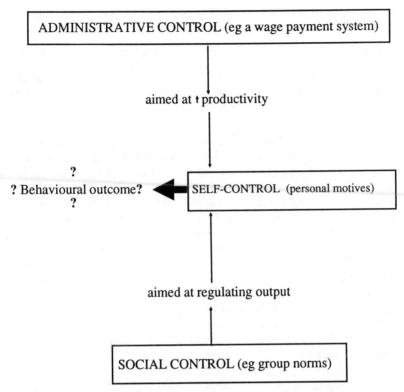

Figure 2.5 An administrative control designed to reward increased productivity

who are exerting the influence on the individual. It therefore involves emotional gratification through emotional attachment to 'significant others'. In contrast to internalization, identification does not necessarily involve the individual developing internal moral imperatives. However, such imperatives may develop as the individual adopts the beliefs, norms and values of the significant others in his or her perceptual world, thereby producing what Kelman specifically defines as internalization. Kanter, in her anthropological discussion of 'Utopian communities' (1968), draws on Kelman's notion of internalization to distinguish what she calls 'mortification' and 'surrender'. While both involve the individual's redefinition of his or her symbolic environment, mortification has relatively negative connotations. Thus, mortification processes involve 'submission':

> the exchanging of a private identity for one provided by the organization . . . [They] provide a new set of criteria for evaluating the self, and they transmit the message that the self is adequate, whole and fulfilled only when it conforms to the model offered by the collectivity . . . [They] strip away aspect of an actor's identity, make him dependent upon authority for direction.
> (Kanter, 1968, pp. 511–12)

This type of internalization involves the development of dependency on the collectivity through the removal of the individual's sense of self-control. According to Kanter, surrender is a much more positive process. It involves

> the attachment of a person's decision making prerogative to a greater power, total involvement with a larger system of authority which gives both meaning and direction to an individual's life . . . personal identity is fused with the social entity so that carrying out system demands becomes a moral necessity for maintenance of the self.
>
> (*Ibid.* pp. 513–14)

Kanter's work is particularly useful because it develops Kelman's three-part system of conforming response, and it also draws our attention to the processes that can disengage the individual from prior social and ideological attachments by redirecting his or her beliefs and norms towards those that predominate in any organizational context – whatever those might be.

In recent research specifically concerned with management control in organizations, internalization is associated with what is referred to as 'commitment' (see Guest, 1987; Coopey and Hartley, 1991). This involves the internalization of management-derived and sanctioned beliefs, norms and values, in the sense that they become part of the core of the individual's perceptual world; thereby they develop into moral obligations (moral involvement) that impel autonomously particular forms of behaviour, and they are highly resistant to change. To Kelman, a crucial factor in promoting this situation is the credibility of the influencer(s) and the individual's motivation to internalize a set of beliefs that are considered correct.

Thus individuals may conform overtly to the injunctions deriving from the social or administrative domains; however, underlying that behaviour may be very different psychological states. All three forms of conformity underpin different forms of self-control, of which internalization (or commitment) is only one possible condition. Indeed, as Brown (1965) claims, the processual nature of moral development may involve movement through different conforming 'states' – the individual initially 'obeys' external demands because of sanctions and then, through various everyday social interactions, emotional attachment develops that eventually leads to identification and then to internalization.

In the example given in Figure 2.5, the individual's subsequent behaviour (that is, which norms embodied in the different control influences impacting on the individual are conformed to) would depend on that individual's evaluation of the rewards on offer, and/or his or her perception of significant others and/ or the state of his or her 'moral development'. Obviously these evaluative and perceptual processes are complex issues that raise, among other problematic areas, the whole subject of motivation – the subject of the next chapter.

Conclusion

In this chapter we have reviewed the three types of control identified by such writers as Hopwood as being of fundamental importance to any organizational context. Largely by following and elaborating upon Hopwood, we have described the different kinds of obtrusive and unobtrusive administrative control consciously designed by hierarchical superiors to control subordinates' behaviour. We demonstrate how these administrative controls are, in many respects, 'socially constructed' in the sense that administrative controls are the vehicles for the assumptions, beliefs and values of their designers and maintainers. Their subsequent impact upon the members' whose behaviour they are supposed to control is further affected because an individual's behaviour may be highly influenced by the various social pressures that occur in organizations. However, whether the norms transmitted by either the administrative or the social controls actually come to be expressed in the individual's self-controlled behaviour, depends largely on some of the issues we consider in Chapter 3, particularly the influence of the individual's attitudes and expectations towards their work in the organization.

Exercise

Think carefully about the kind of job you have, then rank each of the six pairs of (a) and (b) statements given below by awarding a score using the following scale:

My job is very like (a): 1
My job is more like (a) than (b): 2
My job is a mixture of both: 3
My job is more like (b) than (a): 4
My job is very like (b): 5

1(a)   I have a detailed job description that specifies what I should do, how, where and when.

1(b)   While I have a rough description of my responsibilities, how I undertake tasks is left completely to my discretion.

2(a)   My work is largely routine and repetitive; thus I can usually predict what I shall be doing on any particular day of the week.

2(b)   My work is complex and varies considerably from day to day. This lack of routine makes it difficult to predict what I shall be doing at any point in the future.

3(a)   In order to do my job effectively, I rarely need to learn new skills or acquire new areas of knowledge.

3(b)   In order to do my job effectively, I am continually learning new skills and acquiring new areas of knowledge.

4(a)   When there is a problem I cannot resolve, I pass it on to my boss, who then finds a solution and tells me what to do.

4(b)   When there is a problem I cannot resolve, I share it with the people I think may be able to help and, together, we try to find a viable solution.

5(a)   My job performance is evaluated in terms of my compliance with the rules and procedures that govern how my job should be done.

5(b)   My job performance is evaluated in terms of getting tasks done – how I actually achieve this is largely up to me.

6(a)   Interpersonal relationships with my peers and my boss(es) are formal.

6(b)   Interpersonal relationships with my peers and my boss(es) are informal.

Scoring

A score of 6–12 – your organizational role is highly preprogrammed; 13–18 – your organizational role is a mixture of being preprogrammed and not pre-programmed; 18–30 – your organizational role is not preprogrammed and thus you have to exercise considerable discretion.

Try the exercise again, but this time with reference to the type of job you would like to have. Compare the results of what you would like with what your job is actually like. What are the implications of this for your personal feelings of job satisfaction?

Further Reading

Hopwood (1974) and/or Dalton (1971) still provide the most useful introductions to the issues created by the variety of different controls in organizations. Both Ansari (1977) and Flamholtz, Das and Tsui (1985) can be read as important elaborations on this theme. This is particularly so in the case of Flamholtz, Das and Tsui in that they develop lucidly an integrated model of control embedded in the context of organizational structure, organizational culture and the organization's environment. Perrow (1967) and Townley (1989) give important discussions of the operation of different kinds of administrative control, while Ouchi (1980) discusses the contingencies bearing on the type of administrative control that might predomi-nate in any organization. Despite their age, Rose (1962) probably provides one of the best collections of papers that focus on the social influences on human be-haviour. A recent alternative to Rose is section B of Frost *et al.* (1991), entitled 'The Differentiation Perspective'.

3

The Evolution of Motivation Theory

Introduction

A precise operational definition of 'motivation' is rather elusive, since its use varies and the word's meaning is full of ambiguity. However, as a starting-point it is possible to infer from relevant management literature and research that 'motivation' in work organizations refers to the processes by which people are enabled and induced to choose to behave in particular ways. Thus, motivation is often associated with a search for the means by which members' job performance and productivity may be improved or maintained. Such processes entail engendering in members a willingness to expend effort in particular directions to achieve what are taken to be desirable goals.

Central to this understanding of human motivation must be an analysis of the factors that cause an organization's members to behave in the ways they do. Thus much current research and theory about motivation begins by addressing the interrelated issues of human 'needs', 'motives' and 'goals' and how these influence the direction and maintenance of an individual's intentional behaviour.

Needs, Motives and Goals

Human needs are usually identified as being expressed through an individual's feelings or experiences of physiological, psychological or social deprivation, deficiency or imbalance. These feelings create drives or forces that stimulate the individual into channelling energies into modes of behaviour that could reduce the tensions created in the individual by that felt need. The specific behavioural manifestations of such energies are usually considered to be guided by factors called motives. These factors give direction to the aroused energies. By channelling their energies into socially approved courses of action, individuals aim towards goals, whose attainment is seen as enabling the

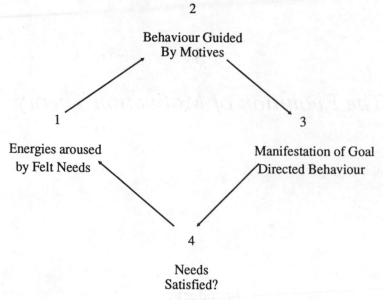

Figure 3.1   Human needs

satisfaction or alleviation of those needs. In this way, motivation is usually described in terms of the forces acting on and in an individual and that cause that individual to behave in a particular goal-directed manner. These processes are illustrated in Figure 3.1.

An individual's felt need may be to have a better standard of living. This may stimulate him or her into pursuing a goal of promotion. However, the individual's actual behaviour in pursuing this goal will be determined largely by what is and what is not socially approved and valued within the organization and in society generally. The assassination of immediate hierarchical superiors could conceivably facilitate the individual's promotion by creating the appropriate vacancies but, given the current norms of most societies and organizations, few people would consider this to be a serious, viable course of action.

An alternative, socially approved course of action would be for the individual to manage his or her 'presentation of self' carefully to hierarchical superiors so that his or her eligibility for promotion (e.g. a competent, hard-working, creative person capable of using initiative and leading others) was evident to them according to the conventions and criteria they use to formulate such a notion. If this course of action meets with success, then such behaviour may be reinforced; in contrast, if the individual sees it fail, he or she is likely to consider alternative courses of action, or even begin to question the goal itself.

The analysis of the nature of these components – needs, motives and goals – forms the main theme of much research concerning motivating people in work organizations. Indeed, it has often been claimed that the issue or 'problem' of motivation is of central concern to management since, if it were possible to understand and explain (and thereby predict) the ways in which people could be motivated at work, it would then be possible, as Handy argues (1985, pp. 26–7), to influence their behaviour by manipulating the components of that motivational process (see also Nadler and Lawler, 1991; Steers and Porter, 1991).

Given this importance, it is not surprising a great deal of theory and research has been generated, all of which attempts to provide, in different ways, the means by which this 'mainspring' of human behaviour may be conceptualized, modelled, analysed and ultimately resolved by various managerial practices in organizations, such as job and payment systems design, appraisal schemes and management style. Much of this work may be seen as being conducted from two somewhat different points of view. One has as its aim studying human motivation in organizations in order to be able to improve management's control of subordinates' behaviour. The other tries to make work inherently more satisfying for human beings by 'humanizing' work and avoiding what are seen as the excesses of certain managerial practices. As more cynical readers may well have observed already, the 'humanizing' orientation may merely be the first dressed in liberal clothes in the sense that it is really about making people feel happier and more fulfilled while making other people richer! Although many proponents of the 'humanizing' standpoint have often claimed 'positive' managerial payoffs (in terms of productivity, etc.) for their approach, we attempt to show that there are significant philosophical tensions in the articulation of the two views.

Motivation Theory

When one reviews the human motivation literature that is specifically concerned with work organizations, one is confronted with what appears to be a bewildering range of approaches that often seem to contradict one another, particularly in their prescriptions for appropriate managerial practice. One reason for this diversity comes from the underlying variations in the assumptions such writers make about the moral and ethical significance work has for people, and with which writers approach their subject of interest. It is important to emphasize that these assumptions have not come about in a haphazard fashion; many can be traced back to the differing significances work has been accorded in different times and cultures. We begin this section by describing some of these interpretations before relating the most significant to the human-motivation theory and literature.

If we take Plato's somewhat disparaging view of skilled artisans as described in his *Republic* as typical of his social peers, the ancient Greeks tended to assign a low social status to anyone who had to work at an occupation all the time. In this way, work was seen as a demeaning necessity best carried out by a slave population until it was possible to abolish work itself (Arendt, 1959, p. 74; Meakin, 1976, p. 2). Prior to the Protestant Reformation, Christianity also had a similarly jaundiced view of work, since it was seen as a necessity for people to work as a penance, a direct result of 'original sin'. As Grint (1991, p. 17) points out, it was in contemplation and otherworldly spirituality, not work, where lay the route to salvation.

Kumar (1984) provides evidence to suggest that, in pre-industrial Europe, people who had to work out of sheer economic necessity appear to have held attitudes towards work that are considerably different from those that are often assumed to characterize modern society. He claims (*ibid.* p. 4) that

> Industrial peoples harbour profound prejudices and illusions about non-industrial peoples, one especially potent one being that they are all bowed down by a lifetime of unremitting toil . . . The ancient Romans . . . so piled up festival days that it is estimated that in the middle of the fourth century AD Roman citizens had 175 days a year off. For the European Middle Ages, contemporary evidence suggests that agricultural workers spent nearly a third of the year in leisure, while Paris craftsmen, for instance, worked for only about 194 days in the year – that is, nearly half the year was leisure time.

However, with the spread of the Protestant Reformation in sixteenth-century Europe, and the subsequent spread of industrialization, a new understanding of the ethical significance of work developed that provided work with the status of moral duty; idleness was hence associated with sinfulness. This elevation in the status of work is closely associated with the Calvinist theological notion of the 'predestined elect'. This doctrine claimed that the individual's salvation or damnation was predetermined by God. This led to an almost neurotic striving to demonstrate that one had God's grace, and was thereby a member of the predestined elect for whom God had predetermined salvation. This election was demonstrated by the believer achieving worldly success (Weber, 1976; Anthony, 1977). Thus it was work rather than spirituality that 'could either save your soul or at least be taken as confirmation that your soul was already saved' (Grint, 1991, pp. 17–18).

This ideological watershed also provided fertile ground for the propagation of a view of science that was based on active intervention in the world (e.g. experimentation), as previously advocated by Francis Bacon (Rattansi, 1972; Tiles, 1987). This new science entailed the moral imperative that 'man' must recover 'his' dominion over nature, which had been lost in the 'Fall'. This in its turn involved the rejection of the previously dominant view of science that was based on Aristotle's teleological perspective: science was a disinterested, passive contemplation of an unchangeable 'natural order'.

Later, especially in the Victorian era, the Protestant ethic was expressed through an ideology that invoked a moral imperative by 'linking the duty to work to religious incantations' (Grint, 1991, p. 18). According to Mathias (1969, p. 208, quoted in Grint, 1991, p. 18), the result was that 'the virtues of hard work . . . saving, thrift, sobriety became the new social imperatives dinned into the heads of the new working classes by their social betters by every known means of communication. They were enshrined in Nonconformist and evangelical doctrine'.

The degree to which this ideology penetrated the British working classes' popular consciousness or, indeed, that of the aristocracy, is of course open to debate (Hobsbawm, 1964). Moreover, several competing ideologies, with alternative webs of philosophical assumptions, were developing at this time. For example, a very different view of the importance of work to human beings emerged during the Enlightenment of eighteenth-century Europe. This period (whose motto, according to Immanuel Kant, was 'dare to know') was characterized by an upheaval in 'thought' (particularly with respect to the possibilities of reason in controlling human life), out of which evolved the new philosophies and new approaches to science. It was also during the Enlightenment that work was begun to be seen both as a means of providing economic necessities and as a potential source of special satisfaction if chosen freely and creative – since such work was seen as an inextricable part of people's humanity and intelligence. In contrast to forced, non-creative work, creative work was seen as an end in itself, natural to human instincts, since it was 'man's' creative interaction with the natural environment that distinguished 'man' from other animals. To an extent this perspective, often called *homo faber*, was expressed in the early work of Karl Marx (e.g. 1973) as well as more recently in the work of both Freud and Jung. Indeed, Jung claimed that such work could form a kind of liberation, but only when 'it is a free act and has nothing of infantile constraint about it' (Jung, quoted in Meakin, 1976, p. 5).

This view of work can be contrasted with the Utilitarian view, which recognized implicitly that with industrialization work was becoming increasingly monotonous, deskilled and intrinsically unrewarding (Kumar, 1984, p. 9). Utilitarianism was articulated by such writers as Adam Smith in *The Wealth of Nations* (1937). Smith saw work as being a necessary evil people will only engage in (and thereby forgo some leisure time for) when they calculate from a vantage point of self-interest some economic or material incentive or compensation. That is, work is something that will only be done to satisfy economic or material needs.

Many aspects of these competing ideologies remain with us today and they are expressed in the way we apprehend the moral and ethical significance of work and what motivates people to work. It is thus hardly surprising that the various philosophical assumptions, beliefs and values that underpin these ideologies have been highly influential on the ways motivation theorists and researchers, as well as management practitioners, have engaged with and continue to engage with human motivation in work organizations. We therefore now turn to these writers and attempt to show the webs of assumptions they apply and the practical ramifications of their subsequent modes of engagement.

It is possible to identify several contrasting approaches to motivation in work organizations, along with their corollary assumptions about their subjects of interest, employees, by following Schein (1965) and Grint (1991). These are illustrated in Figure 3.2.

{1} Scientific Management ⟷ Homo Economicus

{2} Human Relations ⟷ Homo Gregarious

{3} Neo Human Relations ⟷ Homo Actualis

Figure 3.2   Three approaches to motivation in work organizations

Scientific Management: *Homo economicus*

During (and particularly after) the American Civil War, a managerial hierarchy arose in the USA to co-ordinate and control the newly developed mass-
production and distribution enterprises and to supervise such major projects as
the building of railways and the installation of telegraph systems (Chandler,
1977). Important to the development of this managerial cadre was the role
played by engineers, who had graduated from the military academy at West
Point (Hoskin and Macve, 1988). These managers seem to have approached
their managerial duties by applying the disciplinary elements of their own prior
educational experiences. This regime had been developed by Sylvanus Thayer.
According to Hoskin and Macve (*ibid.* p. 66), this nascent managerial cadre
had internalized, during their education, a new system of 'disciplinary organisation and human accountability'. This they proceeded to export to the world
of business through their subsequent careers in the railways and armouries.
Their approach to management engendered a 'new form of disciplinary accountability over men and objects within the factory' (*ibid.*). It is to these men
and to the occupational associations with which they became involved (such as
the American Society of Mechanical Engineers) that it is possible to trace the
sporadic emergence of many accounting procedures (*ibid.*), as well as the
amalgam of disciplinary techniques known as scientific management. Scientific
management was aimed primarily at measuring and controlling people's work
on the shopfloor and this was subsequently codified, theorized and popularized
by Frederick Winslow Taylor during the 1890s (Taylor, 1947).

Many accounts of Taylor's ideas and managerial practices (including his
own) illustrate his fixation for establishing what he saw as efficiency in many
aspects of everyday life, especially work. Instead of following his father in a
legal career, Taylor had embarked upon apprenticeships in pattern-making
and machining before joining the Midvale Steel Company in 1878, apparently
as a labourer. He soon rose to foreman. It was from his experiences on the
shopfloor that Taylor thought he had identified the main sources of inefficiency
in business enterprises.

Taylor begins his analysis by castigating management for what he saw as
their incompetence. He considered management to be far from 'scientific'; it
was instead based on 'rule of thumb' schemes and practices that failed to
control and discipline shopfloor employees. This and its resultant inefficiency
occurred primarily because management did not possess a basic understanding
of what it was employees did in undertaking their work. According to Taylor,
this lack of knowledge about and information on what actually happened on
the shopfloor left management unable to control employee behaviour effectively. Such ignorance left shopfloor activities under the control of operatives
in whose interests it was 'systematically to soldier' – to restrict their output
because of their justifiable fears of rate-cutting and redundancy. To Taylor,
such inefficiencies were further compounded by operatives' employing inefficient working practices and by what he called 'natural soldiering', which he
thought occurred because of the propensity for laziness inherent in human
nature. Thus, as Braverman (1974) implies, scientific management might be
seen initially as an attempt to secure information about the labour process in

order to control it. However, it is the effect of the assumptions with which such people as Taylor pursued their subject that leads to their distinctive approach to the resolution of motivational issues in work organizations.

The key assumptions underpinning the approach to human motivation followed by scientific management are Utilitarian and Hobbesian. As we have shown, according to a Utilitarian approach, people are 'rational-economic' beings motivated primarily by economic reward in the sense that people will only work harder when they are convinced that such expenditure of effort will reward them with money. The Hobbesian approach assumes that people, in their 'natural state', are lazy, aggressive, self-centred, hedonistic and greedy. Driven by these self-seeking and competitive impulses, life according to Hobbes was 'solitary, poor, nasty, brutish and short' as men attempted to acquire dominion over others. Because of these inherent propensities, if it was not for the controls provided by society, Hobbes' 'common wealth' or 'state', life would be a 'war of all against all' (Hobbes, 1964). Hence, when what are perceived as behavioural problems arise in society and its institutions, and these are observed by such people as Taylor through the implicit 'lens' of Hobbesian assumptions, the resulting analysis will tend to emphasize that such problems are caused by a situation of under-control or inappropriate control, which allows the letting loose of human beings' natural instincts. Such a combination of Hobbesian and Utilitarian assumptions are evident in Taylor's understanding of, and his analysis of and prescriptions for, the motivation of shopfloor employees.

The Prescriptions of Scientific Management

Taylor clearly believed that the inefficiencies caused by what he saw as employees' tendencies towards systematic and natural soldiering could be eradicated by management's control of employees' economic rationality. If employees were convinced that only by working harder could they gain greater economic reward, many of the problems he had observed on the shopfloor would be resolved. This leads to two basic prescriptions for management practice:

1. Management must be able to measure the amount of effort an employee is putting into his or her job so that a 'scientific' incentive (cash) can be awarded in proportion to that expended effort, thereby encouraging greater effort.
2. Management must design and specify tasks independently of the jobholder. In so doing, they will be able to identify the most efficient way to do the tasks. Inefficient working practices would thus be avoided, enabling management to gain a clear understanding of the operations any task entails.

These prescriptions were to be operated through several interrelated management practices. To measure effort expended, Taylor thought that it was essential to simplify tasks. The complex tasks done by skilled operatives, which at that time remained largely a mystery to management (thus making the measurement of effort virtually impossible), had to be broken down into their simpler, constituent elements. This would allow management to determine the effort necessary from an 'average worker' to complete such a task. A 'scientific incentive' – cash – could then be related directly to the effort expended. Simplifying tasks also enables tasks to be analysed so that those procedures that would maximize an operative's productivity with minimum expenditure of effort and resources could be identified – 'the one best way'. Taylor considered that, if operatives specialized in doing just a few simplified tasks, they would become much more efficient and productive because of the practice gained through repetition. Taylor's prescriptions for a fragmented and specialized division of labour resonate with Adam Smith's celebrated account of pin manufacture in *The Wealth of Nations*, which was published in 1776. Smith (1937, pp. 3–12) argues that, if one worker is given the task of doing everything necessary to manufacture a pin, even with his utmost industry he would barely be able to make one pin a day. However, if one worker made the wire, another straightened it, a third cut it, a fourth ground the points, with others to make the head and to assemble and finish the resultant product, then ten operatives employed in such a fashion could produce at least 48,000 pins a day! Taylor believed that such a micro-division of labour had the added advantage that labour was, in effect, deskilled; this facilitated the employment of easily replaced, cheaper, unskilled labour, for all parts of a task.

Taylor's attempts at rationalizing individuals' work, by removing the control of how work was done from what he thought the capricious intentions of wilful operatives, are perhaps best illustrated by his own account of the experiments he undertook with a Dutch immigrant he calls 'Schmidt' at the Bethlehem Steel Works. Schmidt was a pig-iron handler, whom Taylor disparaged by likening his mentality to that of an ox and by ridiculing his Dutch accent. Schmidt was in fact called Henry Knolle, a man who had recently built his own house! Perhaps Taylor's jaundiced account of his dealings with Schmidt tells us more about Taylor and his attitudes than about Henry Knolle. After observing and analysing Schmidt's working practices closely, Taylor began to redesign his job by introducing rest breaks, changing his methods of working along the lines described above, and instituting financial incentives. The result was that Schmidt's productivity increased significantly by around 400 per cent while his wages increased from $1.15 to $1.85 a day. When Taylor instituted these changes throughout the pig-iron handling gang, productivity rose by almost 400 per cent and wages rose by around 60 per cent. Thus the cost of pig-iron handling dropped substantially, as did the number of men employed at such tasks – by about 70 per cent.

As already pointed out, an important element in Taylor's approach was the removal of the knowledge previously possessed by the operative – 'conception' was removed from the 'execution' of tasks (see Taylor, 1947, p. 36). Control must be taken from the operative and must become the prerogative and monopoly of management. Management, having identified the 'one best way', had to translate such knowledge into 'rules, laws and formulae' (*ibid.*) and ensure that operatives followed those protocols and procedures in the completion of their tasks, which were considered to be relatively 'fixed'. It was management's duty to select employees with the psychological and physiological characteristics demanded by the tasks they had designed.

Thus the planning, co-ordinating and reintegrating of production processes based on a micro-division of labour became the management's responsibility, with operatives working according to management's detailed instructions. Scientific management thus attacked individual operative's control over their work, as well as the control of subcontracting gang bosses (Littler, 1982). The result was a bureaucratization of the labour process, which allowed management to gain a degree of control over what was done on the shopfloor.

The division of labour in organizations was extended to the extent that tasks were fragmented into their smallest constituent units; this division was further reinforced by the development of piecework payment systems, which notionally related financial rewards directly to operatives' expended effort. In this way, both management and employees would be free to enjoy the fruits of maximum efficiency.

Clearly, Taylor expected that scientific management principles would lead to industrial harmony, since the 'corporate cake' would be larger and everyone would enjoy a larger 'slice'. He believed his 'scientific' way would end disputes about how hard people should work and what constituted equitable financial reward. Although many of his followers saw a role for trade unions in work organizations, for Taylor there was no place for trade unions in his brave new world. Unions regulated financial relations between employers and employees when there was no 'scientific' means of regulating that market relationship; this role was clearly redundant under a regime of his immutable 'scientific laws' that, he claimed, underpinned his approach.

The Failure of Scientific Management?

Since Taylor's death in 1915 it has been argued that, despite resistance from both employees (Friedman, 1977) and management (Gartman, 1979), scientific management – in a variety of guises, such as Fordism (Coriat, 1980) and Bedaux systems (Littler, 1982) – appears to have had a profound influence on management practice and work organization throughout Europe and the USA. Although some writers contest this claim (e.g. Zeitlin, 1983), others have argued that, by the end of the 1930s, most major European countries had experienced the application of some form of scientific management (Fridenson, 1978). Indeed, Littler (1982, pp. 114–15) claims that by 1939 Bedaux systems had become 'the most common system of managerial control'.

Perhaps at the behest of Lenin's injunctions (1968, pp. 413–14), it would seem that scientific management was widely adopted in the Soviet Union (Traub, 1978; Wren, 1980). Haraszti's (1977) poignant account of work in a Hungarian factory also implies that other ostensibly 'communist' countries were similarly affected by the spread of scientific management. Similarly, Kamata's account (1984) of his experiences as an assembly-line worker at Toyota would suggest that even Japanese organizations have not been immune to the growth of scientific management's techniques.

Thus, although there is still much debate about the extent and degree of scientific management's influence on management practice, it would seem that it is not just a phenomenon of mere historical curiosity; rather, it still endures in various forms, often complemented by later developments in managerial thought (Reid, 1978). As such it often appears to serve as an ideological backdrop that influences the form of the organizational change initiatives that accompany technological innovation (Davis and Taylor, 1978; Cooley, 1980; Rosenbrock, 1988). This view led Rosenbrock (1982) to conclude that the pursuit of 'Taylorism' in the past had given rise to poor-quality work, and labour turnover and unrest – all as a result of job fragmentation. These have also become more intensified and widespread through the use of information technology. Cooley (1980) has argued that micro-electronic technology constitutes a 'Trojan Horse' through which Taylorism has been introduced into what was formerly 'intellectual' white-collar work. These conclusions, however, must not deflect our attention from the alternative 'solutions' to motivation and control that have also developed during this century (Friedman, 1977; Littler and Salaman, 1982).

Many of the alternatives to scientific management can be seen as developing from different assumptions about the nature of human beings and their relationships to society and 'its' institutions. They can also be seen as reactions to the behavioural 'problems' associated with the application of scientific management to work organizations. Scientific management, from a managerial point of view, has become increasingly associated with several counter-productive effects and organizational 'problems'. Beynon's (1973) and Chinoy's (1955) accounts of, respectively, the work experiences of British and North American car-assembly workers both provide vivid pictures of the dehumanizing and alienating effects of such a fragmented division of labour. Blauner (1964) also made a useful contribution to understanding alienation by classifying it in four principal ways:

1. 'Powerlessness' is the inability to exert control over work processes.
2. 'Meaninglessness' is the lack of a sense of purpose, since the employee cannot relate his or her role to the overall production process because of the fragmented division of labour.
3. 'Self-estrangement' is the failure to become involved in work as a mode of self-expression.
4. 'Isolation' is the lack of a sense of belonging.

Scientific management's potential to create such alienating jobs can lead to employees' developing highly instrumental attitudes to work – for example, a fixation with the consumer products obtainable with the material rewards employment provides. In other words, scientific management can become a self-fulfilling prophecy: if people are expected to be recalcitrant and economically rational, they are likely to behave in such a fashion (Schein, 1965, p. 49).

However, alienation can also result in more active forms of resistance. As already noted, Blauner (1964) considers one important aspect of alienation to be a feeling of powerlessness in relation to the working environment (e.g. the machinery a worker operates). One active solution may be industrial sabotage, defined by Taylor and Walton (1971, pp. 226–38) as 'that rule breaking which takes the form of conscious action or inaction directed towards the mutilation or destruction of the working environment'. The meanings and motives underlying such behaviour allow three different types of sabotage to be classified (*ibid.* pp. 226–38):

1. To reduce tension and frustration.
2. To facilitate the work process.
3. To assert some form of direct control.

However, there appear to be alternative courses of action other than sabotage that might be caused by the alienating working environments associated with scientific management – one such being the strike (Hyman, 1972). A strike at the State-owned arsenal at Watertown, only several weeks after the introduction of scientific management, led indirectly to the banning of scientific management methods from all government-funded operations between 1916 and 1949 in the USA (Nyland, 1987).

While scientific management has long been associated with behavioural 'problems' at work, it has more recently become associated with inefficiencies arising from inflexibility. It has been argued (e.g. Kelly, 1985) that when an organization has a continuous, standardized and homogeneous throughput, as in the early days of car manufacturing (e.g. the black Model-T Ford motor car), scientific management could be an extremely efficient way of organizing work.

However, where such mass markets do not or no longer exist, and where thus there is a heterogeneous, rapidly changing and unpredictable throughput, tasks are no longer preprogrammable in the manner demanded by scientific management (e.g. under circumstances of variability in customer demand and/or product innovation – Child 1987). What may be required here is a more flexible, committed, itinerant and skilled workforce, capable of exercising discretion so that it can cope with the uncertainties created by fluctuations in product demand and technology. This may not be possible under scientific management or its derivatives (Piore and Sable, 1984; Piore, 1986; Badham and Matthews, 1989). However, some degree of flexibility may be achieved by using new, flexible, production technologies in conjunction with what amounts to scientific management (Coriat, 1980; Smith, 1989). Thus the behavioural and organizational problems associated with scientific management, together with alternative philosophical assumptions about the nature of human beings and their relationships to society's institutions, lead to the development of alternative approaches to human motivation in work organizations.

The Human Relations Movement: *Homo gregarious*

The human relations approach to human motivation can, to some extent, be found first in the work of North American and British industrial psychologists during the First World War. This work, which was concerned with the selection, testing and classification of army recruits, led to the application of psychological approaches to work organizations. Lupton (1971) claims that these initial developments sought both to increase employees' productivity and personal satisfaction by easing the employee's difficulties rather than by the use of sanctions. However, its close relationship to scientific management is illustrated by Sofer's (1973, p. 60) appraisal that its prime concern was increased productivity by reducing friction and control problems by 'helping in the selection and training of people to fit the structure better'. In this sense, this work largely complements scientific management. Its starting point was a series of experiments carried out at the Western Electric Company's Hawthorne plant in Chicago, which led to the development of a model of motivation that is distinct from that underpinning scientific management. At this plant in 1924, a series of experiments was begun aimed at investigating the relationship between different kinds of working conditions (such as illumination, temperature, humidity and the frequency of rest pauses) and employees' productivity (Roethlisberger and Dickson, 1939). Underlying this research was an assumption that, for instance, there was an ideal level of illumination or temperature at which productivity would be maximized. Such physical working conditions were considered independent variables, which were manipulated by the researchers. Any subsequent effects on the dependent variable (employee output) were monitored.

To pursue this research, two groups of employees, matched in terms of productivity, were selected and isolated from the rest of the workforce by being placed in what amounted to laboratory conditions in different parts of the plant. One group, the experimental group, experienced variations in their physical working conditions, while the other group, the control group, did not experience such manipulation. The productivity of each group was then monitored. The rationale behind this was that any discernible difference between the output of each group must be a result of variations in their physical working conditions. The findings were rather unexpected and confusing. For example, output in the experimental group increased, regardless of how illumination was manipulated (*ibid.* pp. 14–15). Even when lighting was dimmed to a flicker, output still increased. Output in the control group also steadily increased, despite the absence of experimental manipulation.

The researchers then conducted a series of experiments in the relay assembly test-room, to facilitate a more detailed investigation of the effects of different physical conditions. These experiments once more entailed segregating a group of employees (whose output had been secretly measured) from other workers, and varying their working conditions while monitoring their output. No matter what the researchers did – even lengthening the working day and reducing rest periods – there appeared to be little effect on an upward trend in productivity.

These events led the researchers to conclude that they were not simply investigating the effects of changing physical conditions on productivity. One explanation was that employees had been made to feel special by being the focus of so much attention. These feelings increased their morale, which in turn led to higher productivity. The researchers considered that, inadvertently, they had investigated employee attitudes, values and norms generated by the experiments themselves – the 'Hawthorne effect'.

Later research, conducted in the early 1930s and which developed out of such findings as these, involved the detailed observation of a group of fourteen men over a seven-month period who worked in the bank wiring-room. This research was far more anthropological in its approach, as the men remained in their normal, everyday work setting. While no physical working conditions were altered, an incentive scheme was introduced to reward group output financially. Although the group appeared not to understand fully how this incentive scheme worked, it was noted that the group appeared to control their output to what they considered a fair day's work – 'the bogey'. This output norm not only restricted output to a maximum (overproducers were castigated by their colleagues as 'ratebusters') but it also deemed what was acceptable to the group as a minimum (underproducers were considered to be 'chisellers'). Indeed, this norm was not only enforced by verbal abuse directed at deviants but there is also evidence to suggest that there was a threat of physical violence. Despite methodological problems in the research designs used (Gill and Johnson, 1991, pp. 48–52), these findings have been credited with raising important questions about motivation and the role of the 'informal' organization (Schein, 1965).

Although Roethlisberger and Dickson (1939) published a detailed account of their research at the Hawthorne plant, it is Elton Mayo's less sophisticated, empirically dubious and rather polemical analysis (1940, 1949) of the substantive research findings that laid down the foundations of human-relations theory and its associated management practices. Important in this interpretation is Mayo's reliance upon the Durkheimian concept of 'anomie'.

Writing during the last quarter of the nineteenth century, Durkheim (1960) argued that one effect of the social and technological changes that had accompanied industrialization and urbanization was the development of an increasingly complex, specialized and differentiated division of labour. A result of this was that the traditional mechanism of a social order based on the subordination of the individual to systems of shared values, beliefs and sentiments embedded in the common experience of an undifferentiated population (mechanical solidarity) had been effectively destroyed. Durkheim felt a new social order, based on contractual relationships engendered by the interdependence of a differentiated division of labour (organic solidarity) had failed to develop properly (Clegg and Dunkerley, 1980a, p. 22). The resulting social disequilibrium, which Durkheim considered transient, was characterized by 'anomie' – people had insufficient or inappropriate norms through which they might, by consensus, determine appropriate behaviour. Merton (1957, p. 162) defines anomie usefully as 'a breakdown in the cultural structure, occurring particularly when there is an acute disjunction between the cultural norms and goals and the socially structured capacities of members of the group to act in accord with them'. The changes Durkheim had observed during the latter part of the nineteenth century had necessarily created a complex and hierarchical division of labour. This increasing differentiation had also sown the seeds of moral anarchy and conflict, particularly in the economic sphere; it had brought about a disintegration of the old moral order that was based on a uniformity of beliefs in society and its institutions (conscience collective). Durkheim believed that new norms of behaviour, expressed as new forms of collective morality and social cohesion, would have to be constructed to regulate social behaviour and to eradicate anomie. This would rectify the still-persistent problems that had been caused by an abnormal or forced division of labour created by the imposition of coercive power.

Armed with this Durkheimian perspective, Mayo drew attention to the role of emotions and sentiments in the regulation of workers' behaviour by arguing that human co-operation at work had always relied on the evolution of a 'nonlogical social code'. However, this code had disintegrated under the pressures generated by the social and technological changes of recent years – particularly the spread of political liberalism with its stress on individualism, as well as the ever-increasing division of labour (Rose, 1975, pp. 120–4). In shopfloor employees, these anomic pressures engendered norms that were inimical to, and effectively subverted, management's aims. To Mayo it was therefore imperative to 'repair social solidarity at the level of the organisation' by instilling in employees a 'sense of its corporate consciousness' (Clegg and Dunkerley, 1980a, p. 122).

Referring to data from the Hawthorne research, Mayo claimed it was possible to reintegrate these isolated individuals by encouraging their conformity to the appropriate norms in work groups that had been socially engineered to create them. A suitably trained managerial élite would control and enable this intervention into this informal aspect of organizational life. As Grint (1991, p. 127) observes, conformity to the norms instigated by management was to be

> the normal path for the mass of non-rational subordinates in organisations who would only become anxious if left to decide for themselves. In short, although the attitudes of workers appeared unpredictable, this merely made the task of the manager more concerned with rooting out such contingencies and ensuring the direction of organisations could be determined by expert managers.

To Mayo, developing management's social skills would be vital to allow a manipulation of workers' non-logical sentiments when replacing the destroyed traditional bonds of community. In particular, Mayo advocated that management and supervisors should develop such communication and interpersonal skills as leadership and counselling to nurture the worker's 'desire and capacity to work better with management' (Mayo, 1949, p. 74–5, quoted in Rose, 1975, p. 122).

In sum, Mayo argued that employee morale and motivation could be 'improved' by managers who were better able to elicit their co-operation by becoming more sensitive to their social needs and who could stimulate therapeutical norms compatible with management's aims and intentions. As Butler (1986, p. 218) puts it, Mayo attributed to the worker a need to belong that is so obsessive it will 'lead him to espouse the cause of any group which has exhibited social concern for him'. He likens Mayo's aims to an attempt to create a social system that has the nesting properties of a Russian doll:

> the informal group captures the individual, and the firm captures the informal group . . . [By] its power to absorb totally the successive smaller dolls of the informal group and the individual, the firm eventually creates a closed system in which it is allegedly able to shape the perceptions of the worker to its own ends. It would do so by making the employee believe that there existed a paternalistic relationship towards him on the part of the firm.
>
> (*Ibid.*)

Management was therefore encouraged to intervene consciously in the informal organization that had developed spontaneously out of members' everyday social interaction to build a new moral order, which would 'create and sustain consent . . . to recreate a sense of community inside the workplace, a call we are again hearing from advocates of corporate culture' (Thompson and McHugh, 1990, p. 81). That many modern writers resonate with Mayo's Durkheimian perspective is shown by their notion that, if the appropriate values and attitudes are internalized, a common sense of purpose or 'moral involvement' activated by emotion and sentiment develops; this makes the constant surveillance of organizational members – as a form of control – redundant (e.g. Pascale and Athos, 1981; Peters and Waterman, 1982). As Mitchell comments – with specific reference to Peters and Waterman's (1982) work – the implicit idea is that it is 'management's job . . . to shape the person and his or her values so that they conform with the values of effort, productivity, teamwork, and striving for excellence . . . management not only manipulates people to believe in certain values; management constructs the values without any real adherence or belief in them' (Mitchell, 1985, pp. 352–5).

The Implications for Motivation Theory and Management Practice

The implications for motivation theory and management practice that emerged from the Hawthorne research were, basically, at odds with those of scientific management. The Hawthorne research appeared to have shown that there was little correlation between economic incentives and productivity. This indicated that economic rationality was not the only influence upon employee be-haviour; it also drew attention to how people derived a source of need satisfaction at work from their sense of belonging and from their opportunities for meaningful relationships provided by their membership of work groups within the organization.

Employee behaviour was seen to be influenced strongly by a series of social and emotional factors. The informal organization, particularly, was a key influence on members' behaviour. Its power seemed such that it could promote productivity, as in the case of the relay assembly test-room; or, as in the case of the bank wiring-room, it could, alternatively, encourage restriction of output. If management could engineer and cultivate sentiments that supported their aims by attending to employees' social and emotional needs, the result would be higher productivity and social harmony.

Thus, scientific management's view of people as socially isolated and econ-omically rational beings was replaced by the belief that human beings were basically social animals who gained a sense of identity from social relation-ships. This implied that management needed to focus its attention on the group rather than the individual. Human relations, therefore, represents a significant departure from scientific management's universalistic economic model of em-ployee behaviour to an equally universalistic socio-emotional model. In effect, *Homo economicus* had been displaced by *Homo gregarious*. As Schein (1965, p. 34) succinctly claims, the Hawthorne studies were 'one of the major forces' that resulted in a concern with how informal associations of groups 'pro-foundly affect the motivation to work, the level of output and the quality of work done'.

The Failure of Human Relations?

The élitist notion that management could and should assume the role of disseminators of social harmony in work organizations (Baritz, 1965) ensured the popularity of human relations approaches among academics and management practitioners in both the USA (Bartell, 1976) and the UK (Child, 1969). For instance, at the University of Michigan, Kurt Lewin appeared to be achieving Mayo's aims by demonstrating that managers (leaders) 'through communications (social skills), could manipulate participation (informal organisation) to produce a superior group climate (morale), thus enhancing satisfaction (integration) with the group life (social system) and improving performance (output)' (Rose, 1975, p. 163). In the UK, human relations led much of British management towards an analysis of employee productivity in terms of social motivations and the role of leadership (Child, 1969). However, in accomplishing this shift away from an analysis of physiological conditions, incentive schemes, work study, etc., to one that concentrated on individuals and interpersonal relations, likely technological, financial and socio-economic constraints bearing on management practice were discounted – an orientation Bennis (1959, p. 260) subsequently labelled as 'people without organisations'.

The human relations movement produced thousands of empirical studies about group motivation, morale and leadership that, in turn, engendered subsequent management practices. Perhaps the most significant aspect of this work was the study of leadership as a means of influencing employee behaviour (Likert, 1961). This work developed specific approaches to leadership training, such as sensitivity or T-group training, which were aimed specifically at modifying values and attitudes (National Training Laboratories, 1953; Argyris, 1962), as well as the promotion of participatory decision-making as a means of promoting a climate to stimulate motivation (Coch and French, 1948). At the same time, there was a concern about how informal group processes in work organizations influenced members' behaviour (Homans, 1950; Zaleznik *et al.*, 1958).

However, nearly all these developments have been, understandably, criticized on both ideological and empirical grounds. As derived from Mayo's original perspective, human relations clearly proposes the need for employees to conform to management-inspired and disseminated norms as the means to ensure social harmony in organizations. Such élitism, informed by its unitary view of organizations that considers any conflict harmful, and this compounded with its social-engineering priorities, was soon identified as a subtle type of manipulation and exploitation that ignored employees' legitimate economic interests (Braverman, 1974, pp. 139–51). Early in the development of human relations, the United Auto Workers described Mayo and his colleagues as 'cow sociologists' seeking to milk employees by making them more contented with their lot (Baritz, 1965, p. 114–15). While such criticisms of human relations' ideological basis are important, perhaps even more devastating was the problem that years of empirical research had failed to demonstrate any clear relationship between such things as leadership style and employee productivity.

Neo-Human Relations: *Homo actualis*

After the Second World War, an approach to work organization closely related to human relations emerged but which was founded on much more sophisticated concepts of human needs and motivation. This school of thought and its derived management practices, often dubbed neo-human relations, shifted the earlier focus of human relations away from an analysis of members' social interaction within working groups to one that emphasized the individual. However in accomplishing this, they maintain a critique of what is perceived as scientific management's overly coercive approach, which they felt was derived from inappropriate assumptions about human needs. The main element of this alternative approach is the desire to integrate individual and 'organizational' goals through a process of 'self-actualization'. This is perhaps best illustrated in the work of one of neo-human relations' exponents, Douglas McGregor.

In *The Human Side of Enterprise* (1960), McGregor argues that the way enterprises were traditionally organized tended to be practical expressions of webs of managerial values and assumptions about human nature and behaviour – which McGregor called 'Theory X'. This philosophy of management has the following elements:

1. It is highly utilitarian in that people are considered to have an inherent dislike of work and they will avoid it if they can.
2. Because of their inherent indolence, people must be coerced to gain their compliance with 'organizational' objectives, to which they would otherwise remain indifferent.
3. Rather than wishing autonomy and responsibility at work, most people prefer to be directed by hierarchical superiors.

McGregor was highly critical of such views and the managerial practices they spawned, not because of some humanitarian impulse but because he saw the model of human motivation that underpinned Theory X to be fundamentally misconceived. In developing an alternative philosophy, which he called 'Theory Y', McGregor implicitly and explicitly drew on the work of two writers, Abraham Maslow (a practising clinical psychologist) and Chris Argyris (a staunch critic of bureaucratic forms of work organization). The alternative philosophy of Theory Y has the following principles:

1. Employees may appear to be recalcitrant and unco-operative, but this is not because of some inherent dislike of work itself – rather it is an outcome of their experience of management's traditional approach to work organization and control.
2. Most people are capable of exercising imagination, ingenuity and creativity in their exercise of self-control, and self-direction in the pursuit of objectives to which they are committed. In most modern organizations, such capacities are under-utilized.
3. Coercion is not the only or the most appropriate motivator. The most significant rewards are intrinsic to work and relate to the satisfaction of higher-order needs.
4. If conditions are right, it is possible to integrate the achievement of

organizational goals with the satisfaction of employees' higher-order needs. One result of this will be that not only will individuals accept responsibility but they will also actively seek it.

In proposing Theory Y as a radical alternative to traditional modes of management and organization, McGregor argued that management's essential task should be to ensure that organizational conditions should be such that people could best achieve their own goals by directing their efforts towards organizational objectives.

In order to understand the repercussions of this on managerial practice, it is necessary to turn to Argyris and Maslow's work. However, before doing so, it is worth pointing out that, in contrast to the Hobbesian assumptions that epitomize Theory X, it is possible to discern in McGregor's Theory Y a very different set of philosophical assumptions about 'human nature' and work's moral and ethical significance to human beings.

Although stripped of any radical critique of capitalist society and its institutions, which might have given McGregor's argument a more overtly Marxian–Hegelian flavour, Theory Y seems to share a concept of alienation with that of Rousseau. Unlike Hobbes, Jean-Jaques Rousseau (1983) regarded human beings in their natural state as 'noble savages' who displayed the qualities of kindliness, altruism, freedom, equality and brotherhood. However, the development of society and its institutions had resulted in inequality, which corrupted human beings' dignity and freedom, and which was a source of social ills and moral depravity. Redemption and the resolution of society's problems was only possible through the re-establishment of the moral worth, freedom and dignity of the individual. Rousseau's philosophy might encourage a romantic yearning for earlier and simpler times as a solution to modern society's corruption of human instincts; alternatively, it could also inform an analysis of the problems of modern work organizations that assumes that a causal factor of the problems is over-control or alienation. Alienation distorts and constrains the inherent human propensities invoked by the notion of the 'noble savage'. This notion is a set of assumptions evident in the work of neo-human-relations theorists. It can be contrasted with the essentially Hobbesian outlook that not only informs scientific management's assumptions but also, through the concept of anomie, much of human relations. Neo-human relations is based on rival assumptions about human nature in the same way that the concepts of alienation and anomie are in opposition. Lukes (1978) is helpful here. While Durkheim sides with Hobbes, Marx sides with Rousseau:

> For the former [Hobbes], man is a bundle of desires, which need to be regulated, tamed, repressed, manipulated and given direction for the sake of social order, whereas for the latter [Rousseau], man is still an angel, rational and good, who requires a rational and good society in which to develop his essential nature . . . For the former, coercion, external authority, and restraint are necessary and desirable for social order and individual happiness; for the latter they are an offence against reason and an attack upon freedom.
> (Lukes, 1978, p. 145)

As the concept of alienation leads to an analysis couched in terms of over-

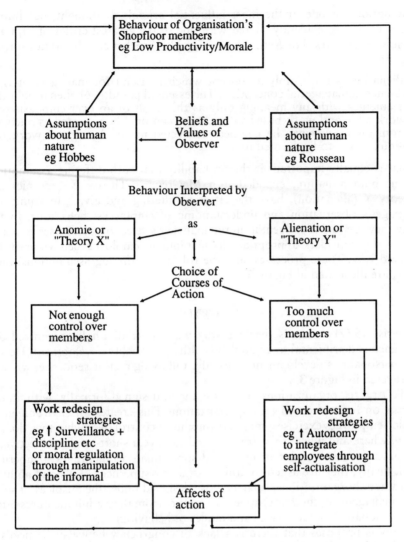

Figure 3.3 How differing assumptions about human nature affect a manager's decisions

control, the concept of anomie leads to an analysis framed in terms of a lack of control – moral or otherwise:

> Whereas anomic man is, for Durkheim, the unregulated man who needs rules to live by, limits to his desires, 'circumscribed tasks' to perform and 'limited horizons' for his thoughts, alienated man is for Marx a man in the grip of a system, who 'cannot escape' from a 'particular exclusive sphere of activity which is forced upon him'.
>
> (*Ibid.* p. 141)

It is thus perhaps one of the greatest paradoxes in management theory that the assumptions of one of the most influential schools of thought, neo-human relations, are so evidently shared with one of the greatest critics of capitalist society, Karl Marx. For Anthony (1977, p. 304) such a paradox is not surprising, since

> alienation is not simply a concept which is useful for managers, it is, in essence, a managerial conception. The essential paradox of alienation is that it emerges with any meaning only as the result of an over-emphasis on a work ethic and work-based values. Man can only be regarded as alienated from his work when he has been subjected to an ideology of work that requires him to be devoted to it.

What is equally important is the probability that such differing assumptions about human nature, encoded into McGregor's Theory X (anomie) and Theory Y (alienation), have the effect of filtering and giving meaning to a manager's observation and understanding of employees' behaviour. In this way they are highly influential in the manager's selection of courses of action he or she considers appropriate to manipulate employee behaviour in the desired way. These processes, and the role such differing assumptions might play, are illustrated in Figure 3.3.

Argyris

Argyris (1957) contends that the way work is traditionally organized and designed is detrimental to an adult's healthy personality development. He sees the personality's development as usually following a clear sequence, which is illustrated in Figure 3.4.

To Argyris, organizations are, in the main, designed formally, with an emphasis on hierarchy and task specialization. This creates an environment in which employees exercise a minimal amount of control over what they do, and how, where and when; they are expected to have a short-term perspective, to be passive, to be dependent upon and subordinate to hierarchical superiors; and, finally, they are asked to utilize just a few superficial skills and abilities. Traditional organizations, such as those designed under the auspices of scientific management, therefore, appear to require from their adult members infantile personality characteristics and modes of behaviour.

Argyris proposes that there is a lack of congruency between the needs of the healthy adult and the demands of this type of formal organization. In such organizations, management tends to try to reduce subordinates' autonomy by creating over-control through job fragmentation and specialization. This, often exacerbated by authoritarian leadership, causes feelings of frustration and failure, and it engenders conflict. McGregor, similarly, considers that Theory X allows only for the same, limited perspective of childhood – the result of which is childish behaviour from the frustrated adult employees.

Maslow

Maslow (1943, 1954) developed his theory of human motivation out of analyses of the biographies of such historical figures as Einstein, and out of his

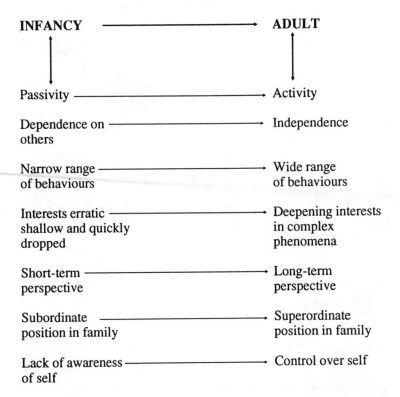

INFANCY ────────────────→ **ADULT**

Passivity ──────────────────→ Activity

Dependence on ──────────────→ Independence
others

Narrow range ───────────────→ Wide range
of behaviours   of behaviours

Interests erratic ──────────→ Deepening interests
shallow and quickly   in complex
dropped   phenomena

Short-term ─────────────────→ Long-term
perspective   perspective

Subordinate ────────────────→ Superordinate
position in family   position in family

Lack of awareness ──────────→ Control over self
of self

Figure 3.4   Argyris's personality development model

own experience as a clinical psychologist. As a clinical psychologist, he selected
and interviewed a number of people on the basis of their not having any
symptoms of neurotic behaviour but feelings of psychological well-being. He
found that these people shared many personality characteristics, which he
considered to be a new personality type, the 'self-actualizing' personality.
Greatly influenced by his humanistic values, he considered human beings to be
rational and purposeful entities, whose actions are initiated by attempts to
satisfy changing needs.

Of considerable significance to Maslow was the idea that unsatisfied needs
serve as 'magnets' that attract efforts to satisfy them; however, once those
needs are satisfied they no longer motivate behaviour – a person's behaviour
then becomes orientated towards other matters: needs as yet unsatisfied. Such
needs occur in a hierarchy of importance, which he called 'prepotency'. Needs
occurring at the higher levels of this hierarchy do not influence behaviour until
lower-level needs have been satisfied. As soon as a lower-level need has been
satisfied, needs on the next hierarchical level become activated, and these serve
as an influence on the individual's behaviour. Thus, as time passes and circumstances change, the needs that motivate an individual's behaviour vary in
importance. It follows from this that motivation is a dynamic force expressed
in individuals by their striving constantly and unconsciously towards the

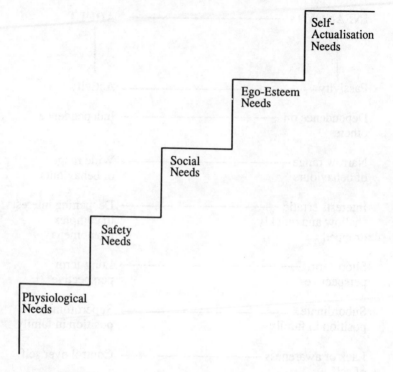

Figure 3.5   Maslow's hierarchy of needs

fulfilment of new, higher-order needs. Maslow considered that this hierarchy of needs, which everyone possesses, consists of five levels – see Figure 3.5.

Physiological needs
Physiological needs refer to the basic need for food, water, oxygen, sleep and sexual gratification, etc., which are the most powerful determinants of be haviour when they are not being satisfied. Organizational factors important in satisfying these needs include such things as pay and working conditions. Once these needs are relatively satisfied, they merge into the background, and the next hierarchical level of needs emerges as an influence on behaviour.

Safety needs
Safety needs concern the achievement of control over some of life's uncertainties and a subsequent reduction in anxiety – for example, the desire for security, and protection from the threat of being deprived of the ability to satisfy physiological needs. Organizational factors important in satisfying these needs include such things as health and safety at work, job security and welfare provision.

Social needs
Social needs reflect human beings' gregarious propensities – their need for friendship, affection, love and a sense of belonging. Organizational factors that allow for the satisfaction of social needs include membership of a cohesive and

supportive work group, as well as friendly interaction with supervisors and managers. Again, according to Maslow, once this level of needs is satisfied, then its influence as a motivator wanes and the next class of needs becomes an important influence.

Ego needs

Ego (or esteem) needs display humans' desire for internal self-esteem and the more externally derived esteem of others. Self-esteem includes the development of a positive self-image, self-confidence and self-respect; external esteem refers to the desire to acquire public respect, prestige, status and acclaim. Key organizational factors that enable the satisfaction of these needs include such things as social recognition, organizational status and positive feedback from others.

Self-actualization

Self-actualization is, for Maslow, the highest and last class of needs in the hierarchy, and it corresponds with ultimate psychological health. However, in a way it is the weakest level since all other classes of needs must be satisfied in order for it to emerge as an influence on behaviour. Maslow describes self-actualization not as a fixed state but as a continuous, unique and highly personal process of becoming whatever an individual is capable of becoming – self-fulfilment. Viewed in this way, unlike other needs it is ultimately insatiable; it is a constant striving to achieve and sustain that which is a person's potentiality. Self-actualization means a process of unfolding potentialities, abilities and competencies any individual possesses but are made actual. Organizational factors that allow for the pursuit of self-fulfilment include the opportunity for creativity, and achievement and advancement in a challenging work environment.

To McGregor, the message for management from this hierarchy of needs was obvious: organizations designed under the influence of Theory X ignored the dynamic nature of human needs. In focusing merely on the material and economic they had inadvertently stimulated employees' higher-order needs; management had no understanding of these, and they did not have the organizational arrangements to satisfy them. The result was that managers found it increasingly difficult to motivate employees. McGregor echoes Maslow's (1943) estimate that the average working adult had satisfied 85 per cent of their physiological needs and 70 per cent of their safety needs – because management had exhausted the only motivator their organizational designs allowed for: providing high standards of living. Although such an inference may imply, dubiously, that there is some absolute level at which Maslow's lower-order needs become satiated, thereby ignoring the likelihood that such levels are socially defined, socially relative and thus variable, McGregor proceeds to conclude that management had to develop the means by which the individual's need for self-actualization could be integrated with the achievement of goals sanctioned by management.

While there are various elaborations on and refinements of Maslow's model of human needs (e.g. Alderfer, 1972), perhaps the most important of these for managerial practice is Herzberg, Mausner and Snyderman's (1959) empirical research.

Herzberg

Herzberg's motivation-hygiene theory of motivation was developed from research into the relationship between job satisfaction and productivity among 200 Pittsburgh engineers and accountants (Herzberg, Mausner and Snyderman, 1959). Herzberg and his colleagues used semi-structured interviews to examine the variables that affected these respondents' feelings about their jobs. They were asked to think about when they felt especially good and especially bad about their work. From the descriptive data gained, Herzberg and his colleagues were able to identify what they thought to be the main factors associated with job satisfaction and job dissatisfaction. The most controversial thing in Herzberg's theory is the idea that certain things (motivator factors) lead to job satisfaction, whereas others (hygiene factors) prevent *dis*satisfaction but cannot engender satisfaction.

Motivators include such factors as the content of the work itself, and the availability of opportunities for responsibility, advancement and recognition for achievement. In other words, factors that are intrinsic to the job. Hygiene factors, in contrast, are extrinsic in that they relate to the context or environment in which an individual does his or her job. Thus they include such factors as the organization's policy and administration, working conditions, salary, supervision and interpersonal relations.

Herzberg argued that, if hygiene factors were bad, they demotivate people and promote job dissatisfaction. However, if they are good, they will not motivate people – they will merely create a neutral condition whereby the individual is neither dissatisfied nor motivated. The implication is that improvements in the extrinsic aspects of work are of limited value in promoting job satisfaction and motivation. At best they can provide only the preconditions for higher productivity.

It is the other set of factors, the motivators, on the other hand, that encourage people to work harder and that thus increase job satisfaction. As Herzberg claimed (*ibid.* p. 70), motivators were 'complex factors leading to this sense of personal growth and self actualization'. Incidentally, he also thought that, if motivators were absent, this would not cause dissatisfaction but would simply create a lack of motivation and job satisfaction. In other words, rather than seeing job satisfaction and dissatisfaction as being opposite poles of the same continuum, Herzberg argues they are really two separate concepts (see Figure. 3.6).

If a manager wanted to motivate his or her subordinates towards higher productivity, while it is important to ensure that the hygiene factors are correct, the manager must manipulate the motivators by attending to job-content issues (e.g. 'job enrichment'). Motivators entail redesigning jobs to make them more interesting and challenging. This 'vertical loading' would include not only reskilling but also provisions for increased responsibility, creativity and autonomy. In effect, such 'job enrichment' could reintegrate jobs that had been fragmented by the specialized division of labour created by scientific management, and restore conception to the execution of tasks.

Herzberg had clearly recast Maslow's hierarchy of needs in terms of a dualism (Figure 3.7). When hygiene factors are present in an employee's working environment, physiological, safety and social needs are likely to be met.

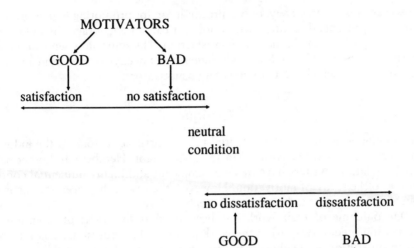

Figure 3.6   Herzberg's motivators and hygiene factors

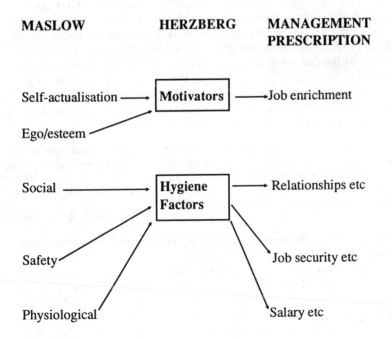

Figure 3.7   The correspondence between Maslow and Herzberg

However, this is, effectively, only a precondition for promoting higher productivity – it prevents discontent with a job but cannot encourage the individual beyond a position of absence of dissatisfaction. The solution when wanting to motivate employees lies in Maslow's higher-order needs of ego/esteem and self-actualization – which relate to Herzberg's motivators.

Critique

By drawing attention to the potential role of intrinsic factors on the individual's organizational behaviour, Maslow, McGregor, Herzberg and other neo-human relations writers have made a significant and highly influential contribution to the study of motivation. However, their work has been the focus of much controversy and the subject of much criticism.

One outcome of their work has been to shift the focus of attention in motivation theory away from the work group and interpersonal relations between supervisors and subordinates to a concentration on the individual's job satisfaction. Management's aims and objectives were no longer to be achieved through the manipulation of employees' collective consciousness; rather, integration with management's goals was now to be secured through the individual's self-actualization. *Homo gregarious* is thus replaced by *Homo actualis*.

Such writers can be regarded as attempting to restore the 'craft ethic' and the intrinsic meaning to work, which had been deskilled by the ravages of scientific management. However, in so doing these writers share with their human-relations forerunners a highly universalistic orientation. They assume their theories of motivation, underpinned by various concepts about human needs, are applicable to all people regardless of historical or social context. To Hollway (1991), such 'psychological universalism' (see also Lupton, 1971, pp. 98–100), with its cavalier approach to generalizability, comes from the legacy of orthodox theories of motivation. In this orthodoxy, human motivation is assumed to be based on the operation of a series of primordial and instinctive needs. Although the number, ordering and content of these needs varies according to the theorist, the legacy of this orthodoxy is that

> it has no way of conceptualising the limits of its generalisability: if it is biological, it can be true of all humanity . . . Maslow's and Herzberg's assumptions about motivation are universalistic despite the fact that they are expressions of American human relations values and assumptions concerning personal commitment to work.

> (Hollway, 1991, pp. 105–6)

Neo-human relations writers, such as McGregor and Herzberg, have clearly assumed work to be a central life interest.

A closer examination of Herzberg's empirical research, however, reveals numerous methodological flaws. As Schein (1965, pp. 56–60) points out, the way Herzberg phrased his questions left respondents with little option but to answer in the way they did. Moreover, his original research was conducted with only professional respondents (engineers and accountants); the production and clerical employees originally included in the sample were dropped without any thorough methodological justification. Hollway (1991) suggests that Herzberg created a biased sample because he was only interested in people who, potentially, were internally committed to their work, since the clerical and production workers 'did not produce the accounts he was seeking, he didn't sample them' (p. 1064). It is ironic that it is precisely those types of employee who were excluded from Herzberg's research who have been the focus of the application of his findings!

It seems that Herzberg extrapolated findings of dubious validity from a biased sample (white, male, North American, middle class). Goldthorpe *et al.* (1968) suggest that such middle-class employees often have a 'bureaucratic orientation' to work, where work is defined as a central life interest and where self-fulfilment, achievement and career advancement are valued. They thus imbue work with a moral dimension often expressed in terms of service and commitment to an organization.

In contrast, from their work in three organizations in Luton, Goldthorpe and his colleagues claim that other types of employee (such as assembly-line workers) have a highly 'instrumental orientation' to work that involves calculative involvement. All these employees want from work is to be able to earn enough money to allow them to enjoy life outside work. Although they did not like the tasks they had to undertake on the assembly lines, they did not associate this with any significant feelings of job dissatisfaction. They sought no intrinsic meaning in work, and they did not perceive it as a site for significant social relationships. Instead, work was merely an instrumental means to an extrinsic end; thus they tried to sell their labour on the market to the highest bidder.

Apart from the instrumental and the bureaucratic, Goldthorpe and his colleagues also identified what they called the 'solidaristic orientation' towards work. Here work is primarily seen as a group activity, from which the individual derives a sense of identity. An important feature of this is the individual's sense of loyalty to the collectivity. Whatever the object of these feelings – trade union, an immediate work group or the whole membership of a small enterprise – maintaining group solidarity overrules other concerns, such as those of economic reward.

This study has been rightly subjected to considerable criticism. One claim in particular has been the subject of much dispute – that workers' orientations appeared to have been generated autonomously of the working environment through the exclusive action of external socio-cultural variables they have brought with them into the workplace. They have gone so far as to argue that, since attitudes towards work are formed outside the workplace, conditions of full employment allow workers to choose a place of work that matches their dispositions. The result of this is a self-selecting workforce that has a shared orientation towards work. But as Daniel (1969) has commented, Goldthorpe and his colleagues were in danger of stopping their analysis at the factory entrance – just as previous researchers had done so at the factory exit. Clearly, any comprehensive analysis must take into account how workers' experiences both within and outside the workplace influence their attitude towards work.

Goldthorpe and colleagues' basic point is, however, important, since it suggests that the universalism of neo-human relations and, by implication, that of human relations and scientific management, is absurd: different socio-economic groups appear to attach different meanings to, or have different orientations towards, work (Parker, 1972; Gallie, 1978; Fineman, 1983). Workers' job satisfaction cannot be considered usefully except in relation to the more basic question of their often highly variable, inconsistent and unstable orientations towards work. Despite the probability that such orientations and meanings are influenced by a multiplicity of contextual factors both internal and external to the workplace (Curran and Stanworth, 1981), until what meaning 'work' has for them is known – the way they 'order their wants and expectations relative to their employment' (Goldthorpe *et al.*, 1968, p. 36) – Goldthorpe claims it is impossible to make any prediction or assessment about job satisfaction. As a social actor, a worker's orientation or definition of the situation, in effect, mediates between what Goldthorpe and his colleagues have called the 'objective features' of the work situation and the nature of his or her response (*ibid.* p. 182).

This has, obviously, devastating implications for motivation theory. It implies that, in order to understand human motivation in work organizations, what is needed is an approach that allows for the variability and complexity of human beings; human beings who self-consciously construct meaningful action, who do not respond to stimuli arising from subconscious needs – subconscious needs that have been adduced by supposedly privileged observers in an a priori manner. The wants, expectations of and attitudes towards work are 'culturally determined variables, not psychological constants' (*ibid.* p. 179). In other words, an approach to motivation compatible with social action is needed (e.g. Silverman, 1970). A social-action approach does not accept that everyone will interpret their work situation in the same way. Instead, this approach sees

> individuals as interpreting their situation in the light of the satisfactions they seek at work and the meaning that work has for them. So that whilst certain kinds of work may prove unacceptable to some workers, they may prove acceptable to others with different goals. The same can be said of management policies. Whilst well-meaning 'human relations' policies on the part of management may appeal to certain groups of workers, they may engender feelings of unwelcome paternalism and claustrophobia in others.
>
> (Stanworth, 1977, p. 19)

It might be argued, therefore, that the motivation theories discussed in this chapter are derived from theorists' a priori assumptions about the moral and ethical significance of work to employees; employees whose subjective propensities and predilections may or may not 'fit' such models. What is needed instead is an approach that avoids imposing the 'observer's' values but allows for the exploration of employees' subjective worlds – wherein, perhaps, lies the key to understanding human motivation in work organizations. In Chapter 4 we turn to a way of studying motivation that, when suitably reformulated, appears to be largely in accord with these aims and perspectives: expectancy theory.

Further Reading

Meakin (1976), Anthony (1977) and Kumar (1984) all provide accessible and interesting accounts of how the moral, ethical and ideological significance of work has varied through history and in different cultures. While there is a voluminous literature on scientific management and its impact on work organizations, perhaps the most detailed, readable and theoretically significant account is still the work of Braverman (1974), which is best read in conjunction with the important critiques provided by Littler and Salaman (1982) and Kelly (1985).

Hollway (1991) presents an incisive and critical review of human-relations and neo-human-relations literature and empirical research, while Ray (1986) relates these schools of thought to current approaches to management.

Silverman (1970) and Gallie (1978) both provide interesting accounts of the social-action approach, while a critical review of the literature on 'work meanings' is provided by Fineman (1983). Rose (1985) provides a valuable account of how the moral and ethical significance of work is changing in different ways, and at different rates, for different occupational groups.

Finally, excellent overviews of the areas covered by this chapter are to be found in Grint (1991) and in Butler's (1986) highly original contribution.

4

Motivation and Output Controls

Introduction

In the previous chapter we looked at a number of approaches to understanding human motivation in work organizations. These were criticized primarily because they share a universalistic orientation: each assumes that the particular theory it promotes (underpinned as it is by a particular concept of fundamental human 'needs') is applicable to all people – regardless of historical or social context. As we tried to demonstrate, such a 'psychological universalism' fails to take account of the cultural diversity within and between societies and their institutions, a diversity that results in different social groups attaching different meanings to (and projecting different expectations towards) work.

In order to understand these motivational *processes* better, it is necessary to apply a theoretical model that allows for this diversity and complexity by enabling an exploration of organization members' subjective worlds. Hence the first part of this chapter considers expectancy theory, which has arisen largely out of a response to this. Expectancy theory permits an analysis of human variability by concentrating specifically on how individuals make sense of the work situations that confront them and how individuals act in accordance with those meanings. Later in the chapter we use expectancy theory to analyse the design and operation of what we have previously called output-based control systems.

Expectancy Theory

Though closely related to the work of Lewin (1951) and though a considerable elaboration on the work of Georgeopoulos *et al.* (1957), expectancy theory was first formulated explicitly by Vroom (1964). Expectancy theory has since been subject to much revision and development by various theoreticians (e.g. Straw, 1977; Zeldeck, 1977), among whom the contributions of Lawler and his colleagues seem to be the most significant (Porter and Lawler, 1968; Lawler, 1973; Lawler and Rhode, 1976). Expectancy theory begins by questioning the assumption that people have fixed sets of needs; instead it attempts to take into account human variability and complexity. At the same time, it presents a model that allows for, and is commensurable with, the impact of human subjectivity upon motivational processes.

To understand this approach, one first needs to consider the assumptions underlying it. Porter and Lawler (1968) criticize what they consider to be the erroneous assumptions of the theories discussed in the previous chapter. They argue that, whether it be scientific management, neo-human relations and so on, each theory assumes that employees are simply *alike* – all are motivated by economic rewards or all aspire to self-actualization. Depending on the theory, attached to these universal concepts of employee motivation are specific courses of action (e.g. job enrichment or the administration of cash incentives), which rectify motivational 'problems' and which are applicable to any situation. The solutions put forward are decided by the particular theory, which, because of their universal nature, create the principle that there is 'one best way' regardless of the situation.

By contrast, Nadler and Lawler (*ibid.* pp. 100–1) try to explain the assumptions of expectancy theory. These can be summarized as follows:

1. People make conscious decisions about their own behaviour in organizations, especially with regard to the amount of effort they are prepared to direct towards performing their jobs.
2. Different people have different attitudes and orientations towards work, which are expressed as different needs, desires and goals, and which can be systematically analysed.
3. People make choices between the possible alternative modes of behaviour of which they are aware. They consider the degree to which a particular course of action will lead to outcomes they desire, or at least which they think are likely to lead to such outcomes.
4. Essential to understanding human motivation in work organizations is the need to discover the different meanings people attach to work and their working environments.

These assumptions have been combined to produce a model of motivation that focuses on organization members' orientations towards work, their abilities and their interpretations of the situation. The result is a theory that comes near to such 'cognitive' theories as attribution theory and equity theory. Central to its whole approach are two important concepts: expectancy and valency.

Expectancy

Vroom (1964) defines expectancy as the beliefs an individual holds about the outcomes likely to result from a given work behaviour or performance. It is thus the individual's subjective appraisal of the associations between different possible actions and the outcomes of those actions. It refers to such questions in the individual's mind as 'If I achieve that level of performance, what rewards will I receive?' 'How much effort must I expend in order to achieve that level of performance?' The individual's prior experience of the interaction between actions and outcomes, as well as the individual's level of self-esteem, influence his or her subjective appraisal of these relationships and his or her subjective estimation of the probability that a particular course of action will lead to particular outcomes (Lawler, 1973).

Valency

Vroom (1964) uses the term 'valence' to refer to the attractiveness (or affective orientation) people attach to the various outcomes they see as resulting from particular levels of performance or modes of action. Valency refers to the level of satisfaction or dissatisfaction an individual expects to receive from a particular outcome. 'Negative' valency describes the perceived outcomes the individual would prefer to avoid; 'positive valency' describes the outcomes the individual finds desirable.

Expectancy theorists do not assume that positive and negative valencies are shared universally; such preferences and aversions are variable or contingent, and it is thus important to find out what they might be rather than to make a priori assumptions. An individual's attitudes and orientations towards work will be a significant influence on what they perceive as desirable and undesirable. Since expectancy theory allows for variability in human perception, and since it focuses our attention on perceptual processes, at first sight expectancy theory seems commensurable with the social-action critique of the 'content' theorists, such as Maslow and Herzberg and as discussed in the previous chapter.

According to expectancy theory, therefore, motivation is the result of the interaction between expectancies and outcomes and so, to put it bluntly, the management implications are that, if they want high levels of employee job performance, they must ensure that outcomes employees perceive as positively valent are also seen by those employees as being tied to the achievement of those prescribed levels of job performance. Conversely, those same employees must also see that negative valencies are tied to low levels of job performance.

This interaction between expectancies and outcomes has been explored by many researchers (e.g. Galbraith and Cummings, 1967; Graen, 1969). The result has been several variations on a main theme, which is best illustrated by the model developed by Lawler and Porter (1969). This model extends Vroom's understanding of motivational processes by incorporating further variables and feedback loops.

The key to this model is a sequence of subjective processes Porter and Lawler (*ibid.*) consider individuals engage in when deciding whether or not to try out a certain behaviour, such as working harder (see also Lawler, 1973):

1. They consider whether or not the expenditure of effort will actually lead to the level of performance he or she desires. This particular means–ends relationship is known as the effort–performance relationship or expectancy.
2. They identify what the probable outcomes that will result from attaining that level of performance are. This particular means–ends relationship is known as the performance–outcome relationship or expectancy.

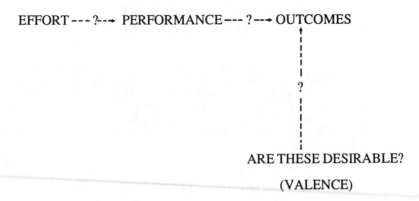

EFFORT --- ?--→ PERFORMANCE --- ?--→ OUTCOMES

?

ARE THESE DESIRABLE?

(VALENCE)

Figure 4.1   The subjective processes in decision-making

3. They consider the degree of attractiveness or desirability (valency) each of these perceived likely outcomes holds.

These processes are illustrated in Figure 4.1. The basic idea is that people will not be motivated to expend extra effort in their work unless they value the outcomes they believe to be attached to a higher level of performance positively, and unless they believe such extra efforts will actually lead to a higher level of performance.

This raises a number of questions that must be considered when predicting whether or not an individual will choose to work harder. Does the individual feel it is possible to attain a higher level of performance? Will the expenditure of extra effort be reflected in a higher level of performance? What outcomes does the individual associate with that higher level of performance? Are these outcomes attractive to the individual?

If the individual does not believe there is a relationship between extra effort and the attainment of higher levels of performance, or the individual finds the perceived outcomes to be unattractive, expectancy theory argues that individual's motivation to expend extra effort to perform the tasks would be low.

It might be possible here to accuse expectancy theorists of having an overly deterministic and rationalized view of human decision-making – that people calculate and choose consciously the behavioural options that maximize their desired pay-offs (Langer, 1981). However, many theorists are at pains to dismiss such criticism (e.g. Lawler and Rhode, 1976; Nadler and Lawler, 1991). Instead they argue that, although expectancy theory does emphasize the link between how people continuously make choices between behavioural options and motivation (even though the decision-making is habitual rather than conscious), in making choices people do not have a complete knowledge of the results of their behavioural options. Also, they are not aware of the full range of options available to them; nor do they necessarily have a comprehensive and consistent scale of values with which they might evaluate the valence of the various outcomes they are able to identify. Their choices are based on imperfect judgement and imperfect knowledge – their 'bounded rationality' (Simon, 1957). Thus, 'beauty is in the eye of the beholder', and this leads to a consideration of the culture people defer to when making such choices when we analyse motivation (Cooke and Slack, 1985). As Lawler and Rhode (1976, p. 26) argue,

> Experiencing the environment is an active process in which people try to make sense out of their environment. In this active process individuals selectively notice different aspects of the environment, appraise what they see in terms of their own past experience, and evaluate what they experience in terms of their own needs and values . . It is not safe to assume that the same management policy, practice, or decision will be seen in the same way by members of an organisation.

Attribution Theory

It is in this context that it is possible to locate attribution theory's contribution to understanding motivation. Attribution theory, generally, is concerned with the relationship between personal perceptions and behaviour. It stresses the individual's interpretation of the causes and explanations of past events and the prediction of future events through his or her perception of self, as well as of others and of events in his or her environment (Heider, 1958).

One's personal perception of self (i.e. personal attributes, such as ability) and one's perceptions of the attributes of one's personal environment (e.g. management control systems) combine to influence subsequent behaviour. While much research in this vein has investigated how individuals make causal inferences about others' behaviour (e.g. Jones *et al.*, 1972; Kelly, 1972), what is most relevant to a consideration of expectancy theory is work that considers the ways people attempt to explain what has happened to them in terms of successful and unsuccessful job performance.

Explanations of job performance lie either in the individual's own behaviour and attributions or with reference to the individual's personal environment. Own behaviour and attributions is known as an 'internal locus of control'; personal environment is known as an 'external locus of control' (Weiner *et al.*, 1971; Miller, Kets de Vries and Toulouse, 1982). The result of this research has been, to some extent, to illustrate how such causal attributions of success and failure affect people's appraisal of the likelihood of future success and failure and how this, consequently, affects their subsequent behaviour.

Important here is how this variation in the perceived locus of control seems to correlate with variations in expectancies. People functioning under an internal locus of control often feel they can influence their job performance personally by exercising their ability and by expending effort. In contrast, those who see themselves operating under an external locus of control often feel their job performance is beyond their personal influence; they are thus less likely to exercise their own ability and expend effort. These observations reinforce the concept of self-control, which has already been referred to in Chapter 2 and is explored further in Chapter 6.

Attribution theory, therefore, gives some analytical depth to the arguments of expectancy theorists. However, it is important to emphasize that an individual's expenditure of effort might not necessarily lead to the desired level of job performance: the individual's skills and abilities must influence the effect of such an expenditure of effort. Similarly, the effort's effectiveness is also influenced by the individual's perception and interpretation of his or her organization role and the activities necessary to attain the desired level of performance. If the individual is unclear about what his or her organizational role is, or does not understand how to direct effort so that it is reflected in subsequent job performance, it is likely that these will have a detrimental effect on job performance.

According to expectancy theory, job satisfaction occurs when the resulting outcomes are valued by the individual and are perceived as fair and equitable in return for the effort expended. This raises the issue of what kinds of outcome are available to people in work situations. Expectancy theorists usually discuss these primarily in terms of intrinsic and extrinsic rewards.

Intrinsic and Extrinsic Rewards

Intrinsic rewards are outcomes given to the individual by him or herself. They refer to outcomes derived purely from task performance itself and include such individual feelings as achievement, challenge, competence and personal worthiness, etc. The organizational context in which an individual works cannot give or remove these rewards – it can only make them possible or more likely.

In contrast, extrinsic rewards are outcomes that derive from the organizational context in which an individual works – for example, positive or negative outcomes from an organization's reward systems, fellow employees or hierarchical superiors. These are rewards administered by agents external to the individual; thus they include payment systems, promotion, fringe benefits, acceptance by co-workers and job security etc.

However, how people evaluate the attractiveness of the intrinsic and extrinsic rewards they perceive as available varies. Unlike neo-human-relations theory, expectancy theory does not assume that work is a central life interest for everyone. Similarly, it is not possible to assume, as with scientific management, that all people are 'economically rational'. Intrinsic and extrinsic aspects of work may vary according to socio-economic background, age, gender, educational attainment and so on. Employees' social background, particularly, can significantly affect their evaluation of different kinds of reward. Some employees might strive for improved social status and have a delayed gratification ethos, while others might have a highly instrumental and short-term orientation towards work. The message of expectancy theory is that the nature of such valencies vary. If this is the case, then management approaches to motivation should also vary – 'it all depends'. So it is in this sense that expectancy theory is a highly contingent approach to human motivation in work organizations.

As has already been pointed out, while feelings of job satisfaction depend on people valuing the rewards they receive, such rewards must 'meet or exceed the perceived equitable level of rewards' (Porter and Lawler, 1969, p. 31). The equity or fairness of the rewards are relative to the level of job performance the individual feels he or she has attained, and are important factors affecting feelings of job satisfaction. People compare what they have put into a job with what they receive (i.e. the ratio of inputs to outputs) and will adjust their behaviour or, indeed, their cognitions, to correct any perceived imbalance or feelings of inequity.

Expectancy theory, therefore, incorporates many of the ideas put forward by equity theory, as formulated by Adams (1965), and, more recently, by Mowday (1991). Equity theory argues that perceived feelings of inequity stimulate dissatisfaction, and the resulting tension motivates people to reduce and, ultimately, to remove that felt inequity. This might be achieved by altering inputs, outputs or the balance between inputs and outputs cognitively, or even by engaging in flight from the source of inequity through absenteeism or resignation. The way a relationship between inputs and outputs is considered to be fair is influenced by comparisons the individual makes with a reference group. Hence, feelings of equity or inequity about the balance between inputs and outputs are not constructed with reference to some absolute standard – they are socially relative and are made through social comparison with a group, or groups, of significant others.

Summary

A summary of Porter and Lawler's (1968) expectancy model of motivation is given in Figure 4.2. This model demonstrates how a variety of factors affect the amount of effort a person is prepared to put into the performance of the tasks allotted to him or her through an organization's vertical and horizontal differentiations. As we have shown, these factors include the extent to which that individual believes the effort will be reflected in performance; the extent to which a particular level of performance will lead to the attainment of rewards; and the value the individual places on the rewards he or she associates with

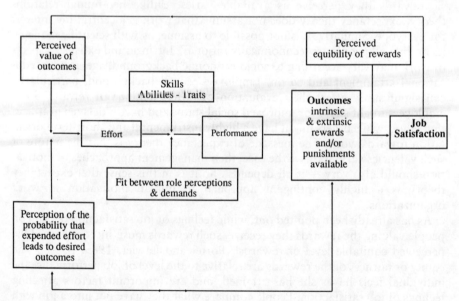

Figure 4.2   The expectancy model of motivation (Porter and Lawler, 1968, p. 165)

that performance in contrast to the negative outcomes he or she associates with such an expenditure of effort. Other factors influence the effort's effectiveness, and these include the individual's abilities and traits, as well as his or her perception of role and so on. Job satisfaction arises when the intrinsic and/or extrinsic rewards that are provided as a result of job performance are valued by the individual, and perceived as a fair and equitable return for the effort expended (*ibid.*).

Expectancy theory is still the subject of much debate and controversy as researchers attempt to find the appropriate methodology by which they might test, empirically, the theory and its predictions (Campbell and Pritchard, 1976; Harrell and Stahl, 1986; Miller and Grush, 1988; Kernan and Lord, 1990). For example, Campbell and Pritchard (1976) argue that much of the research that questioned expectancy theory's validity was characterized by numerous conceptual and methodological flaws that make the findings dubious. These issues have led Pinder (1991, p. 156) to conclude that, although there have been many studies that ostensibly test the validity of expectancy theory, 'only recently have there been many appropriately-conducted studies, leaving us with grounds for optimism that the theory is a reasonably valid model of the causes of work behaviour'. Clearly, expectancy theory will be the subject of continuing debate and theoretical refinement. Expectancy theory's robustness probably lies in its ability to incorporate successfully the insights of other 'process' theories of motivation, such as equity theory, as well as the contributions of researchers who have been concerned to explore how people perceive their surroundings and how they act on the basis of those subjective processes.

However, despite Luthans' (1981, p. 189) rather suspect claim to the contrary, perhaps some of the most important aspects of expectancy theory relate to its analytical and practical utility when it comes to the design and redesign of control systems. In the second part of this chapter we attempt to demonstrate this by using expectancy theory to review the behavioural context – how human behaviour is affected by and simultaneously affects – the operation of what we have termed output-based administrative control systems. This will also serve to analyse some recent thinking about the design and operation of these organizational phenomena. However, before we can do this, it is important to have a thorough model of the elements and relationships that combine to create this form of organizational control. Although other models do exist (Swinth, 1974; Lawler and Rhode, 1976), a particularly useful model is provided by Otley and Berry (1980).

Otley and Berry's Cybernetic Model of Administrative Control

Otley and Berry (1980) provide a good starting-point for considering how output-based controls operate when they begin their analysis by using a systems model to represent whatever it is that is being controlled. For our purposes, this systems model will be used to represent an activity or series of tasks undertaken by an individual or a group (the controlled), which someone else purposively is attempting to control (the controller). This activity is shown in Figure 4.3, which demonstrates how various resources or inputs are combined together and are hence changed to create various outcomes or outputs.

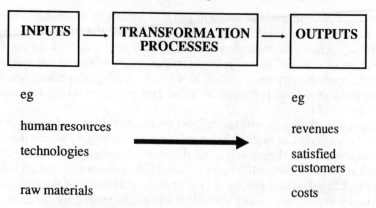

Figure 4.3   An organizational activity as a system

Otley and Berry (*ibid.* pp. 236–7) argue that, in order for such an activity to be controlled, at least four necessary conditions must be met:

1. Objectives must exist for the activity being controlled; without a purpose, control has no meaning, since it would be aimless.
2. The activity's outputs must be measurable by using relevant criteria or indicators, which, when applied, allow the assessment of the extent to which the activity is attaining the objectives defined in (1).
3. A 'predictive' model of the activity being controlled is required so that the causes of any non-attainment of objectives can be determined, and the effects of any possible actions to correct the situation forecasted and evaluated, so that the most appropriate might be identified.
4. There must be some capacity for taking action, so that deviations in attainment (outputs) – relative to the objectives set for the activity – can be reduced.

If any of these four conditions are missing, the activity over which control is being attempted will be out of control. The relationship of these four conditions to a systems model of organizational activity is shown in Figure 4.4.

The sequence of control in Figure 4.4 begins with the comparison (3) of the objectives (1) set for the activity under control, with observations or measures of the output's activity (2) (Otley and Berry, 1980). If the comparison between what has actually happened (a reality judgement) and what should have happened (a value judgement) generates a mismatch or deviation, then this signals the person who is attempting to control the activity to instigate some form of corrective action. In order to decide what might be the most appropriate corrective action (4), the 'controller' has to interrogate his or her predictive model of the activity he or she is trying to control. The information provided by such a model derives from the individual's knowledge of the activity being controlled (i.e. in terms of inputs, transformation processes and outputs), as well as the individual's understanding of the objectives being brought into action and imposed by the control system. Such a predictive model analyses the causes of the deviation(s) as well as the likely outcomes of available potentially

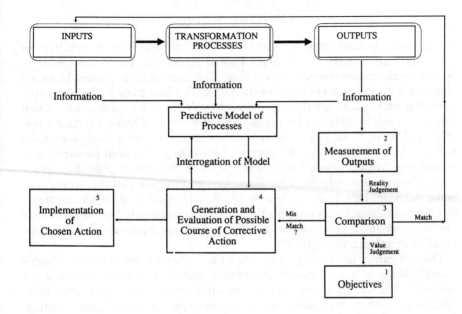

Figure 4.4 A cybernetic model of control (Otley and Berry, 1980, p. 263)

corrective actions. Finally, a corrective action is chosen, implemented (5) and its effects on the activity under control monitored.

Although Otley and Berry suggest that this 'cybernetic' model of control (with some modification) could be applied to analyse such phenomena as self and social control, here we use it to consider specifically what we have called output-based administrative controls. It is possible to summarize the operation of such an output-based administrative control system in terms of the following behavioural factors:

1. Objective setting.
2. Performance/output measurement.
3. Comparison of outputs with objectives.
4. Generation and evaluation of corrective actions.
5. Implementation of corrective actions.

Underpinning the operation of such an output-based control system must be the intrinsic and extrinsic rewards available to the person being controlled. Although this element is not represented in Otley and Berry's original model, the operation of intrinsic and extrinsic rewards could be represented as a separate feedback loop between the comparison element and the inputs to the activity under control (as illustrated in Figure 4.4), in circumstances where a match between outputs and objectives (rather than a mismatch) has been registered. However, by focusing merely on this feedback loop, we would tend to limit our consideration of reward issues seriously. Therefore, in order to accommodate the all-pervading influence of such rewards, we consider their differing impacts by referring to each element of Otley and Berry's original model. It is to each of these five elements that we now turn.

Objective Setting

Management writers often tend to see organizations as having objectives or goals that exist independently of the human actors who combine together to constitute the organization's membership. This type of management literature abounds with the concept 'organizational goal', often going as far as to consider that such 'goals' are the key characteristics of work organizations in that they have been 'established for the explicit purposes of achieving certain goals' (Blau and Scott, 1962, p. 1). This type of 'reification' involves giving essentially human characteristics (e.g. the power of thought and action) to social constructs (e.g. 'organizations') (Silverman, 1970, p. 9). This implies that organizations exist separately from the intentions and purposes of the people who make them up. However, surely only people have goals and objectives; therefore one can consider an organization as having goals only 'where there is an ongoing consensus between the members of the organisation about the purposes of their interaction' (*ibid.*).

This reificatory tendency perhaps has a use in that it helps to create a myth – a myth that obscures a possibly threatening reality: most work organizations are not based on consensus. Another possible outcome of this, on the other hand, is that it may lead people into being incapable of seeing human relationships as other than things (i.e. fetishes). In other words, changing social relationships and activities into 'things' that seem to exist independently of the actors who engage in their production and reproduction, as well as transforming what is historical and relative into something that appears immutable and absolute. Moreover, such writers as Katz and Kahn (1978, p. 481) argue that this propensity to treat an organization as if it were a person oversimplifies organizational behaviour, since there is no 'organizational equivalent of the single unitary nervous system of the individual'. As Gouldner (1959, p. 420) points out, 'an organization as such cannot be said to be orientated toward a goal. A statement that an organization is orientated toward certain goals often means no more than these are the goals of its top administrators'.

Therefore since it is people who come together to make up an organization and who have goals, etc., unless there is some ongoing consensus among that membership those considerations must lead us to view work organizations as being composed of different individuals and groups with varying (and often conflicting) objectives with regard to their involvement in the organization.

Pfeffer and Salancik (1978, p. 36) use the term 'coalition of interests' to describe this situation, where each person attempts to 'obtain something from the collectivity by interacting with others, and each with its own preferences and objectives'. Organizational life must be seen as a continuous process of conflict, negotiation and, indeed, co-operation between people who have a multiplicity of goals, perceived interests and purposes. If everyone shared the same objectives there would probably be no need for the kinds of control systems discussed here.

Control systems may be seen as social and technical arrangements whereby the objectives or goals of a particular group or individual are brought into action and imposed on others so that these individuals' actions and decisions are directed towards the attainment of those objectives. Indeed, it is through objective setting that Simons (1991) argued that control systems should reflect the strategic orientation of those occupying the higher echelons of organizations.

In Figure 4.4 the objectives for the activities being controlled represent performance standards or explicit goals that reflect normative expectations about what constitutes the achievement of successful task performance. There is considerable evidence to suggest that clear and specific objectives will reduce subsequent variability in performance and help to engender higher performance by ensuring 'goal clarity' (e.g. Kenis, 1979). However, the substantive nature of an objective can vary considerably – for instance, it might be in the form of production targets, sales targets or budgetary standards. Regardless of the actual form these objectives take, the intention behind their creation is to channel the efforts of an individual or group towards the controller's ends, since various extrinsic and intrinsic rewards may be tied to the achievement of those standards. In this context the roles of intrinsic and extrinsic rewards tend to be rather different (but often their implications for designing this element tend to coincide).

Whether people are motivated primarily by extrinsic or intrinsic rewards, expectancy theory seems to suggest that people are not prepared to expend effort in the pursuit of objectives they perceive to be unachievable. This has implications for how difficult the objectives should be, and who should be involved in the objective-setting process. With regard to how difficult objectives should be, a considerable amount of research focuses specifically on the motivational effects of budgetary standards. At the risk of over-simplification, this research demonstrates how the highest levels of performance were achieved in situations where budgetary standards were difficult but attainable (Kenis, 1979; Merchant, 1981). Much lower levels of performance, however, tended to occur where the 'controlled' saw the standards as being either easily attainable or unattainable (Hofstede, 1967; Otley, 1977). This implies that, from the controller's point of view, objectives should be difficult but perceived as attainable by those whose job performance it is the system is attempting to control (Latham *et al.*, 1978). Ronen and Livingstone (1975) found that, when objectives are set close to but above the individual's aspiration levels, the aspiration levels will tend to rise. This has implications for the processes by which objectives are set, and may be understood in terms of the extent to which the controlled are involved in the objective-setting process. Again at the risk of over-simplification, this presents a choice between imposing an objective or negotiating an objective through the participation of both the controller and the controlled. There is a considerable body of research on the effects of such participation on employee motivation.

Early research and theory, which was usually based in a human-relations or neo-human-relations approach, generally tends to support the contention that such participation is conducive to engendering higher morale, and the acceptance of – and desire to achieve – objectives (Argyris, 1964; Likert, 1967), albeit often mediated by the attitudes of those being controlled (Becker and Green, 1962). Since this research, several studies seem to confirm that budgetary participation improves job satisfaction (Kenis, 1979; Chenhall, 1986), but does not necessarily improve job performance (Chenhall and Brownell, 1988).

However, this is not to suggest that participation is some kind of universal panacea: research undertaken using expectancy theory suggests a much more ambiguous situation. Ronen and Livingstone (1975) found that participation can enhance the attractiveness of both intrinsic and extrinsic rewards by providing a means of communicating expectations about what constitutes successful performance – provided the controlleds' norms are supportive of participation. To an extent this agrees with the arguments presented by Lawler and Rhode (1976), who claim that, where objectives are imposed, this can lead unintentionally to the creation of unreasonable objectives. It leaves out of the decision-making process the people who will often have the greatest understanding of what it is that is possible and reasonable to achieve in their jobs. Moreover, it ignores the importance of letting the controlled understand why such objectives have been set. It is thus argued that participation in objective-setting is more likely to ensure feelings of equity and acceptance and, hence, that the promised extrinsic rewards are actually available.

Similarly, where people are primarily motivated by intrinsic rewards, it is argued that such outcomes as feelings of competence and self-esteem are related to achieving the set objectives, but only when those objectives have been accepted as legitimate. To create and maintain those feelings, it is important that people think they can (and actually do) achieve those standards. In such circumstances, participation in objective-setting can encourage someone to accept the objectives by creating feelings of personal investment and, thereby, stimulating that person's commitment to attaining them (*ibid.*). In this sense people can, through their participation in objective-setting, become 'ego-involved' with a budget (see Collins, 1982).

By implication, Brownell and McInnes' (1986) research tests some of these conjectures. Intriguingly, they found that where there was participation in objective-setting, the valency of intrinsic rewards fell. They attempted to explain this very surprising finding by pointing to how participation, in the objective-setting process, tends to strengthen expectations of extrinsic reward based on objective attainment; thus participation created the motive for the controlled to negotiate easy objectives and thereby trade off intrinsic for extrinsic valencies. This raises the whole question of how people attempt to build in 'slack' during objective setting processes.

Building 'slack' into an objective entails the person whose activities are to be controlled providing false or misleading data during the objective-setting process. While this can happen accidentally, particularly in situations of high uncertainty (Otley and Berry, 1979), Schiff and Lewin (1970) have noted how, during the development of a budget, subordinate managers might try to use their intimate 'local' knowledge to protect their perceived vested interests by attempting to dupe their controllers. They might achieve this by, for example, deliberately inflating their estimates of predicted costs and/or reducing predicted revenues. The question this raises is whether or not participation in the objective-setting process increases the probability that this phenomenon will occur. Both Onsi (1973) and Camman (1976) have conducted research into budgeting that focuses on this area. Their findings suggest that, where the controlled were able to participate in the objective-setting process, their propensity to build in slack was reduced. However, Merchant (1985) indicates that certain variables affect this relationship. He found that where the controller had the ability to detect slack, there tended to be a greater emphasis on meeting budgetary objectives but, at the same time, the controlled were allowed greater participation and their propensity to build in slack was reduced.

The whole situation seems to be complicated further by the controlleds' personality characteristics, which seem to intervene by affecting how they respond to participation. Brownell (1981), whose findings are reinforced by Collins' earlier work (1978), reports that those with an internal locus of control learned faster and achieved higher levels of performance and satisfaction where there was participation in budgeting; however those with an external locus of control learned faster and had higher levels of performance and satisfaction where participation was considered to be low.

To summarize, the effects of participation are varied and very complex, since they are influenced by the interaction of an array of social, psychological and organizational factors (see Merchant, 1984; Chenhall and Brownell, 1988). One thing, however, soon becomes apparent: it is naïve to assume that the opportunity to participate in objective-setting will automatically result in the controlled becoming more highly motivated to achieve the resulting objective(s). Yet in some of the circumstances discussed previously, a participative approach to objective-setting can produce higher motivation and job satisfaction but, ironically, this might be through building slack into these objectives and thus achieving lower performances. As Brownell (1982) so elegantly describes the situation, impersonal factors might determine the need for participation, but personal factors determine its effects. It is with this in mind that we now turn to a further set of important issues that affect objective-setting, factors that derive from what is known as double-loop learning.

Otley and Berry's model of control is 'error' based in the sense that once a deviation or mismatch between the actual outcomes of the organizational activity under control and the objectives set for that activity is observed, this causes a control action to be implemented to reduce or remove that error. This ability to identify and correct deviations from an a priori objective or standard enables controllers to keep those activities 'on course' (Morgan, 1982, 1986). Hence comes the term 'cybernetic', which derives from the Greek word *kubernetes* meaning 'steersman'. This process is called 'single-loop' learning. In contrast, 'double-loop' learning involves the ability to question and evaluate whether or not the objectives being imposed by the control system are appropriate. A significant problem with output-based control systems is that the objectives imposed on the activity being controlled may have become inappropriate; thus the control system is operating, through 'single-loop' learning, to keep the activities on the wrong course. To Morgan, the facility for 'double-loop' learning is hindered by several issues arising in work organizations. In very hierarchical organizations, particularly where people are rewarded for success and punished for failure, people will tend to engage in defensive forms of 'impression management' in order to appear competent in terms of the criteria deriving from the set objectives (Morgan, 1986, pp. 89–91). Problems that might threaten this presentation of self are avoided, obscured or rationalized away. The result of these modes of behaviour may be that people are unable to cope with uncertainty and ambiguity. People thereby cannot challenge, or have become afraid of challenging, the continuing relevance of a particular objective that has become the taken-for-granted norm through which control over their job performance is instituted. Indeed, those who are prepared to challenge current practices and operating norms are likely to be seen as subversive, as 'suspect in overall values and orientation' (*ibid.* p. 90). Accordingly, they endanger their survival within the organization.

Where organizational activities involve undertaking variable or non-routine tasks, and these activities take place in complex and rapidly changing environments, the activities become characterized by high degrees of uncertainty and unpredictability. In these circumstances there is the danger that the objectives of this type of control system become rapidly out of date, or they may have been inappropriate from the outset. In such circumstances, people tend to engage in a form of 'bureaucratic behaviour' in that they attempt to fulfil the expectations contained within those objectives for the sake of doing so and to gain the rewards they consider to be still tied to that attainment – despite the probability that such objectives are no longer relevant to their effective job performance. It is in the context of this problem that certain innovations in budgetary control-system design can be understood.

Traditionally, budgetary control involves establishing performance standards for the controlled based on past experience and the allocation of resources to them to enable the achievement of those standards. In this way they tend to operate to preserve the status quo. They act as a stabilizing force, thus creating organizational inertia rather than encouraging adaption through recognizing changed circumstances and evaluating previous practices. Once established, such performance standards are often difficult to change and they engender inflexibility (Hedberg and Jonsson, 1978). This might not be a problem where tasks are routine and unchanging or where there is environmental stability, but this situation does appear to be inappropriate in situations of uncertainty created by environmental instability and non-routine tasks (Amigoni, 1978; Emmanuel and Otley, 1986, p. 153). If output controls are to be used in these circumstances, they must stimulate innovation, experimentation and flexibility – by sensitizing members to instability and change – rather than creating the tendency towards rigidity and complacency, by filtering out ambiguity and uncertainty (Argyris, 1977). Accounting researchers (e.g. Hedberg and Jonsson, 1978; Williams, 1981) have attempted to tackle this problem by considering how ambiguity may be introduced into control systems by making performance standards subject to continuous review and change. They argue that control systems need to be designed in such a way that they do not build in resistance to change by setting performance standards that refer to the past. Instead, controls should allow for 'learning, unlearning and relearning' through innovations that result in 'semi-confused budgeting', such as zero-base budgeting. In Morgan's terms, this means that, rather than imposing predetermined objectives, double-loop learning is facilitated by processes in which the limits that are placed on action are continuously subject to question. This has important managerial implications, since

> whereas the traditional philosophy is to produce a master plan with clear-cut targets . . . it may be systematically wiser to focus upon defining and

challenging constraints [that] involves a choice of limits (the negative-feedback 'noxiants' one wishes to avoid) rather than just a choice of ends. The effect . . . is to define an evolving space of possible actions that satisfy critical limits. This leaves room for specific action plans to be generated on an ongoing basis and tested against these constraints for viability.

(Morgan, 1986, p. 92)

Morgan also considers that double-loop learning may be facilitated further by encouraging people to accept the problematic nature of the uncertain situations they confront. An important aspect of this is a philosophy that allows people 'to write off legitimate error against experience' (*ibid.* p. 91) and enables people to approach issues and problems from as many perspectives as possible. Despite its problematic effects, this might necessitate the controlleds' participation in the objective-setting process.

Performance/Output Measurement

Measurement involves shaping the objectives set for the activities under control into a set of criteria or indicators that allow observation and measurement of the activities' outputs. The form this measurement process takes largely depends on the nature of the objectives being brought into action. At a prescriptive level, the resulting measures must allow for the assessment of the extent to which those activities are attaining those objectives. However, this state of affairs is very difficult to achieve in practice.

According to expectancy theory, the controlled will direct their efforts to aspects of their work they perceive as being measured, provided they feel desirable rewards are tied to that notion and level of job performance. Hence it follows that the measurement process has a crucial influence on motivation. The measures cybernetic systems apply to job performance can be analysed in three ways: completeness, objectivity and influenceability (Lawler and Rhode, 1976). We consider each of these in turn.

Completeness

Completeness refers to the extent to which the behaviours necessary to perform the activity under control adequately are fully revealed and captured by the control system's measurement elements. The less completely a control system measures those behaviours, the more likely it is to encourage behaviour the controller sees as dysfunctional (Lawler and Rhode, 1976). This is because these measures, in effect, define good and poor job performance. Where the controlled are primarily motivated by extrinsic rewards, they will be motivated to concentrate their efforts on the measured aspects of their roles; hence, they will appear competent in the terms of the incomplete measure, since performing well in these aspects leads to those rewards. Where people are primarily motivated by intrinsic rewards, incomplete measures may obviously cause the individual to be unable to see a connection between performing well (in terms of the measure) and the availability of such intrinsic rewards as feelings of competence and achievement. They can thus become demotivated.

This is highlighted by the current vogue in higher education to evaluate lecturers' qualities in terms of 'customer satisfaction'. This is often achieved through questionnaires, etc., that attempt to measure the degree to which students are satisfied with a particular course. The lecturer is usually aware that aspects of his or her classroom behaviour are going to be revealed to and inspected by hierarchical 'superiors'. Although the effects of this process will be affected by the lecturer's orientation to work, he or she will, possibly, attempt to modify their behaviour accordingly – especially in an organization where the customer is 'king'. The result might be a fixation with the presentational aspects of being a lecturer. However, this fixation can, at the same time, cause a decline in content and educational standards. Students might be regarded by the lecturer as good adjudicators of presentation, but they usually lack the knowledge to evaluate the content of lectures. Moreover, in order to be popular with students and, by implication, to satisfy them, there may be a temptation to avoid making courses difficult in terms of content and assessment standards. Thus, through the application of an incomplete measure and, consequently, through poorly thought-out objectives, certain kinds of dysfunctional behaviour can be encouraged, even though the person appears to have their behaviour under control and *appears* to be performing their job to a high standard. As Kerr (1975) has pointed out, the behaviour that is rewarded is the behaviour that can be expected. This raises the whole issue of the inevitable partiality of output-based control systems.

Objectivity

Whether measures of output are objective refers to the extent to which they measure what they are supposed to measure (i.e. valid), and to the extent to which, if different people did the measuring, their subsequent findings would be consistent (i.e. reliable). According to Lawler and Rhode (1976), for either intrinsic or extrinsic motivation to be present, the controlled must understand how the measure operates and regard the measure (and the measurement processes) to be fair and unbiased. In either case, the controlled must be able to see the connection between their expenditure of effort and how well they perform in terms of the measure. When validity and reliability are not overtly seen as present, people may doubt there is any clear relationship between their efforts and their subsequent 'scores' on the measure. This situation can only have a detrimental effect on intrinsic feelings of achievement and accomplishment or on people's belief that promised extrinsic rewards will be forthcoming. However, as Lawler and Rhode (*ibid.*) point out, since expectancy theory emphasizes the fact that 'beauty is in the eye of the beholder', this state of affairs will probably be influenced by the degree of 'trust' that exists in the organization. In other words, if the controlled trust those who do the measuring, it may be possible to maintain extrinsic and/or intrinsic motivations, despite the use of invalid and unreliable measures. By implication, the converse might also hold in situations of low trust – despite the application of highly objective measures of performance.

Influenceability

One problem invalid measures can create is that many ostensibly objective measures of task performance are not very influenceable by individuals. How well they undertake their personal duties and tasks may have little bearing on the scores they subsequently receive on measures that only notionally focus on the outputs of their task performance. This might often be the result of extraneous influences acting on the measure, which are outside the control of the person being measured. In other words, measures that seem very objective (e.g. corporate profits) may not respond to members doing their tasks well: scores are the result of a variety of influences beyond members' control. They are thus non-influenceable by job performance.

Comparison

How output is measured varies according to the nature of the activity over which control is being attempted. The motivational implications of those processes are, in turn, affected by the controlleds' expectations and aspirations. Once some form of measurement has been undertaken, it is possible to compare these 'reality judgements' with the 'value judgements' encoded in the objectives previously planned for the activity during standard-setting processes.

The result of this is what is called 'feedback control'. If a deviation or mismatch between the result of an organizational activity and the objectives set for that activity is detected, a corrective action is implemented to reduce or remove the deviation. One problem that might possibly be created by this approach is that a deviation has to occur before corrective action is implemented. To avoid this problem, control can be based on 'feedforward' control. Instead of control involving a comparison of actual outputs with objectives, predictions are made about what outputs might be in the future. If these predictions differ from what is desired, control actions can be implemented to pre-empt and minimize deviations before they occur.

It is in the various advantages that might accrue from using 'feedforward control' that we can locate what is called the 'time span of discretion' (Jaques, 1967; Lawler and Rhode, 1976). This refers to the time difference between when a task is performed and when inadequate performance is detectable. Every task has a particular time span of discretion (Jaques, 1967). For example, for people working on an assembly line the time span of discretion may be only a matter of minutes. However, for the managers who originally made the decision to invest in that assembly-line technology, the time span of discretion for that particular task might be a matter of years.

If performance is measured and compared to objectives on a timescale shorter than the time span of discretion, this can lead to feelings of inequity, since the quality of task performance is being evaluated before it is discernible (Lawler and Rhode, 1976). The effect is that people cannot see a relationship between the efforts they expend and how well they perform according to the signals they receive as a result of comparison processes. For these controls to engender either intrinsic or extrinsic motivation, the controlled must consider the comparison processes to be credible. When credibility is threatened, the controlled will question whether or not there is a relationship between effort, performance and reward.

If no mismatch is signalled during the comparison process, this means that those undertaking the activities must have met the objectives set for that activity. Otley and Berry's original model (1980) tends to ignore what might happen in this situation. It concentrates on error detection and deletion as opposed to reinforcing the behaviour that achieved a match between outputs and objectives. This is where the 'cybernetic' or 'steersman' analogy begins to break down. According to this analogy, there is no need to take action if something is 'on course' – a notion that is rather inappropriate to human behaviour. There is thus a need to add to their original model a loop that represents the processes by which behaviour (that is, meeting objectives) might be reinforced. In Figure 4.4 this is shown by a loop linking comparison processes, via a registration of a match between reality and value judgements, and the inputs to the activities under control. This loop represents the intrinsic and extrinsic rewards that might be available to those undertaking the activities successfully. Here expectancy theory leads us to consider the kinds of rewards available to those people, whether or not they were attractive to them and whether or not people felt they were equitable, given the effort they have had to expend, in the light of social comparison with relevant significant others.

The effectiveness of intrinsic and extrinsic rewards is further influenced by the extent to which people accept the fairness and veracity of these comparison processes. Where the outcomes of comparison are judged to be inequitable and so capricious that they are unable to see a relationship between the rewards they experience and the efforts they expend, the efficacy of such rewards in channelling behaviour will be considerably reduced.

Where a mismatch between outputs and objectives is registered by the comparison processes, this leads the controller to begin to examine the reasons why such a situation has occurred, and to generate and evaluate possible courses of action (*ibid.*).

The Generation and Evaluation of Courses of Action

When a controller attempts to correct the mismatch signalled by the comparison process, he or she will inevitably engage with the situation by projecting onto it a predictive model. Although such models are bound to be to some degree imprecise and partial, their application involves the controller trying to analyse why the deviation has occurred, and tying to that causal analysis remedial courses of action, the effects of which the controller has tried to predict.

As we have seen, attribution theory generally concerns the ways in which we relate causes and explanations to the various events we experience. While we have focused on that strand of attribution theory that considers the ways people attempt to explain what has happened to them, this theory also considers the ways in which people observe others' behaviour and attribute causes to it. Hence it is important to understand how courses of action to correct deviations are generated and evaluated.

As with the individual's perception of self, a central question raised by attribution theory concerns how people determine whether or not another person's behaviour derives from internal or external causes. When evaluating the causes of the non-attainment of objectives through interrogating a 'predictive model of processes', a controller attempts to establish the extent to which that 'deviant' behaviour was caused by internal or external causes. Internal explanations explain that behaviour in terms of such causes as the person's personality, emotions, motives, knowledge, skill and ability – factors that person controls. External explanations focus on factors beyond the individual's control: other people, a problematic situation and/or bad luck.

Obviously, the controller's prejudices can be important factors influencing whether the controller sees the causes of non-attainment as being internal or external. Bearing this in mind, it is useful to consider Kelly's (1972) model, which tries to explain the processes by which people establish the reasons for others' behaviour. This model suggests that people analyse variations in others' behaviour by constructing causal inferences. It states that, in making attributions, people take into consideration three important dimensions of that variability.

Consensus

Consensus is the degree of difference in behaviour of a person under observation from the behaviour of others faced with a similar situation. The lower the difference, the higher the consensus, and vice versa. High consensus suggests that the observer is more likely to attach an external attribution to a particular individual's behaviour. When a deviation in the task performance of a particular individual is reported by the comparison process, and similar reports are apparent for other individuals doing similar jobs, it is more likely the observer will attribute an external cause – i.e. it is not his or her fault. However, if a situation of low consensus were observed, the observer is more likely to attribute an internal cause.

Distinctiveness

Distinctiveness is the extent to which an observed person behaves in the same manner in different situations. When an individual's behaviour is considered to be highly distinctive relative to their behaviour elsewhere, the observer is more likely to attribute an external cause. Alternatively, where that behaviour is not considered unique but similar to behaviour exhibited by that individual elsewhere, an internal attribution is more likely.

Consistency

Consistency refers to how unusual or different someone's behaviour is from their previous behaviour when facing similar situations. Where consistency is high, the observer will be more likely to attribute the behaviour to an internal cause. Where consistency is perceived to be low, this can lead to the attribution of external causes.

What is important here is that the observer's perceptions will influence his or her subsequent response. When a controller attributes an individual's failure to achieve preset objectives to an internal cause, their subsequent consideration of corrective actions will be very different from that in a situation where they have attributed an external cause (Mitchell and Wood, 1980). However, this is not to suggest that people enter into a full review of the three dimensions of behavioural variability listed above; rather, people often make use of their limited experience and understanding in making judgements. This process might involve rationalizing away ambiguities that derive from incomplete or contradictory data (Kelly, 1972). The extent to which the controlled see the resulting feedback (via corrective actions) to be appropriate and fair may, indeed, be influenced by the extent to which it matches their own explanations of failure (in terms of internal or external loci of control).

Implementation of Chosen Actions

For control to be possible, corrective actions must be available (Otley and Berry, 1979, p. 241). Four types of corrective action are identified:

1. Actions that change the inputs to the activity under control. This is called first-order control.
2. Actions that change the objectives or change the expected level of attainment for the activity under control. This is called second-order control or double-loop learning.
3. Actions that change one or more of the following: the predictive model of the activity in use; the measurement processes; and the comparison processes. This is called internal learning.
4. Actions that change the activity under control itself. This is called adaptive or systemic learning.

As Otley and Berry (*ibid.*) point out, the information that signifies a corrective action is needed is usually in the form of the registration of a mismatch between objectives and outputs. Although this information might draw members' attention to the need to take action, it does not indicate what action should be taken. Inevitably the identification, evaluation and selection of viable corrective actions are interpretative processes in which the problem-solvers, in trying to make sense of the complexity that confronts them, project onto the situation all kinds of a priori assumptions, meanings and values. Although attribution theory allows us to consider some of these issues, the impact of these processes further draws our attention to the all-pervading importance of culture in understanding people's organizational behaviour – whether they are the controlled or the controllers.

Conclusions

We have tried to show in this chapter that the design and operation of output-based control systems should be based on the analysis and consideration of numerous interrelated behavioural issues. These were identified, through expectancy theory, and the elements Otley and Berry (1979) consider as combining together to constitute an output-based or cybernetic control. This supports the need for a contingent approach to the design and operation of such controls since, from a managerial point of view, there is evidently not one best way to approach these problems.

At a more critical level, our discussion has demonstrated how these organizational phenomena are inevitably partial and partisan social constructions, despite their superficial appearance of objectivity. Thompson (1967), although referring specifically to accountancy, is particularly helpful on these matters. He argues that accounting controls and, by implication, output-based controls generally, might be seen as systems of signs that convey meaning. That is, they are signifiers that have been 'stabilized' by being inserted into a particular 'gaze' so that they are congruent with particular objectives, which, in turn, express the interests of dominant coalitions (*ibid.* pp. 534–6). This 'gaze' gives prominence and visibility to particular aspects of organizational life, and thereby makes them available for inspection and evaluation. This provides a means by which hierarchical superiors might discipline and control those in subordinate positions. The 'gaze' adopted defines what is important by promoting particular patterns of visibility and surveillance, which embody particular objectives and interests. At the same time, alternative potential 'gazes', objectives and interests are submerged. Questions of power must be central to any analysis of the 're-presentational' practices that are enmeshed in any output-based control.

In following Otley and Berry's (1979) model we have tried to show how these controls are based on establishing objectives (or norms, standards or goals – the terminology varies) and methods of intervention when deviations are identified through measurement, comparison and various analytical and interpretive processes. Several researchers (Roberts and Scapens, 1985; Boland, 1987; Miller and O'Leary, 1987; Hoskin and Macve, 1988) have recently begun to apply the work of Michel Foucault (1979, 1981) to these issues. Foucault traced the processes by which, in the nineteenth century, the 'governable person' had been constructed in relation to sexuality, crime and punishment. To Foucault this had occurred by making people's behaviour visible to the inspection of controllers, who compared such observations to a model of 'normality'. Anyone deviating from that model became the subject of further analysis by these judges of 'normality'. By applying Foucault's ideas to work organizations, it is possible to see how output controls are based on 'disciplinary power' rather than 'sovereign power'. Sovereign power involves direct confrontation between hierarchical subordinates and superiors (Roberts and Scapens, 1985), in a similar way to what was previously called entrepreneurial control. Disciplinary power, on the other hand, involves employees becoming 'surrounded by calculative norms and standards', which enmesh people in a 'web of calculative practices' (*ibid.* pp. 239–41) by making it 'possible to attach to every individual within the firm norms and standards of behaviour [and] rendered susceptible to a continuous process of judgement' (*ibid.* p. 242).

In this way, an 'epistemic structure' is created that traps members 'within a calculus of efficiency [and] expectations of behaviour', which constructs, potentially, the governable person by making people the object of knowledge by the social construction of such 'normalising judgements' (*ibid.* pp. 253–4). Thus it is argued that, despite appearances to the contrary, output-based controls are socially constructed phenomena that create and purvey, rather than reflect passively, organizational realities. They create and express expectations encoded into objectives and standards that shape members' perceptions of what is important and to what they should turn their efforts. As such, what is 'accounted for' (Burchell *et al.*, 1980) gives a particular and partisan version of reality amongst members, by defining 'success' and 'failure' as well as 'problems' and their possible modes of resolution. In this way, members' perceptions of themselves, others and events are limited to particular 'gazes' or forms of visibility. By highlighting certain aspects of organizational reality, output controls exclude and deny possible alternatives by casting them into shadow (Covaleski and Dirsmith, 1988; Hines, 1988).

These issues are explored in subsequent chapters, particularly when considering culture and power. However, it is worth considering here the conditions in which output controls appear to be so problematic as to become highly dysfunctional from the controllers' point of view. This, in effect, takes us back to our discussion of different types of administrative control in Chapter 2. There we noted how controls that are purposively designed to influence members' preferences and cognitions, and thereby influence their value premises of behaviour, may tend to occur in certain organizational situations.

In looking at the behavioural aspects of output controls, we have emphasized the ways in which output controls try to ensure goal congruency by monitoring the outcomes of organizational activities. As Ouchi (1977, 1979) points out, in contrast to what he calls 'behavioural controls', such output control does not require controllers to observe subordinates' behaviour directly. Behavioural controls are administrative controls, which, instead of focusing outputs, involve the direct observation of people as they undertake organizational tasks in order to ensure they follow the 'correct' procedures. Ouchi (*ibid.*) demonstrates how these behavioural controls must therefore entail prior knowledge of cause and effect (i.e. means-ends) relationships to make possible the pre-programming of how tasks must be undertaken through the codification of a body of rules. Thus controllers observe, guide and order subordinates' organizational behaviour in terms of these rules. Provided they ensure that subordinates follow those rules, their successful task performance will be almost guaranteed. In order for these behavioural controls to 'work', controllers must have expert knowledge of how tasks should be undertaken (see also Eisenhardt, 1985). Ouchi (1977, 1979) calls this 'perfect knowledge of the transformation process'. Ouchi argues that, in contrast, output controls can only 'work' in circumstances where the outputs of members' organizational activities are measurable. In this way Ouchi identifies two contextual factors whose interaction influences which form of administrative control is appropriate. This interaction is represented by a matrix, which creates a very useful analytical tool (Figure 4.5).

In quadrant 1, knowledge of the transformation process is perfect and outputs are measurable. Hence, both output and behavioural controls are suitable. Production lines designed under the guise of scientific management would be examples of this kind of situation. In quadrant 2, knowledge of the transformation process is imperfect, but outputs are measurable. Because tasks are not pre-programmable, only output controls are suitable in this situation. The selling of goods or services, such as double-glazing or insurance, are examples of this situation. In quadrant 3, knowledge of the transformation process is perfect, but outputs are not measurable. Only behavioural controls are suitable. Much clerical and administrative work constitutes examples of this, although one of the impacts of information technology may be to make outputs more measurable. It is in quadrant 4 where we find the most problematic

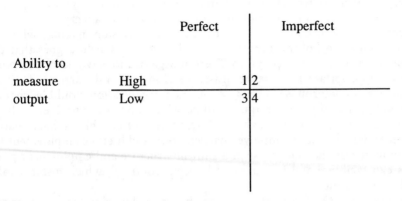

Figure 4.5   Factors affecting choice of administrative control (adapted from Ouchi, 1979, p. 843)

situation, since the ability to measure output is low and knowledge of the transformation process is imperfect. Therefore both output and behavioural controls are unsuitable. Many organizational tasks, such as research and development, are characterized by this situation, since they are not pre-programmable and outputs are very difficult to measure in a meaningful manner. This is not, of course, to suggest that attempts to control aspects of the organizational behaviour of those who perform such tasks are not made through the use of behavioural and output controls; rather, the question is one of the viability and consequences of such attempts. According to Ouchi (1979), it is under these conditions that what we have called control through influencing the value-premises of behaviour becomes the only viable means of administrative control. These he calls 'clan controls', which are characterized by members' commitment to a collectivity or organization on the basis of shared values and beliefs, the internalization of goals and strong feelings of solidarity.

In later work, Ouchi (1981) argues that what makes 'clan controls' possible are members' expectations of long-term employment and the belief that their future careers are closely linked to the company's future success. The commitment created by those beliefs is reinforced by, and offers the opportunity for, management's investment in the development of member's (often company-specific) knowledge and skills. Ouchi (*ibid.*) calls this approach to management and control 'Theory Z'. This is based on the notion that Western organizations can learn from their Japanese counterparts. However, in doing so he claims that Japanese organizational forms cannot be adopted easily in the USA. Ouchi's notion of Theory Z is ostensibly a compromise between what he takes to be the characteristics of North American (Theory A) and Japanese (Theory J) organizational forms (*ibid.* pp. 57–70). He typifies many North American firms as being characterized by short-term employment; explicit behavioural and output controls; rapid performance evaluation and promotion; and specialized organizational roles and career paths with individual responsibility and decision-making that, in effect, create parochial perspectives and concerns.

In contrast, Ouchi considers that Japanese firms stress lifetime employment, implicit control through shared norms and values, gradual performance evaluation and promotion, non-specialized organization roles and career paths with collective responsibility and decision-making, which is closely linked to holistic perspectives and concerns. Ouchi argues that the wholesale transfer of Theory J to Western organizations would not be possible or appropriate because of resistance from cultural barriers. Thus he constructs a compromise, Theory Z. Such an organization would be characterized by the egalitarian devolution of decision-making and problem-solving to teams of employees through the development of non-hierarchical matrix organizations based on employee participation and lifetime employment for many members. For Ouchi, such a shift in structure and employment practices can facilitate and is facilitated by 'clan controls', which foster loyalty and commitment.

At first sight, Ouchi's work appears to be closely linked to that of Peters and Waterman (1982) and Deal and Kennedy (1982), particularly given their shared emphasis on control by influencing the value-premises of members' behaviour. However, these writers tend to de-emphasize the importance of underlying structural form, job redesign and long-term organizational attachments, etc. Instead, they approach their concern to create shared (i.e. homogenized) organizational cultures by what we have noted as being a slightly revamped version of a human-relations perspective, albeit couched in a new idiom, which emphasizes management's role as manipulators of cultural symbols and meanings.

This raises the whole issue of cultures in organizations and its relationship to both administrative control and social control. This, and the possibility of developing cultural homogenization, are the subjects of the following chapter.

Exercises

1. Use expectancy theory (see Figures 4.1 and 4.2) to analyse your decision-making regarding whether or not to expend extra effort in undertaking a task, such as writing an assignment. To do this it may be helpful to start by identifying and considering the following:

   (a) The effort–performance relationship.
   (b) The performance–outcome relationship.
   (c) The balance between the positive and negative valencies you attach to these outcomes.

2. By using Otley and Berry's (1979) model (see Figure 4.4), identify the following features of an output-based control with which you are familiar (e.g. an examination):

   (1) Objective/standard setting.
   (2) Performance/output measurement.
   (3) Comparison processes.
   (4) Generation and evaluation of corrective actions.
   (5) Implementation of corrective actions.
   (6) The rewards provided by the control system.

With reference to Ouchi's (1979) model (see Figure 4.5), is this output-based control appropriate?

Further Reading

Porter and Lawler (1968) still provide one of the best accounts of expectancy theory, although it is probably best considered with reference to the collection of articles reproduced in Steers and Porter (1991). Klein (1989) argues for a model of motivation that integrates expectancy elements with cybernetic concepts in a way different from, but by no means incommensurable with, the approach outlined here. Euske (1984) presents an alternative and highly detailed analysis of output-based controls.

Morgan (1982) examines the epistemological bases and contribution of cybernetics, which he extends in later work by considering the metaphor of organizations as 'brains' (1986). For an amusing account that includes examples of how poorly designed output controls caused various kinds of dysfunctional behaviour in the (former) Soviet Union, see Nove (1977).

Smart's work (1985) on the thought of Michel Foucault is still probably one of the best-available introductions but, for an excellent application of these ideas to organizations, see Burrell (1988).

5

Culture and Control

Introduction

This chapter examines managerial attempts to control organizations by managing, intentionally, their corporate cultures. This management is designed to influence the value premises on which member's organizational behaviour is based. It has become fashionable in consulting circles to sell what is, essentially, culture change in much the same way as, for example, management by objectives and organization development were once sold – particularly when incorporated into such packaged consulting approaches as total-quality management. The manner in which each consulting package claims successively to be the panacea for the organizational ills managements are trying to cure is a fundamental feature of the values underlying much management practice. These packages are preoccupied with instant solutions, need to be seen to be in fashion and have an impatient disregard of thorough diagnosis (Gill and Whittle, 1993). The trend to control by managing culture has been influenced by such best-selling books as Peters and Waterman (1982) and Ouchi (1981). Ouchi's book, in particular, draws heavily on Japanese examples.

As we saw in chapter 3, there appear to be three broad ways open to managers to motivate employees and so to control organizations. The earliest was the bureaucratic approach, where employees were rewarded according to their expenditure of effort, which, in turn, was believed to give rise to improved productivity (rational/competitive man or *Homo economicus*). There then followed the human-relations approach, with its belief that a socially satisfying work life would lead to improved employee loyalty and so to increased productivity (sociable/co-operative man or *Homo gregarious*). A later phase, which seems to develop from human relations, was neo-human relations or *Homo actualis*. This approach seeks to change the variables that affect behaviour, such as organization structure or the employees' conditions of service, and through these changes to influence organizational behaviour.

Finally, although earlier forms co-exist with others, we seem currently to be in the corporate-culture phase, where a 'strong' culture is considered to lead to a love of the organization by its employees, which, again, is assumed to create improved productivity. However, as we said in chapter 3, managing culture by manipulating members' socio-emotional states is basically a regression to human-relations assumptions (Figure 5.1).

However, as we shall see, after more than a decade of popularity, culture as a form of organizational control is increasingly becoming subject to criticism, particularly its capacity for useful, practical application. Indeed, such critiques have even recently become a subject of press comment (Trapp, 1992).

This chapter gives some explanations of the complex term, 'culture', and it discusses the nature of organizational subcultures. This is necessary before any assessment can be made of the possibility of administrative control through the

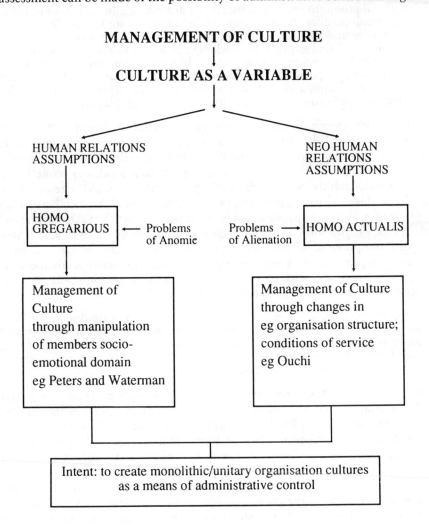

Figure 5.1   The management of organizational culture

management and manipulation of culture. It is also necessary because of the threat subcultures may pose to managements, who attempt to manage cultures at the organizational level. Next we consider how cultures are formed, particularly with reference to small-group developmental processes. We go on to discuss the development of organizational cultures and attempts to change and reinforce these through identification, socialization and indoctrination. Finally we offer a critique of attempts to manage cultures as the most recent approach to ways of controlling human resources and behaviour in organizations.

Defining Organizational Culture

Becker and Geer (1960, p. 134) describe organization culture as follows:

> Any social group, to the extent that it is a distinctive unit, will have to some degree a culture differing from that of other groups, a somewhat different set of common understandings around which action is organised, and these differences will find expression in a language whose nuances are peculiar to that group. Members of churches speak differently from members of tavern groups; more importantly, members of any particular church or tavern group have cultures, and languages in which they are expressed, which differ somewhat from those of other groups of the same general type.

Focused more specifically on the organizational context, Schein (1985) considers that, while behavioural regularities and norms evolve among people who work together, and dominant values and philosophies are the hallmarks of an organization, reflecting aspects of organizational cultures, none is the very essence of culture. Schein believes the term 'culture' should be reserved for the deeper level of basic assumptions and beliefs shared by members of an organization, and that operate unconsciously in defining in a taken-for-granted manner an organization's view of itself in relation to its environment. These deeper assumptions and beliefs are responses learnt over time, which have been successful repeatedly in helping members cope with its external environment on the one hand, and with its problems of internal integration on the other. Accordingly, Schein (*ibid.* p. 9) defines culture as

> a pattern of basic assumptions – invented, discovered or developed by a given group as it learns to cope with its problems of external adaptation and internal integration that has worked well enough to be considered valid and, therefore, to be taught to new members as the correct way to perceive, think, and feel in relation to those problems.

Schein distinguishes these basic underlying assumptions from values and visible artefacts, such as architecture. Basic assumptions are like theories-in-use (Argyris and Schon, 1974). Such assumptions, because they are taken for granted, are much more difficult to locate than values and artefacts and, perhaps, this point is best illustrated by reference to national cultural differences.

As Morgan (1986) points out, much of the interest in organization cultures has been stimulated by the successes of Japanese companies in world markets and consequent attempts to transfer cultural factors that seem to account for these successes to Western work organizations. Basic assumptions are, however, embedded in historical factors, some of which may have evolved over centuries, and the difficulties in transplanting and imitating cultures are, accordingly, often under-estimated. As an example, Morgan (*ibid.*) cites Murray Sayle (1982), who accounts for Japanese culture's solidarity (its collaborative spirit, interdependence, lifelong commitments to work organizations and paternalistic and deferential authority relations) as grounded in history. Sayle considers that Japanese organizations combine the work culture of the rice-field with the spirit of service of the samurai. Rice growing was, and still is, a highly collaborative activity; rice farmers are willing to share their crop with the samurai in exchange for protection, which is now paralleled by the managerial élites found at the top of Japanese corporations. In contrast, in Britain generations of class conflict and an individualistic culture have given rise to antagonistic workplace relations and competition. In Japan and Britain, different cultures have evolved slowly and their roots are deep in history; nevertheless, relationships may be equally paternalistic, and working conditions just as distasteful as, for example, Kamata (1984) describes. The difference appears to be that, in Japan, history has produced a national culture that allows workers to achieve self-respect within the system, whereas, in Britain and other Western countries, an individualistic culture leads workers to gain self-respect by competing against and confronting authority. These are examples of the basic cultural assumptions Schein refers to.

The means Schein employs to analyse these deeper assumptions are developed from a major cultural study by Kluckholn and Strodtbeck (1961): knowledge of the norms and beliefs about the nature of human beings; the relationship between organizations and their members; the nature of organizations in society; and the way key organizational members, in particular, see the relationship the organization has to its environment as one of, for example, dominance or submission. These are basic to an understanding of how cultural variables influence any of Hopwood's (1974) forms of control.

Kluckholn and Strodtbeck (1961) suggest that human nature may be conceived of as innately good, or as a mixture of good and evil, or as evil – depending on the values and beliefs held by members of the particular culture. These differences have important consequences for control. An evil orientation implies that external administrative control is essential to achieve goodness. On the other hand, a good orientation suggests that goodness is fundamentally desired and, therefore, does not require such external controls to produce it. The belief that human nature is basically evil yet perfectable is part of the Puritan tradition of Western countries, whereas studies of Japanese organizations (e.g. Dore, 1973) suggest they are characterized by inherently good orientations. As a consequence, Western managers' assumptions often lead to controls that are designed to correct what are regarded as inherently lazy individual tendencies through performance measures, rewards and punishments that reinforce them. On the other hand, in Japanese work organizations less emphasis is placed on control, as it is believed that the individual is sufficiently committed to the organization's objectives to make individual sanctions less important. More attention is accordingly paid to creating conditions for co-operation.

Corporate Cultures and Subcultures

So far we have discussed the impact of national cultures on organizational cultures. However, within national cultures there is, of course, cultural variety among organizations. In just the same way, within organizations there are subcultures and even what are often called countercultures. Subcultures have long been crucial to the analyses of organizational life developed by such writers as Gouldner (1954), Dalton (1959), Sayles (1965), Nichols and Beynon (1977), Raelin (1985), Gill and Frame (1990) and Sackmann (1991). Subcultural variety, clearly, has much bearing on organizational control. Van Maanen and Barley (1985, p. 33) have suggested that, while the concept of a unitary culture is primarily an anthropological notion, the idea of subcultures is predominantly sociological, and that 'culture can be understood as a set of solutions devised by a group of people to meet specific problems posed by the situations they face in common'.

Subcultural divisions generally arise from the competing value and status systems of different occupational groups – for example, in work organizations accountants, marketing people, maintenance engineers, process workers, academics, administrators, trade unionists, supervisors and managers. Such divisions frequently result in power struggles by occupational groups for control over what is in effect the corporate culture.

Accordingly, organizational subculture may be defined as 'a subset of an organization's members who interact regularly with one another, identify themselves as a distinct group within the organization, share a set of problems commonly defined to be the problems of all, and routinely take action on the basis of collective understandings unique to the group' (*ibid.* p. 38).

In this analysis, culture may be seen as a differentiating rather than an integrating mechanism, and so may pose threats to organizational control and cultural unity. Subcultures may lie relatively dormant until some major organizational change or crisis brings them into prominence and delineates them. For example, the well-known departmental subdivisions in local-authority social-work functions were brought into greater prominence and became more conflicting when one such department was subjected to cutbacks in resources (Gill and Frame, 1990). Indeed, major changes, such as those in technology, may also give rise to culture clashes as evidenced, for example, by Barley (1984) in his study of two radiology departments. In this case the introduction of new body scanners brought latent subcultural differences into the open.

Subcultural differences within organizations may sometimes become ideological and, indeed, conflicting, giving rise to closer affiliations with groups and institutions lying outside the work organization. For example, academics in professional bureaucracies often have greater commitment to their professional bodies than to the academic institutions in which they are employed (Mintzberg, 1979a). Similarly Raelin, (1985, p. 1) in his appropriately titled book, *The Clash of Cultures*, explores the 'inherent conflict between managers and professionals [which] results basically from a clash of cultures: the corporate culture which captures the commitment of managers, and the professional culture, which socializes professionals. Both cultures are further sustained by the wider social culture'.

However, perhaps most threatening among organizational subcultures to those seeking cultural uniformity as a means of control are those brought into being by trade unions. By their very existence, these subcultures exemplify the view that the interests of employer and employee are not synonymous.

To draw this discussion together, Smith (1992) cites the contributions of Meyerson and Martin (1987) and Martin and Meyerson (1988), who provide useful overviews of approaches to organization culture, which they describe as integration, differentiation and ambiguity.

The first – integration – regards culture as an integrating mechanism with an emphasis on harmony, homogenization and consensus. Writers working within this paradigm are Deal and Kennedy (1982) and Peters and Waterman (1982), who stress the importance to cultural uniformity of the espoused values of senior management in the organization. Others are concerned more with the role of formal and informal practices, such as decision-making procedures (e.g. Ouchi, 1981; Schall, 1983) or with the role of rituals and rites (e.g. Beyer and Trice, 1987).

As Smith (1992, p. 11) contends,

> it is not surprising to find that this approach to organisational culture has been associated with the idea that by 'controlling' and 'managing' the organisation's culture, management can achieve increased managerial control, whilst at the same time achieving improved employee commitment and motivation, resulting in increased organisational efficiency, effectiveness and competitiveness.

It is therefore not too surprising that an increasingly large output of books and articles presents this message for managers.

Differentiation contrasts sharply with a view of culture as an integrative mechanism in that it acknowledges that organizational cultures may reflect a variety of values and beliefs typical of most contemporary, complex organizations. Gregory (1983, p. 359), for example, argues that 'many organisations are most accurately viewed as multicultural. Subgroups with different occupational, divisional, ethnic, or other cultures approach organisational interactions with their own meanings and sense of priorities'. The differentiation approach to culture accordingly throws considerable doubt on the notion that management control can be achieved through manipulating organizational culture simply by using various techniques, such as recruitment and selection, job redesign or the reward system. Meek (1988, p. 462) observes that, although one can perceive the culture of the modern organization as a form of social control, 'it is not a form of social control created and manipulated by management, but a process in which management, workers and the community at large participate alike'. In other words, he is distinguishing the internal manipulation and homogenization of organizational cultures as an administrative control on the one hand, and on the other, he is viewing culture as developing spontaneously within organizations as a social control.

Finally, Martin and Meyerson's (1988) third paradigm of the ambiguous nature of culture contrasts with the integrative approach to organizational culture, with its emphasis on consensus, co-operation and harmony and denial of ambiguity. It also, to some degree, contrasts with their second paradigm of differentiation. A view of culture as a differentiating mechanism acknowledges the presence of ambiguity in organizations, but their third paradigm, by contrast, accepts ambiguity as an integral and central part of organizational reality:

> individuals share some viewpoints, disagree about some, and are ignorant of, or indifferent to, others. Consensus, dissensus, and confusion coexist, making it difficult to draw cultural and subcultural boundaries. An ambiguity paradigmic view of culture then, would have no universally shared, integrating set of values, save one: an awareness of ambiguity itself.
>
> *(Ibid.* p. 117)

What is being suggested is that an individual in an organization may make use of a number of cultural paradigms as a means of interpreting, negotiating and so making sense of their organizational reality. In the context of managerial control, a picture is emerging of culture as a spontaneously arising social control, a mediating variable rather than the conventional managerial view of culture as an instrument of administrative control.

Culture Formation

Before moving on to consider the ways advocated for changing and managing organizational cultures as instruments of administrative control, it is necessary first to look at how cultures form. A great deal of research has focused on cultural-formation processes in small groups, and this is summarized to shed some light on how organization cultures originate. However, organizations differ from small groups not only in size but also in the roles founders, leaders and managers play in creating larger systems (Louis, 1980b; Schein, 1985).

Group dynamics theory is founded on laboratory research and on detailed observations of small groups engaged in work organizations or in training and therapy (Bennis and Schein, 1965) and its application to organizations (e.g. Jaques, 1955; Bion, 1959; Reed and Palmer, 1972; Kets de Vries and Miller, 1984).

In examining cultural formation in the small group, Schein (1985) is careful to make it clear that organizations are not simply aggregates of small groups. Converting the dynamics of small groups to the organization needs to be done cautiously, particularly by considering the part managers may play in creating larger systems. Nevertheless, observing the small group as a simpler unit than the more complex organization is helpful, as this helps us understand the cultural development and dynamics of larger social groupings. This is especially the case when considering such things as conformity, compliance, identification, internalization and deviancy – all of which have been researched in small-group contexts, and which underlie many of the crucial matters of organizational control.

When groups first form, the dominant factor is one of dependence as each member struggles with such personal issues and anxieties as inclusion, identity, authority and intimacy. The focus at first is not on the group but on individual anxieties and how these might be relieved by dependence on some authority figure. During this early phase, members either compete for leadership to retain control of self-orientated desires or withdraw – behaviours Bion (1959) labelled 'fight or flight'. Group-behaviour norms are formed at this early stage; that is, informal rules are set that, at the cognitive level, deal with the primary task and, at the emotional level, with authority and influence in order that the task may be addressed.

Some writers (e.g. Tuckman, 1965; Turquet, 1973) refer to stages through which groups move in their development and, while it is misleading to regard such stages as rigidly defined and necessarily sequential as they often blend into each other and early phases may reappear as groups regress, nevertheless, the notion of phases of growth is useful. Tuckman (1965) describes a late phase of group development as 'norming', while Turquet (1973) uses the term 'fusion' in a similar way to indicate the strong individual need to deny internal differences. Consequently, a lack of harmony is ignored, suppressed or punished, and an image of solidarity presented. Norms are a fundamental cultural element; they emerge as crises in the group's development and they are confronted and tackled successfully, becoming assumptions that are taken for granted. The need for group solidarity, conformity and compliance is particularly strong at this time, but it is always a feature of emerging group processes and may be especially prevalent when groups feel themselves to be under external threat.

Many experiments in decision-making have shown that pressure both to conform to the group and to comply with authority are powerful even without external threats, and that deviants are put under group pressure to follow majority decisions (e.g. Asch, 1951; Milgram, 1963; 1974; Hinton and Reitz, 1971). Such dynamics have, of course, implications for management control.

Stages of group development (Tuckman's (1965) 'performing' stage) focus on the work of the group and, as Schein (1985, p. 205) makes clear,

> the work of the group gradually attracts more and more of the members' attention, with the periods of regression into dependence, fusion, fight-flight, or pairing becoming less frequent as the group evolves a culture, stabilizes its ways of working, and thus releases energy for the task in hand. At the same time, if this model is correct, it warns us that the quickest way for the group to lose its ability to work productively is to question some of its cultural assumptions, because such a threat re-arouses the primary anxieties that the cultural solutions dealt with in the first place.

The Management of Corporate Cultures

Any examination of the management of culture and organizational control is affected crucially by the various ways in which culture may be understood in organizational analysis. This is considered, for example, by both Smircich (1983) and Ray (1986). Smircich distinguishes five ways in which culture has been conceptualized by researchers. Two of these see culture as an organizational variable, while the remaining three consider culture as a root metaphor for understanding an organization. Some theorists who hold a view of culture as metaphor regard culture as something an organization 'is' rather than something an organization 'has': 'culture as a root metaphor goes beyond the instrumental view of organizations derived from the machine metaphor and beyond the adaptive view derived from the organismic metaphor' (Smircich, 1983, p. 347).

Researchers who take a symbolic perspective may regard an organization as a pattern of symbolic discourse (e.g. Turner, 1983). As Smircich (1983, p. 351) makes clear, 'theorists and practitioners are both concerned with such practical matters as how to create and maintain a sense of organization, and how to achieve common interpretations of situations so that coordinated action is possible'. Indeed, some work from this perspective suggests that leadership is best understood as the management of meaning (Peters, 1987) or the management of culture (Schein, 1985). Hence, while culture as a root metaphor is significant for any consideration of managerial attempts to manage culture as a means of administrative control, those taking this position generally believe that culture cannot be managed. Rather, it emerges spontaneously, often over considerable periods of time, and is an expression of people's deepest needs and assumptions. On the other hand, perspectives that recognize culture as a variable are generally based on a systems-theory framework. Martin, Sitkin and Boehm (1985) refer to this group as 'cultural pragmatists', who argue that culture can and should be managed. We now turn to ways that have been advocated to manage cultures by those who take this view.

'Active' Culture Management

Those who advocate the active management of cultures, particularly those who have their origins in consulting practices (e.g. Deal and Kennedy, 1982; Pascale and Athos, 1982; Peters and Waterman, 1982; Plant and Ryan, 1988) take an active, pragmatic stance to the management of culture, as do some academics (Tichy, 1983; Schein, 1985). At the other extreme of this group are those who take a relatively passive position; these regard culture as something that, largely, cannot be influenced and more likely to be a factor only in resisting strategic change (e.g. Dyer, 1984; Martin, Sitkin and Boehm, 1985).

Of those taking a pragmatic position in the management of culture, the most direct antecedents are organization development practitioners; indeed, Schein and Tichy are both particularly associated with this pioneering group. French and Bell (1973) suggest that the term 'organization development' (or OD) probably originated in the USA in laboratory training. Participants learnt from unstructured small-group processes, which became institutionalized as a change technology when the National Training Laboratories (NTL) were founded at Bethel, Maine, in 1947. Pettigrew (1985) regards Lewin (1951) and Rogers' (1951) work, which focuses on the here and now, as the intellectual foundation of OD, and the NTL and the Centre for Group Dynamics as the institutionalized form. The pioneers of OD were McGregor, Sheppard, Blake and Mouton, as well as well-known academic consultants, such as Argyris, Bennis, Beckhard, Likert and Schein, who developed Lewin and Rogers' ideas in organizational settings. Indeed, Bennis (1966), in an early contribution, argued that the only way to change organizations was to change their cultures.

Early OD was part of the liberal agenda of the Fifties and Sixties, which later incorporated work humanization. Its techniques were participative and anti-bureaucratic, and the management of change was initially based on small-group processes as a training activity through which aggregates of groups – that is, organizations – might be changed. Its assumptions were that organizational hindrances to humans' capacity for growth needed to be unblocked if organizations were to be healthy and effective. Shared values were openness, trust and creativity (e.g. French and Bell, 1973). By the late Seventies, the OD movement seemed to be in decline (Harrison, 1984), as in many cases its claims to transform organizations had proved over-optimistic, and costs apparently exceeded benefits.

In the Eighties the wider social and economic environment had changed: competitive pressures, recession and changes in political ideology in the West had given rise to a movement away from liberal-humanistic values to a tougher managerial ideology. Silver (1987) suggests that this movement may partially account for the popularity of the 'excellence' cult exemplified by Peters and Waterman (1982). Nevertheless, OD still finds a prominent place in some company human-resource management functions, the term human resource management (HRM) signifying a change from traditional personnel management. Although there is some debate about the nature of these changes (Legge, 1989; Keenoy, 1990), normative features of HRM that apparently distinguish it from personnel management include the human resource as an integral part of business strategy in that it is vested in line management, which is responsible for directing all resources in business units. In particular, it is apparently concerned with the quality of the product or service, and with achieving 'bottom-line' results. In order to achieve all this it seems that a further distinguishing feature of HRM is its emphasis on the management of culture as a central activity of senior management (Legge, 1989). We return to these issues in our concluding chapter.

The Founding of Organizations and Cultural Control

As we saw in Chapter 2, any organization's basis is established when a founding leader or entrepreneur identifies a goal or mission that is achievable only by a group of people (Mintzberg, 1983, Chaps. 11 and 12; and Martin, Sitkin and Boehm, 1985; Schein, 1985, Chap. 9). At this stage there may be an exciting sense of mission for, as Mintzberg (1983) suggests, a new organization is unbounded by tradition and, accordingly, offers wide latitude for manoeuvre. Because these are small organizations they offer members the luxury of close, personal relationships and, frequently, strong, basic, shared beliefs. There may also be close identification and strong devotion to the founder and what he or she wishes to accomplish.

At this stage, founders will be most influential, for their prior experiences will have caused them to form assumptions about how to solve early organizational problems – assumptions around which cultures will form. Schein (1985, p. 224) terms this formative process 'embedding and transmitting'. Its most powerful elements, he believes, are

1. the things to which leaders pay attention;
2. leader reactions to organizational crises;
3. role modelling and coaching;
4. criteria for allocating rewards; and

5. criteria for recruitment, selection, promotion, retirement and
   'excommunication'.

Founders establish organizational culture to a crucial degree, but, it is argued,
what we see at this stage is culture being created rather than consciously
managed – even though leaders inevitably play a key part in the formative
process. Schein sees managers' role at this time as a monitoring and influencing
one, through the same five mechanisms referred to above.

Research on the organizational life-cycle, as we saw in the case of the small
group considered earlier, is concerned particularly with the transitions through
which organizations proceed, such as the change from youth to maturity (Kimberly, Miles and associates, 1980). Some speculate that it is at these times that
the management of culture is most easily facilitated (e.g. Siehl, 1985). Others
(for example, Schein (1985) and Deal and Kennedy (1982)), however, take an
even more proactive position, arguing for leadership in culture creation at an
early stage when the 'leadership externalizes its own assumptions and embeds
them gradually and consistently in the mission, goals structures and working
procedures of the group' (Schein, 1985, p. 317). This distinguishes leaders
from managers who, in Schein's view, need to give culture its due whereas, he
believes, the essence of leadership is to manage culture as a transformational
process. This position is taken by a number of writers, some of whom have
backgrounds in OD (e.g. Zaleznik, 1977; Burns, 1978; Bennis and Nanus,
1985; Tichy and Devanna, 1986; Conger and Kanungo, 1988).

Organizations in Mid-Life and Cultural Control

As an organization establishes itself, its 'actions become diffused with value.
When these forces are strong enough, ideology begins to emerge' (Mintzberg,
1983, p. 153). This is expressed through a number of different mechanisms,
such as special languages (Hirsch and Andrews, 1983), organizational stories
(Wilkins, 1983), rituals and ceremonies (Deal and Kennedy, 1982), sagas
(Clark, 1972) and physical arrangements, such as dress (Pfeffer, 1981a).

As organizations reach maturity, important cultural elements in the growth
period become institutionalized and taken for granted in the organization's
major processes. It may also be felt at this stage that the culture is no longer appropriate, given changing environmental or internal forces. At this stage 'flexible' cultures may be more appropriate than 'strong', monolithic cultures. As a
consequence, much attention has been given to ways of managing cultural change
at this stage in the organizational life-cycle, and prescriptions for it abound.

Deal and Kennedy (1982), generalizing from a case from the North American public sector, suggest that a seven-step approach should be followed. They
recommend that a 'hero', who is committed to the change, should be put in
charge of the process; however, for significant cultural changes to get under-
way, good reasons for making changes are needed. The greater the threat, and
the more clearly and widely the threat is recognized, the more likely an inappropriate culture can be turned round and the more likely organizational
members will accept leaders' authority as potential saviours. Deal and Kennedy (1982, p. 175) advocate transitional rituals as pivotal elements of change:

within the process people mourn old ways, renegotiate new values and relationships and anoint heroes. This helps people understand, accept, and believe in the new order. In one sense the process becomes a temporary culture much like a mourning rite. It prevents people from returning to old patterns or rushing thoughtlessly into unfamiliar new terrain.

Provision of training in new values and behaviour patterns helps people to move from one culture to another. 'Consultants from the outside bring their own magic. They help provide lightning rods to diffuse conflict as the change enfolds [*sic*] beacons for where the change is heading and talismans that the change will really work (*ibid*. p. 176). Finally, it is suggested that new directions should be signalled – for example, by structural changes – and that the workforce's resistance should be reduced through an assurance of long-term security.

In a similar, somewhat mechanistic and prescriptive fashion, O'Reilly (1989) suggests four 'mechanisms' for developing culture and four 'steps' to understanding its management. Unremarkably, these mechanisms include management as symbolic action – that is, visible actions on the part of management in support of the cultural values. Management, accordingly, somewhat paternalistically interprets events for the organization's members, for 'over time people may lose a clear sense for what the superordinate goals are and why their job is important' (*ibid*. p. 21). In particular, O'Reilly's prescription suggests management should not only say what is important but also behave consistently in ways that support that message: espoused theories and theories in use should coincide. O'Reilly also advocates the use of reward systems in the widest sense to reinforce appropriate behaviour. Such reinforcement is considered especially effective if the desired behaviour is rewarded close to its occurrence.

O'Reilly also suggests that participation and information from others are powerful mechanisms. Employee participation has a long history as ways of achieving identification with and commitment to the organization, but most methods are highly manipulative and are, generally, narrowly restricted to, for example, decisions about production processes rather than such fundamental matters as the determination of the organization's goals (Ashworth and Johnson, 1991). Information from others is expressed in a particularly manipulative, if not coercive, manner by referring to after-work socializing that is particularly common in Japanese organizations as a means of isolating organizational members from family and friends. As O'Reilly (*ibid*. p. 22) advocates, 'sixty hour work weeks can isolate people from competing interpretations . . . with this commitment of time workers may be as isolated as if they had joined a cult'.

Identification, Internalization, Indoctrination and Socialization

Other processes are also at work for, as individuals enter organizations, the culture is reinforced through identification, which may be managed or may be a much less overt process as we have already seen in Chapter 2 as internalization. Mintzberg (1983), for example, sees the identification process as on a continuum of, at one extreme, weak identification through the bureaucratically managed control system to strong identification through naturally occurring processes for which we use the term internalization. Mintzberg suggests that, in the case of weak identification, this is likely to be 'calculated' and may not therefore be internalized; however, at the other extreme, for example in religious organizations, individuals are attracted to the organization's culture and internalization is, accordingly, not problematic. Naturally occurring internalization is the strongest, most enduring form, while individual identification with the organization, which relies on formal management techniques and the use of authority, is likely to be relatively weak and ephemeral. Identification is expressed through the extent to which the individual and the organization reconcile such matters as the goals, the means by which these goals are attained, the role to which the new member is assigned and the role's required behaviour patterns.

However, as Mintzberg (*ibid.*) acknowledges, many organizations do not rely solely on internalization that develops naturally. Internalization and identification may be influenced through recruitment and promotion policies, and through various socialization and indoctrination techniques. All these are believed to lie somewhere between natural controls, on the one hand, and bureaucratic controls on the other, according to their strength in integrating individual and organization.

As we noted in Chapter 2, Townley (1991) suggests that the growing trend in the use of systematic selection and appraisal schemes not only seeks to improve competitive strength and efficiency but also, and more importantly, seeks to control employees' attitudinal and behavioural characteristics. Such practices are being introduced to a wider variety of employees than formerly, and are, apparently, no longer confined to white-collar staff. White and Trevor (1983), for example, suggest that perhaps one of the most significant aspects of the management of Japanese subsidiaries is the investment by these companies in sophisticated selection and recruitment policies and senior management's commitment to these practices. Emphasis is in particular placed on 'loyalty', 'seriousness', 'commitment' and 'responsibility'. Similar practices are also evident in North American companies, with the 'strong cultures' supposedly found in many of Peters and Waterman's (1982) 'excellent' sample. It is not surprising that many of these companies seek to recruit a pre-socialized, manipulable, non-union workforce, often with the help of consultants and such techniques as bio-data and psychometric tests.

Such performance appraisal is also being extended to groups and sectors not previously included. Such criteria as 'dependability', 'flexibility' and the individual's commitment to the company rather than to the group are becoming increasingly common – all of which are cultural norms, not easily identifiable, technical, job characteristics (Long, 1986). The emphasis on individual appraisal, in particular, conflicts with norms of co-operation and effective communication in 'excellent' companies. Some writers have suggested that the latter is for external consumption while individual appraisal is closer to internal managerial values and the control system (e.g. Anthony, 1990).

As Mintzberg (1983, p. 156) notes,

> in many cases natural and selected identification do not satisfy organizational needs for loyalty . . . [The] organization may therefore try to evoke the necessary identification, and at the same time, to reduce outside identifications that might interfere with the employee's ability to serve it. In this

regard two processes can be relied upon, an explicit one called indoctrination and an implicit one called socialization.

A narrow distinction is thus made between indoctrination (the use of formal techniques to develop identifications on the part of the organization's members) and socialization, which is largely spontaneous, informal and implicit, and so may be more powerful. These important distinctions are often blurred. Pascale (1985, pp. 37–8) uses the term socialization to cover selection; this is followed by 'humility inducing experiences', reminiscent of informal initiation ceremonies in some organizations and formal procedures in, for example, military organizations. These are designed towards accepting the organization's norms and values and much else included here under indoctrination. Pascale subtitles his paper, 'reconciling ourselves to socialization', as he seems to be embarrassed by the notion of social controls, 'even when some measure of them may be in our [*sic*] best interests'.

Indoctrination may take extreme forms where loyalty is at issue, particularly when it is employed, for example, by religious orders and the military: the indoctrination of American prisoners in Korea is often cited as an example (Schein, 1956; Lifton, 1956). Business organizations may, as well, use programmes of indoctrination, albeit milder ones – house magazines, company ties and 'cultural extravaganza'. An example of cultural extravaganza is described enthusiastically by Deal and Kennedy (1982, p. 74).

Mary Kay Cosmetics stages 'seminars' that are lavish multimillion dollar events at the Dallas convention center . . . awards for the best sales are given – pink Buicks and Cadillacs. One year the cars simply 'floated' down onto the stage from a 'cloud' – a weighty touch of hoopla that produced overwhelming response from the crowd. At the end of this extravaganza everyone understands that the challenge of the company is sales.

Finally we come to organizational socialization, which is defined as the process by which an individual, spontaneously, comes to appreciate the values, the abilities and the expected behaviours essential for an organizational role and for participating as an organizational member (van Maanen, 1976; Louis, 1980a). It is clear that these processes are by no means clear cut and that their content may be best defined by the socializer's intent. Schein (1984a), for example, describes the process of socialization as the way in which new members learn about the organization from such sources as key role models, including the individual's superior (who is promoted and rewarded) and long-serving employees (who offer advice on the realities of organizational life and who explain bizarre behaviour, which has often come to be taken for granted and is only explicable through some accident of history unknown to a newcomer). Newcomers to organizations are thus socialized by their observation of, and search for, cues, which reveal such matters as what desirable behaviour really is if one's career is to be advanced and how to keep out of trouble.

Such cues may, of course, run counter to official pronouncements. Argyris and Schon (1978) have called these unofficial pronouncements 'theories-in-use' the official pronouncements being known as 'espoused theories'. In parts of the English polytechnic sector that is being raised to the status of universities, for example, the importance of academic research is stressed as an espoused theory in most institutions' mission statements. However, even a casual inspection of those selected and rewarded reveals to staff (who are searching to understand the theories-in-use and how these may affect their careers) that research competence is, in reality, relatively unimportant as a criterion for advancement.

Can Culture be Managed as a Means of Control?

The answer to the question posed in the heading to this section seems to be that cultures can be purposively managed only to a limited extent. Many of the prescriptions for cultural control through creating 'strong' cultures as a means of manipulating members is, as already noted, somewhat crude, unsophisticated and touching only on the surface manifestations of organizational life. At worst, the management of culture emphasizes the role leaders and managers play when managing the socio-emotional domain as advocated by Peters and Waterman (1982), which, as we saw in Chapter 2, is heavily dependent on human-relations assumptions, albeit dressed up in new clothes. The evidence that there is a correlation between 'strong' cultures and excellence, as Peters and Waterman and their co-workers suggest, is dubious (Silver, 1987; Thompson and McHugh, 1990). At best, the management of cultures is derived from neo-human relations that, for example, emphasizes structural reorganization to promote cultural change (see Figure 5.1).

The main criticism of those who advocate cultural control is that it is not possible to manage and control cultures closely by their very nature and, further, that the more extreme and mechanistic prescriptions for managing cultures are, then, often the more manipulative, coercive and patronizing and these are likely to be counterproductive in the longer term.

Cultures often evolve gradually over long periods in multiple and diverse ways. In Smircich's (1983) oft-cited paper, cultures may be seen as either what organizations 'are' or as what an organization 'has' – 'has' being a variable that may be manipulated. However, as Smircich makes clear, ideas of culture as either a root metaphor or a variable may both be of use to those wishing to influence cultures, but the cultural control this implies is more subtle and less mechanistic. O'Reilly (1989) contends that such phrases as 'IBM means service' communicate central values around which different organizations build and symbolize important aspects of corporate philosophy. However, as we have seen, an organization's culture always runs much deeper than this: 'The slogans, evocative language, symbols, stories, myths, ceremonies, rituals, and patterns of tribal behaviour that decorate the surface of organizational life merely give clues to the existence of an all-pervasive system of meaning' (Morgan, 1986, p. 133).

Cultural control does not seem possible in the mechanistic ways prescribed by such advocates as, for example, Peters and Waterman (1982) and Deal and Kennedy (1982). As Pascale (1985) suggests, the mechanisms put forward are often distasteful, coercive and manipulative. Frequently, other forms of control are not superseded by cultural control, as formal structures and mechanisms often exist alongside the management of meaning and may often be in conflict with them. The espoused cultural norms of high-quality communication and trust said to be exemplified by open-plan offices may not co-exist smoothly with an emphasis on individual appraisal, secrecy about the level of rewards and non-unionism. Such ambiguity was well portrayed in the Channel 4 documentary about Hewlett Packard, appropriately entitled 'The Gilded Cage'.

The managerial view that what is good for the organization is good for the employee has always been an underlying feature of work organizations. However, the idea that this can be imposed by social processes involving, for example, brain-washing and totalitarianism is disturbing and, naturally, can cause alienation and a strong feeling of resistance. However, this may be an unduly pessimistic observation. As Anthony (1990, p. 3) contends, the belief system, values and meanings of the managed organization are 'never' transmitted successfully 'beyond the boundaries of management to the intended receptor'. The result is the isolation of managers of organizational culture who, Anthony believes, become locked into a deeper commitment to values that are not widely shared – in other words, 'he who leads is lost'. Second, manipulative and insincere behaviour is readily detectable for what it is and is often satirized. An example of this is the UK's former nationalized electricity industry and its statutory requirement to 'consult' its employees through local advisory committees (LACs), which were known to the workforce as 'let's all cuddle'. Such cynical, pointed jokes are very powerful in helping to destroy the very practices to which they are directed.

There is some firm evidence that creating changes in organizational culture is difficult; indeed, the decline in the organizational development movement in the late Seventies was largely a consequence of its inability to deliver its promises. Much of the recent spate of anecdotal material claiming the efficacy of cultural change in improving organizational effectiveness is short on evidence. As Smith and Peterson (1988, p. 121) point out, detailed published case studies of organizations 'within which major changes in culture have been successfully accomplished do exist but they are rare'.

Two recent research-based cases confirm the contention that resistance to attempts to change organizational culture is likely to be strong, and that any changes occurring are unlikely to be internalized and permanent (Ackroyd and Crowdy, 1990; Ogbonna and Wilson, 1990). A third case of sophisticated action research in British Rail that acknowledged all these difficulties is, perhaps, more optimistic by suggesting that the use of the 'culture concept' can bring about appropriate changes (Bate, 1990).

Ackroyd and Crowdy (1990), in a study of a group of slaughtermen, demonstrate that the work cultures they studied are highly distinctive, resilient and difficult to control or change and, further, that these slaughtermen apparently worked in groups the cultures of which, in many ways, typified 'excellent' companies. These cultures had emerged naturally without management action, and were in many respects in opposition to managerial policies. As Ackroyd and Crowdy point out, such work cultures are to be found in many organizations: they result in effective work performance but often in contradiction to senior management's instructions. In other words, the espoused theories differ from theories-in-use. This raises the important issue of whether 'democratic leaders' might 'let the reality of the situation evolve from the definitions of the situation offered by their colleagues, listening to what is being said, summoning and integrating key themes, and evoking and developing imagery that captures the essence of the emergent system of meaning' (Morgan, 1985, p. 136).

Ogbonna and Wilson (1990) examined attempts to change the super-market's culture to one of being more customer centred or, as the authors put it, from being one of customer as 'punter' to customer as 'king'. They concluded that supermarket and shopfloor staff have not taken on board the values and assumptions espoused by their senior managers, which had been promulgated largely by training courses and films, and that there had been little internalization. A campaign directed towards cashout operatives, to get them to smile at customers, was attacked by an official of the trade union, USDAW, who 'was devastated about the assumptions management has of the workers . . . [They] should be treated like adults and not children in a play-school' (*ibid.* p. 14). Some of the more bizarre practices of North American 'excellent companies' are similarly and comprehensively demolished by Silver (1987), who regards such practices as 'silly' and degrading.

Bate's (1990) study of a three-year organization development project in British Rail, in contrast, uses a differentiated analysis of culture as its conceptual focus to a strategy for change. To move the project from design to implementation (i.e. to attempt culture change), the following theoretical propositions emerged:

1. Cultures are produced interactively and can therefore only be changed interactively.
2. The interaction's quality will be reflected in the quality of the relationships and in the dialogue within and among different interest groups and subcultures, both inside and outside the organization.
3. Cultural adaptation and change is, therefore, a network development process. The network, not the formal authority structure, is the basic unit of cultural production and adaptation.

Bate (*ibid.* p. 104) claims that, as a consequence of an intervention based on these propositions, people in British Rail were able to think culturally about their everyday reality and began 'to put labels on it'. The language culture that was based on the way people talked to one another also seemed to be changing, as did the ways people seemed to be influencing one another. Bate (*ibid.* p. 83) concluded after three years' work that 'the culture perspective can be used to develop novel insights into organisational problems, new directions for change, and appropriate strategic processes'.

Conclusion

Managing culture as a means of control seems possible if organization is seen to rest in shared systems of meaning. Influencing the norms that communicate key objectives is the action suggested, managers being symbolic actors who foster desirable patterns of meaning. However, when we look at the processes by which this may be achieved, we are looking at a much more demanding, subtle and democratic activity on the part of management than the literature suggests.

Even if democratically inclined, thoughtful managers find that cultures as systems of control are not capable of being managed mechanistically in the manner of, say, the financial reward system. As we have seen, such procedural advice is based on a faulty diagnosis of the nature of organizational culture and the ways it develops. This diagnosis is also probably a symptom of the consultant's need to develop packaged material to ensure large sales. These features, as well, seem to arise from internal staff's need to be seen to be energetic; they generate forms and paperwork which emphasize controlling the organization rather than facilitating the necessary changes (Gill and Whittle, 1993).

This brings us to the paradox in much management literature. A shallow understanding of social organization and its culture, as put forward in a number of popular management books, is probably as unhelpful to managing culture as no understanding at all. It may well be at odds with the very managerial objectives being pursued. However, a deep understanding of organizational culture as a precursor to influencing it with subtlety runs counter to the current vogue articulated by the culture gurus such as Peters and Waterman. It also runs counter to the prevailing managerial values of being biased towards direction, firm action and speedy decision-making – that is, it runs counter to one of the principal values held by managerial culture.

Further Reading

Useful general introductions to organizational culture are to be found in Frost *et al.* (1985) and its successor, Frost *et al.* (1991). From a managerialist perspective we have also found Schein (1985) useful. We would also draw attention to Gregory (1983), Smircich (1983), Allaire and Firsirotu (1984) and Sackmann (1991) – all of which provide insights on methods of investigating organizational cultures.

On the subject of managing and changing organizational cultures, and of culture as a means of managerial control, we suggest reading different perspectives. Using Meyerson and Martin's (1987) classification, authors writing from an integrative standpoint are Ouchi (1981), Deal and Kennedy (1982) and Schein (1984a, 1985). From a differentiation perspective we suggest Meek (1988), Martin and Meyerson (1988) and, particularly, Bate (1990).

6

Leadership, Self-Management and Self-Control

Introduction

So far we have largely been concerned with control as an external phenomenon: the control of individuals through rewards, punishments and the control of the work environment, which is administered down hierarchies by superiors. The very nature of leadership in most cases implies control of subordinates, either directly or indirectly.

As we saw in Chapter 5, leadership through cultural control is usually defined as charismatic or transformational. This is a popular theme with some academics and practitioners (e.g. Burns, 1978; Bass, 1985; Bennis and Nanus, 1985; Tichy and Devanna, 1986; Bryman, 1992). However, as we have already suggested, this is difficult to achieve as the very management of culture is, itself, problematic. Additionally, the leader as a charismatic figure may have negative consequences, inducing in subordinates a dysfunctional dependence that stifles creativity and initiative.

Accordingly, in this chapter we review first some approaches to leadership and control and then make a case for what we term 'self-leadership' as a means of achieving self-controlling organizations. This conforms with Hopwood's (1974) belief that control over employees is ultimately self-imposed, and that external controls are likely to lead only to minimal compliance unless they are designed, in the main, to stimulate and facilitate an employee's own internal influence and energy.

It is, however, necessary to point out that control and self-control are ambiguous concepts (Thomas, 1984), and that there are many ways of classifying and defining them. In Chapter 2 we presented Hopwood's (1974) threefold classification of controls in organizations: administrative, social and self-control. This is probably an extension of others' work, for example, Dalton and Lawrence (1971), who classify controls in organizations depending on the locus of administration: organizational, informal group and individual.

Control deriving from the informal group comes from mutual commitment and is measured against group norms. Signals for the need of corrective action are indicated by deviation from group norms, rewards are contained in continuing membership of the group and punishments by various forms of ostracism. Finally, control by individuals or self-control derive from individuals' goals and aspirations, are directed by self-expectations and corrected when targets are missed. Rewards are the satisfactions gained from being in control and punishments the sense of disappointment and feeling of failure in missing targets. In Chapter 2 we differentiated between compliance-based self-control and commitment-based self-control. Here we are concerned with commitment-based self-control.

Leadership and Control

Early work on the nature of the manager's job suggest that it is concerned with a set of composite functions. Fayol (1914), who has been described by Mintzberg (1973) as the father of the classical school, considered that there were five basic managerial functions: planning, organizing, co-ordinating, commanding and controlling. Similarly Urwick (1943), who was formerly a distinguished soldier and, later, a founder of an influential consultancy, continued this tradition in Britain by regarding the essential managerial functions as forecasting, planning, co-ordinating, commanding and controlling. The 'principles' of the last two functions (command and control), he contended, 'is to secure the general interest and to see that it is not interfered with by individual interests' (*ibid.* p. 78).

Mintzberg's (1973) contribution was (at least in part) to build on the work of Carlson (1951) in addressing what managers actually do at work rather than describing either what it is considered they do or what they say they do. To investigate this, Mintzberg gathered data by systematically observing and recording managers' activities, a method he later termed 'direct' research (Mintzberg, 1979b). This he contrasted with Carlson's method, which was to collect data by asking the managers he surveyed to keep diaries. This is somewhat incidental to our discussion, but the point it is necessary to make is that the classical school fulfilled managers' need to know what they should be doing when management was a pseudo-profession struggling for professional recognition. The classical school's assumptions still block the search for a deeper understanding of the manager's work but, more importantly for the discussion here, this has also led to a belief among managers that this is not only what a manager does but also what he or she should do.

Despite the fact that Mintzberg, with Lewis and Stewart (1958), exploded the classical view of managerial work (in which they were followed by others, e.g. Kotter, 1982), there is always a considerable time lag before new ideas are accepted; especially so if, as in this case, other powerful forces are present that cause resistance to change. In some quarters managers are still taught management principles, and books (e.g. Koontz and O'Donnell, 1972) were until recently still published on which lecture courses were based. It is therefore natural that managers regard controlling as one of the principal behaviours to engage in if they are to be seen as 'managing'. The assertion that managing primarily involves commanding and controlling is still strongly held, and this help, in part, to explain the influence of former military men in senior positions in organizations – British Rail being, until recently, a notable example (Bate, 1990).

Leadership theory and managers' continuing fascination with what makes an effective leader has also reinforced the idea that a great deal of managing is concerned with controlling subordinates directly and closely. There seems to be some support for the view that the concept of leadership functions as a social construct to reinforce existing social beliefs and structures about the necessity of hierarchy and leaders in organizations (Gemmill and Oakley, 1992).

The persistence of attempts to determine the nature of effective leadership is probably accounted for by subconscious psychodynamic forces of the sort hinted at above. As Smith and Peterson (1988, p. 11) point out, 'there has been a period of about 70 or so years during which researchers into leadership acted as though they were medieval alchemists in search of the philosopher's stone'. The earliest attempt to find an explanation of effective leadership was the study of the association between particular individual traits (such as intelligence) and effective leadership, especially during the period when psychometric assessment tests and procedures were being developed. However, the relationships between most of the traits and effective leaders ('great men') appeared weak, and effectiveness also seemed to depend on contexts (Mann, 1959; Stogdill, 1974). In the late 1940s the trait approach was replaced by theories that derived largely from group or laboratory methods – though both, as we shall see, were concerned to suggest universal rather than contingent applications.

Classic studies of leadership as a universal behavioural style were carried out by Lewin, Lippitt and White (1939), who examined the impact of three different leadership styles in boys' clubs. Three club leaders role played each leader style in turn, and what they described as democratic (supportive), *laissez-faire* (vacillating) and autocratic (controlling) styles were compared for effectiveness. As Smith and Peterson (1988) make clear, however, the reporting of the work's results was influenced by the political climate of the late 1930s, and the study did not reveal the effectiveness of the democratic style in all respects only that it was effective in certain dimensions. Also, when the research was replicated in other parts of the world entirely different results were produced in other cultures.

During the 1950s and 1960s many attempts were made to define effective leadership styles by using research designs that took data by means of questionnaires from managers and subordinates actually in organizations. Perhaps the largest project of this kind was that based at the Ohio State University. This work (which became known as the Ohio State leadership studies – Stogdill and Coons, 1957) described leadership style as varying in two ways: 'consideration' and 'initiating structure'. Consideration was defined as behaviours, such as consultation, which encouraged mutual trust between leader and led. Initiating structure included behaviours that resulted directly in the speedy completion of tasks, such as defining and ordering. Thus effective leaders were those who behaved towards others in a considerate manner but who also provided an appropriate structure to enable tasks to be completed expeditiously. 'Consideration' and 'initiating structure' are, roughly, synonymous with 'support' and 'control'.

These studies were replicated in small groups by, for example, Cartwright and Zander (1953), Likert (1961) and Blake and Mouton (1964). Blake and Mouton drew on the work of the Ohio researchers but treated consideration (support) and initiating structure (control) as interrelated rather than separate elements in that, in their concept, effective managers were those who showed high concern for task performance and also for those with whom they worked; that is, both controlling and supportive behaviours.

However these early studies failed to take into account the circumstances or contingencies in which leadership acts occurred and, accordingly, the same criticisms of universality levelled at the trait approach were also made of behavioural approaches to leadership style.

One of the earliest contingency theories of leadership effectiveness was put forward by Fiedler in 1967. Fiedler's measure of leader personality is constructed around the 'least preferred co-worker' scale, which rests on the assumption that the person the leader has most difficulty working with reflects a basic leadership style. Fiedler's second assumption is that the leader's implicit behavioural style, which contributes most to group performance, varies according to the nature of the situation – which is seen to change according to three factors. These factors are the quality of the leader's relationship with subordinates, the leader's formal position, power and the degree of task structure. The last two variables are the direct exercise of managerial control. Task-orientated leaders will do best, Fiedler believes, in situations that are highly favourable and also in situations that are very unfavourable. In intermediate situations, the relationship-orientated leader is expected to do better. While there is some empirical support for Fiedler's theory, many consider he relies on a personality measure of doubtful validity and, indeed, that his findings are somewhat ambiguous (Feldman and Arnold, 1986).

Subsequently, path-goal theories of leadership have been developed, which assert that leaders must first ensure that subordinates understand how to accomplish leaders' goals and that then, as far as is possible, subordinates will achieve their personal goals in the process (House, 1971). The leader's task is, therefore, very directive and high on control in that he or she ascertains the task environment and then selects those behaviours that will ensure that subordinates are motivated towards organizational goals. However, empirical tests of the path-goal model in different work situations have produced highly variable findings, which have yielded mixed support for the model (Schriesheim and Von Glinow, 1977).

More recently, House (1984) has attempted to widen the scope of contingency theories by drawing on the work of contingency theorists more broadly in the field of organizational behaviour. On this basis, House makes sixty propositions about the personal and organizational circumstances that would cause a particular leader to choose a specific style. House suggests that a principal factor in the leader's choice of style is expectations about how subordinates will respond to them.

In general, early leadership theorists took what might be termed a managerialist position. This is also a more widely held position than the leadership literature in Vroom and Yetton's (1973) work on decision-making. Here a contingency theory of decision-making is presented, which focuses on leadership acts in settings requiring explicit decisions, including the extent to which subordinates should be involved in the process. Heilmann *et al.* (1984), when testing the Vroom-Yetton model, found that it was supported when students took the manager's perspective but not when they took the subordinate's. Subordinates apparently preferred to participate in all decisions regardless of their nature. Thus Jago (1982, p. 315), after reviewing leadership research over the years, complained that

> although thousands of empirical investigations of leaders have been conducted in the last seventy-five years no clear and equivocal understanding exists as to what distinguishes leaders from nonleaders and perhaps more importantly what distinguishes effective from ineffective leaders . . . Although behavioural scientists have granted few topical areas greater research attention the results of these efforts remain a bewildering melange for even the most serious student of organisations.

In summary, traditional leadership theory has focused at least in part on the leader as controller over aspects of the followers' environment, such as rewards, punishments and authority relations.

The disillusionment with the confusions inherent in earlier approaches to leadership study has led to a revival of Weber's (1947) notion of charismatic leadership. This stresses the leader's personal qualities, 'resting on devotion to specific and exceptional sanctity, heroism or exemplary character of an individual person, and of the normative patterns or order revealed or ordained by him' (*ibid.* p. 328).

In the late 1970s, House (1977) and Burns (1978) revived this idea. House (1977) offers seven propositions about aspects of charismatic leadership in complex organizations. Among these are the following:

1. Charismatic effects are dominance and self-confidence, need for influence and a strong conviction of the moral righteousness of their beliefs.
2. The more favorable the perceptions of the potential follower towards a leader the more the follower will model (a) the values of the leader; (b) the expectations of the leader that effective performance will result in desired or undesired outcomes for the follower; (c) the emotional responses of the leader to work-related stimuli; (d) the attitudes of the leader to work and the organization.
3. Leaders who have charismatic effects are more likely to engage in behaviors designed to create the impression of competence and success than leaders who do not have such effects.
4. Leaders who have charismatic effects are more likely to engage in behaviors that arouse motives relevant to the accomplishment of the mission than are leaders who do not have charismatic effects.

(*Ibid.* pp. 194–205)

On the other hand, Burns' (1978) analysis was based largely on the study of major political leaders. His primary interest was in what has come to be known as 'transformational leadership', which he contrasts with transactional leadership. In transactional leadership a mutual exchange is judged to have taken place between leader and follower as long as both derive benefit from it;

in other words, the subordinate agrees to accept leadership in exchange for extrinsic rewards. Burns (*ibid*. p. 20) contrasts this with transforming leadership, in which 'leaders and followers raise one another to higher levels of motivation and morality'. It is also suggested that transformational leaders go beyond such basic emotions as fear and greed to appeal to such ideals and moral values as justice and liberty. As House, Spangler and Woycke (1990, p. 364) put it,

> Charismatic leaders transform the needs, values, preferences and aspirations of followers. These leaders motivate followers to make significant personal sacrifices in the interest of some mission and to perform above and beyond the call of duty. Followers become less motivated by self-interest and more motivated to serve the interests of the larger collective.

Charismatic leadership theories thus focus on the emotional and motivational arousal of followers by engaging the followers' self-esteem and confidence in the leader – values that are all important to followers' intrinsic motivation.

Bass (1985) attempted to distinguish between transactional and transformational leadership by using questionnaire measures in different cultures. These suggest that subordinates who rate their superiors high on the transformational scales also rate them high on effectiveness; however, those rated high on the transactional scales are regarded as less effective. A number of methodological criticisms have been made of Bass's work (e.g. Hunt, 1991), but further work by House, Spangler and Woycke (1990) has found considerable support for House's (1977) theory. Zaleznik (1977, 1989) also distinguishes transactional and transformational leadership by contrasting managers who are interested in maintaining a smoothly running organization with leaders who are concerned to bring about change.

The Burns' study has been instrumental to many others, described by Kets de Vries (1990, p. 755) 'as a movement back to basics i.e. a renewed interest in the observation of leaders in action'. Accordingly, recently there has been a large number of studies of the charismatic leader in context (e.g. Bennis and Nanus, 1985; Tichy and Devanna, 1986; Kotter, 1988; Conger and Kanungo, 1988; and a useful summary review by Bryman, 1992).

Tichy and Devanna's (1986) study is typical of these. It refers to the accelerating rate of change and the key to global competitiveness as being companies' ability to transform themselves continually. In order to achieve this, Tichy and Devanna see a need for transformational leadership at all levels of the organization. Their work draws on Zaleznik's (1989) comparison of managers and leaders, their study, for the most part, being based on interviews with twelve leaders in a wide variety of organizations. They admit they are not concerned with a representative sample but want their work to be

> a challenge to our academic colleagues interested in leadership and change. We have taken positions in this book which are really hypotheses. We do not have a large systematic sample that we have followed over a long period of time with data from multiple sources; instead we have a small number of clinical cases based on individual interviews with limited data from others in their organizations.
>
> (Tichy and Devanna, 1986, p. xiv)

Tichy and Devanna's analysis is, then, typical of many books written recently primarily for managers in that the data is presented in an attractive, albeit racy, style, and their prescriptions are based on limited data. It is, nevertheless, appropriate to outline their conclusions briefly.

They present the transformational 'drama' in three 'acts'. The first is to recognize the need for revitalization – it recognizes the challenges the leader faces when attempting to alert the organization to threats from the environment. The second 'act' is the process of creating a new vision involving the leaders' attempts to focus the organization on a mission that is motivating and positive. Finally, in the third act the leader institutionalizes the change or transformation so that it will be long lasting.

In their conclusion, Tichy and Devanna review the common characteristics that differentiate their sample of transformational from transactional managers. These characteristics, they believe, are the conscious identification of themselves as change agents; their courage; their clear articulation of their value position and its congruence with their behaviour; their view of mistakes not as failures but as learning experiences; their ability to deal with complexity, ambiguity and uncertainty; and their sense of vision. These are all, clearly, important attributes, but they all suggest implicitly superhuman qualities and the subordinates' dependency on the leader, which may induce a lack of employee creativity and initiative and pose survival problems when the leader is no longer available.

Pauchant (1991), while reminding us that research on charismatic leadership is sparse and inconclusive, suggests that it has its 'darker' side. Using a psychoanalytic analysis, Pauchant constructs a hypothesized typology of 'transferential' leadership dependent on a complex of leader–follower attributes and relationships. He concludes that 'one of the most destructive potentials of this type of leadership seems to emerge from the psychic unit where the leader is self-inflated and the followers self-deflated' (*ibid.* p. 523). He therefore cautions against too ready an acceptance of the notion of charismatic leadership's beneficial effects, especially as he cites evidence of self-deflation in organizations and society (e.g. Rogers, 1980). He also suggests that self-inflated managers seem to be gaining positions of power in organizations – a view supported, for example, by Lasch (1979) and Gill and Whittle (1992). The result from introducing charismatic leadership in this analysis may, therefore, be an excessive reliance on the leader and a consequent stifling of creativity and initiative in subordinates. As social despair, helplessness and anomie increase so the need for a messiah and a magical rescue by a heroic leader increase. We agree with Gemmill and Oakley (1992) and Krantz and Gilmore (1990) that the charisma's significance may be in its meaning as a social delusion and maladaptive response in conditions of uncertainty and turbulence that allows followers to escape responsibility for their own actions and inactions.

There are, therefore, a number of forces that may dispose managers to be obsessed by control. Pioneer writers on the nature of management and leadership theorists have contributed to the belief that much of management is fundamentally concerned with control. An additional, powerful, underlying factor is the stressful nature of managerial work and the neurotic and compulsive behaviour which may ensue. Managers often feel insecure; frequently they may feel they are superfluous, and they know with their employees that the organization seems to run more smoothly when they are missing from it. Such anxieties may be expressed in frantic, controlling activities.

Here we are reminded of Kets de Vries and Miller's (1984) speculative typology of neurotic styles and organizational dysfunctioning and, in particular, of their compulsive organization, where there is an emphasis on formal controls and information systems to ensure the organization operates smoothly. However, things are so programmed in these organizations that bureaucratic dysfunctions, inflexibility and inappropriate responses become common. The organization becomes poor at managing differences, as such behaviour requires flexibility and the capacity to cope with ambiguity. In such situations, managers are likely to become alienated because initiatives are stifled, and they lack influence and discretion.

Our belief is that there are many practical examples of the dysfunctions already referred to. Here we illustrate the difficulties by discussing just two cases – one from the public sector and one from the private.

Polytechnics in England have undergone radical change in that they recently left local authority control and became independent corporate entities. The latest stage in the movement to give them greater autonomy is the conferment of university status. The external control of the quality of much of polytechnics' work exercised for more than twenty years by the Council of National Academic Awards (CNAA) has been relinquished. The CNAA is to be disbanded in early 1993. Accordingly, the controls exercised by the CNAA are being replaced by new external controls and internal controls. These changes are bringing control in these institutions into even greater prominence.

Mintzberg (1979a) has described higher educational institutions as good examples of professional bureaucracies along with, for example, hospitals. Using his own university, McGill in Montreal, as his main example, he suggests that the prime co-ordinating mechanism is the standardization of skills, which is maintained by hiring accredited professionals who staff the decentralized operating core and whose standards originate in self-governing professional associations with colleagues in other professional bureaucracies. The operating core is the chief component in the professional bureaucracy and, subservient to it, is the only other large element: the support staff whose function is to serve it. In Mintzberg's formulation, the planning and work formalization functions are not well developed as the operating core largely looks after these matters. There is, as a consequence, little need for close supervision and management of work by middle management as there is in the machine bureaucracy.

However, as was discovered in research into public-sector higher education when it was experiencing the trauma of cutbacks in the 1980s, a polytechnic's organization varies considerably from Mintzberg's generalized type of the professional bureaucracy based on the large university (Gill and Pratt, 1986; Gill and Frame, 1990). The reasons for these differences probably lie in the cultural history of polytechnics, particularly their origins as technical teaching institutions producing standardized course outputs and their very close relationship with local authority bureaucracies. So it has, until recently, been the case that most polytechnics were more centralized than the typical Mintzberg professional bureaucracy and the bureaucratic component was at least as powerful as the professional academic operating core. Or, to put it more crudely, they were, at least in their origins, more like schools than universities, and the essential features of these cultures linger on.

At the present there seems to be a struggle in polytechnics for power – between the academic system on the one hand and the technostructure on the other. The recent changes in external control have heightened these differences and, to fill the control void left by the CNAA, the centralized, internal control functions have been strengthened. One consequence has been an increasing tension between a more decentralized academic system on the lines of the typical university and a centralized administrative system concerned with replacing the CNAA's close control of quality. These conflicts are experienced in the operating units (faculties or schools) as power struggles for greater independence and, in the administrative system, as a need to exert greater control over wayward academics. The academic component of the system believes it is not being left to manage towards overall targets in the particular circumstances of the decentralized faculty or school but is being subjected to inappropriate central control. Where, as in many cases, polytechnics are multi-site, these conflicts may be exacerbated.

Public-sector higher education in England is, of course, not unique in these difficulties. The brewing industry is also undergoing rapid change as individual brewing companies seek to reduce costs as a result of the Monopolies and Mergers Commission Report, *The Supply of Beer* (1989). The industry, traditionally, has been conservatively minded and has had no pressing need to change because, in part, it has been so profitable. The industry is, however, becoming much more competitive and, in many companies, steps are being taken to improve profitability.

Research in one company is being conducted into the distribution function, which is concerned with the delivery of beer to licensed premises (Gill and Farrar, 1992). Policies are being introduced to improve the function's efficiency by such measures as the restructuring and merging of distribution depots and reductions in manning; the introduction of total quality management; a review of payment systems and attempts to introduce staff-status schemes; and the introduction of distribution information systems using new technology.

However, such measures are being introduced largely from the centre through three senior intermediate levels between chief executive and the depot manager on what is, by its very nature, a highly decentralized organization. Distribution depots are geographically dispersed and located in very different environments, and they have long, idiosyncratic histories. Not surprisingly, they exhibit much subcultural variety.

The depot manager (who is located in the classic middle-management role between senior managements served by technical specialists and the shopfloor) is being asked to manage changes introduced from the centre that the manager not only has had little part in designing but that also often seem inappropriate in the culture of the particular depot.

As with the academic management of faculties in polytechnics, the distribution depot managers often consider that they would prefer to be involved in the negotiation of targets on which to manage in the particular culture in which the depot is located. This they would prefer to having uniform policies and controls imposed from the centre. As Zaleznik and Kets de Vries (1975) make clear, the three levels of rationality in organizations (the total organization, the group and the individual) are often in conflict. Powerful corporate staffs are often the non-rational response of chief executives to their control needs. An impressive group of studies suggests a shift from pyramidical to flat structures to achieve wider participation and so commitment, with the objective of improving decision quality and output. However, in conflict with this aim is the effect of reducing senior managements' power.

An approach that departs to some extent from this, and which is one of the main conclusions of this chapter, suggests remedial action that places less dependence on the leader and also, incidentally, prescribes a less demanding, controlling leadership role. This considers leadership and the control of organizations as being achieved by encouraging the commitment-based self-control of individuals throughout the organization. This approach is based on the belief that the only real control is through intrinsic individual motivation; the role of extrinsic control is to set the scene and to create the conditions for the design and introduction of appropriate intrinsic controls. It is suggested that the effectiveness of extrinsic organizational control mechanisms should be judged by the way they influence self-control systems based on the internalization of norms within individual organizational members:

> Organizational standards will not significantly influence employee behavior if they are not accepted. Similarly organizational rewards will not produce their desired effects if they are not valued by the employees receiving the rewards. Regardless of how employee performance is appraised the performance evaluation that will carry most weight will be the evaluations that employees make of themselves . . . All this suggests that to be effective a leader must successfully influence the way people influence themselves. A tight external control system may at the very best produce compliance. Commitment to excellence however flows from the powerful leadership potential within.
>
> (Manz and Sims, 1989, p. 7)

This is a somewhat different form of leadership from that developed earlier, and we discuss this below. First, however, it is necessary to consider some basic findings about the nature of individual motivation and, in particular, to distinguish intrinsic and extrinsic motivation. It should be pointed out at this stage that intrinsic motivation will be based upon commitment to shared norms however these are derived – whether from senior management or otherwise. We then apply these findings to leadership and management, whose function we conceptualize as creating self-controlling and self-motivating organizations.

Intrinsic and Extrinsic Motivation

As we saw in Chapter 3, intrinsic motivation is thought to be motivation resulting from an individual's need to be competent and self-determining (Deci, 1975). Intrinsically motivated tasks are therefore those that are interesting and enjoyable to perform, irrespective of such extrinsic rewards as cash.

When behaviour is intrinsically motivated, individuals are believed to feel that task accomplishment is under their own control and, under these circumstances, they will engage in these activities for intrinsic rewards. On the other hand, when individuals receive extrinsic rewards for task accomplishment, they will see the locus of causality to be external and will engage in those activities only when they believe they will receive extrinsic rewards. Many management theorists who have a behavioural-science orientation have based much of their work on the belief that people can exercise commitment-based self-control. For example, McGregor (1960) considers internal motivation and control as one of the principal assumptions underlying his Theory Y.

Similarly, Argyris (1964) and Tannenbaum (1968) provide many examples of intrinsically motivated behaviour. As we saw in Chapter 4, there is some evidence that control based on extrinsic rewards may be too potent in the sense that it results in people becoming too responsive to the control system; this, in turn, may lead to a number of undesirable consequences. Commitment-based self-control represents a possible alternative strategy because it may make external controls superfluous.

Staw (1976) explored the case for a negative relationship between intrinsic and extrinsic motivation. The basis of such a prediction stems from an assumption that individuals may work backwards from their own actions and so seek out the sources of their causation. For example, if the external pressures on an individual are so great that they would cause him or her to perform a task regardless of its internal characteristics, that individual might infer logically that he or she is extrinsically motivated. On the other hand, if external rewards are very low the individual might then infer that his or her behaviour is intrinsically motivated.

In situations where there is insufficient justification for a person's actions (for example, where intrinsic rewards for an activity are very low, such as might be the case with an uninteresting task and there are no compensating extrinsic rewards – i.e. cash), the individual might re-evaluate the intrinsic characteristics of the task ('it was not so bad after all') to justify his or her behaviour. On the other hand, both extrinsic and intrinsic rewards may be high in that the task may be very interesting and the payment very lavish. In this case the theory predicts that the individual may re-evaluate the task in a downward direction. The individual may mistakenly conclude that he or she was extrinsically motivated to perform the activity by the size of the external reward, and that the task was not very satisfying.

There are thus two stable situations:

1. External rewards are high and internal rewards, associated with the task itself, are low.
2. The task is, itself, rewarding, and intrinsic rewards are consequently high and external rewards low.

Unstable situations are those where there is insufficient justification: where intrinsic and extrinsic rewards are both low or where there is over-sufficient justification in cases where both extrinsic and intrinsic rewards are high. In both of these last two cases, the consequent attributional instability is resolved by individuals altering their perceptions of the intrinsic rewards associated with the task itself.

Individuals apparently resolve unstable attribution states by cognitively re-evaluating tasks in terms of their intrinsic rewards rather than changing their perceptions of extrinsic factors. The reason for this may lie in the comparative clarity of extrinsic compared with intrinsic rewards. Extrinsic rewards are relatively clear cut and evident, whereas an individual must judge the intrinsic reward for him or herself, and this is comparatively subjective. Accordingly, shifts in perception are most likely to occur in the intrinsic factor.

Deci, Nezlek and Sheinman (1981) suggest that reinforcers can be modified to express either external or internal control by taking the controlling or informational aspects of a reinforcer. It was demonstrated empirically that children were more intrinsically motivated and developed higher self-esteem when their teachers used rewards as information rather than as controls. One strategy for linking external control with internal motivation may be to use rewards as a source of information rather than as a source of control. Laboratory experiments and natural-field or quasi-experiments have been conducted to test these theories and, broadly, they seem to have force (e.g. Festinger and Carlsmith, 1959; Deci, 1971; Calder and Staw, 1975).

In summary, extrinsic rewards may motivate task activity and provide satisfactions and, similarly, intrinsic rewards may also motivate. However, the joint effect of intrinsic and extrinsic rewards may be quite complex in that, in some cases, the interaction of intrinsic and extrinsic factors may motivate positively under some conditions and, under others, the effect may be negative.

Implications for Control in Work Organizations

There are many circumstances where it is difficult to arrange for extrinsically motivated control systems to operate functionally. For example, many members of voluntary-work organizations and educational organizations are often considered to be intrinsically motivated to perform their tasks and, generally, extrinsic rewards in such organizations are not necessary to induce the performance of desired behaviours. Further, if extrinsic rewards were to be offered to employees of voluntary organizations, we might expect, on the basis of the research cited above, that there would be a decrease in intrinsic motivation.

On the other hand, in many industrial organizations a large number of jobs are still not inherently interesting enough to foster high intrinsic motivation, although it may be true that the numbers of such tasks are diminishing with increasing automation. There are also, of course, powerful social and legal norms for extrinsic payment. In these situations it may not be particularly appropriate even to consider ways of engendering commitment-based self-control on the assumption that there is little scope in such organizations for job or organizational redesign. However, the key concern is to discover which situations are most appropriate for self-control to operate effectively.

Some research seems to suggest that such self-controlling systems operate most effectively when they provide feedback, allow participation and where tasks are moderately difficult to attain. We now discuss each of these factors in turn (e.g. Manz and Sims, 1987).

Feedback

Feedback seems to be crucial to the exercise of self-control as it performs two important functions. First, it gives the individual the information needed to correct his or her behaviour when it deviates from a standard. Second, it can provide the intrinsic motivation that will lead a person to perform in a more effective way. Feedback therefore not only makes it possible for someone to exercise self-control by providing necessary information but it also provides the conditions for commitment-based self-control to be exercised.

Information may be provided in two forms: first, as information about how individuals are performing at the time they are performing (Vroom, 1964) and, second, as feedback about performance after the task has been performed. Feedback is necessary if commitment-based self-control is to operate effectively because, without it, the person will not know how to correct his or her behaviour. Further, there is some empirical evidence to suggest that feedback can contribute to intrinsic motivation and so to a person's willingness to exercise commitment-based self-control (Hackman and Lawler, 1971).

Participation

Tannenbaum (1968) has argued that, in participative cultures, there is likely to be greater control because influence attempts made in such cultures are more effective and because there is self-control. Given participative leadership styles, control increases from the manager's point of view because subordinates can be expected to be committed to what has been agreed on. Under other leadership styles there may be less certainty that tasks will be performed – at least with enthusiasm. With participation, subordinates feel they have more control because they have the opportunity to influence what they are going to do and are, therefore, more likely to be committed to the task. For the same reason managers, too, may feel they have more control under these circumstances. The argument seems to be that, when people at lower levels of organizations have the opportunity to participate, they have more influence. This awareness causes them to be more likely to exercise commitment-based self-control that, in turn, may increase organizational effectiveness.

Difficulty

As we discussed in detail in Chapter 4, work on achievement motivation suggests that motivation is highest on those tasks that participants see as moderatively difficult (McClelland, 1961). When people are performing tasks they believe they have a fifty-per-cent chance of success at, effective performance is considered as achievable and is, accordingly, attractive and rewarding – it is associated with feelings of competence and achievement. It would seem that control system goals regarded as moderately difficult to achieve will be most individually rewarding in terms of their intrinsic motivation.

On the other hand, if goals are set so high it is thought there is little chance of achieving them, people will abandon any hope of reaching apparently unattainable goals. Conversely, if goals are set so low to be easily achievable and are so regarded as unchallenging, there is likely to be little possibility of individuals being intrinsically motivated. Of course, motivation in this case may still be high when people are extrinsically motivated – something found frequently in many work organizations (Lawler, 1971).

Many field experiments have been conducted to test these notions. These have largely confirmed that when difficult goals are set (for example, tight budgetary standards) and the task is considered very difficult if not impossible, performance tends to be lower than when goals are perceived as attainable but challenging and moderately difficult. Experiments have also suggested that very difficult-to-attain goals seem to have a positive effect on performance only when they are accepted (Locke and Bryan, 1967; Hofstede, 1968; Latham and Yukl, 1975; Latham and Locke, 1979; Erez and Kanfer, 1983).

In sum, self-control is likely to be exercised and people to be intrinsically motivated to perform effectively when they undertake tasks that provide feedback and that have moderately difficult, acceptable goals. Commitment-based self-control also seems to be most likely in people who desire intrinsic rewards and who are comfortable with participation in decision-making. We now consider in more detail the possibility of introducing, through appropriate leadership and management, increased commitment-based self-control in organizations.

Towards Self-Controlling Organizations

Management has rightly been considered to be obsessed with control (Mintzberg, 1989) – control that, paradoxically, is in any case probably illusory (Dermer and Lucas, 1986). Mintzberg (1989) describes the final chapter of his book as a pessimistic polemic in which he contends that the structural form he earlier (1979a) labelled the 'machine bureaucracy' dominates our thinking about how organizations should be constructed. The central driving force in these structures he describes as an obsession with control:

> control of workers, control of markets, control of the future, control of whatever might control them, including, if necessary, owners and elected governments. Bringing things under control is exactly what their planning systems are designed to do . . . (in fact it is the obsession with planning as a form of control that explains all the fuss in our society about 'turbulent' conditions . . . what they really mean is that something happened which was not anticipated by their inflexible systems).
>
> (Mintzberg, 1989, p. 341)

Mintzberg then goes on to argue that professional management has been dehumanized and, in turn, that it has dehumanized its organizations by making them so 'rational' and efficient that they cease to function effectively – by emphasizing calculation commitment has been driven out.

However, it is likely that this is compounded by an illusion of control. Managerial beliefs that their assumptions about measurability and compliance are in use throughout an organization are, in fact, in large part wishful thinking. Such illusions are functional. Dermer and Lucas (1986) make the point that, for example, mission statements created by senior managements are accommodated organizationally by being subsumed in a variety of other missions held by other groups in organizations; hence, a composite global vision tends to become institutionalized over time. Such possibilities are ignored by those wedded to conventional control systems. Undesirable outcomes are attributed to deficiencies in the control systems themselves, which are consequently modified and perpetuated (Hofstede, 1978; Wildavsky, 1978).

The conventional managerial control model assumes that control involves the exercise of authority to achieve compliance, and that management is the dominant controlling force: 'Strategy expresses management's expectations which in turn serve as a reference point for management control' (Dermer, 1988, p. 26). In contrast to the conventional approach, the 'consensual' approach (e.g. Tannenbaum, 1968) differs in that the expectations on which control is determined are arrived at by interdependent relationships rather than by a unidirectional imposition of authority. The consensual approach emphasizes the sharing of control and the building of a consensual organization through various forms of participative management. The autonomous activity engaged in by stakeholders is a means of reconciling the contradictions they see between management strategy and conditions in practice (Hedberg, Nystrom and Starbuck, 1976). The traditional management model (based on functionalism, strategy and cybernetics) needs, on the basis of this argument, to be augmented by an approach that recognizes the importance of the autonomous activity of self-interested participants.

This moves us closely to commitment-based self-controlling organizations based on intrinsically motivated individuals supported by a carefully constructed external organizational environment. This environment is one in which managerial leadership and control is based not on control through command and authority but on more subtle, supportive processes that encourage employees to lead and control themselves. Such a view involves the democratization of work organizations and this is, clearly, rather a tall order but one we feel in the long run will be inevitable. As we have argued, not only are attempts to rely solely on unilaterally imposed, external controls dehumanizing and bureaucratizing but also all this effort as a sure means of control is in any case probably illusory.

Thomas (1984) tries to clarify the nature of self-control by reviewing its use in the literature, especially regarding the conditions in which it may be an effective means of organizational control. He takes a somewhat pessimistic view of the extent to which there can necessarily be goal congruence between individual and organizational objectives, and doubts whether administrative and social controls have to be internalized to be effective, as is suggested by some authors (e.g. Hopwood, 1974). We address these issues later in this section.

The advocates of commitment-based self-control as an effective means of organizational control suggest there are organizational conditions that, when present, will have the strong possibility of resulting in self-motivating individuals and, importantly, that this is likely to result in a more committed, productive and creative workforce (e.g. Mills, 1983; Manz and Sims, 1989; Manz, 1991). While the expectancy approach to motivation outlined in Chapter 4 warns against a normative and universal approach to human motivation as propounded by neo-human relations, it does, nevertheless, seem to be the case that trends outlined below may be reinforcing approaches to control based on commitment-based self-control, and that this may be a likely development. The important point is to see the self-influence system as the ultimate system of control and one with which other control systems are compatible and supportive. All organizations have control systems designed to exert influence on their employees, but these do not exert influence directly. They have an impact to the extent that they act in intended or unintended ways on organizational members' self-control systems. Recognizing and facilitating employee self-regulating mechanisms suggests a more realistic view of control than control based solely on external influence. Over-reliance on external control may lead to dysfunctional, rigid, bureaucratic behaviours.

As an illustration of some of the difficulties of this, we discuss approaches to formal systems of performance appraisal and goal-setting. Such processes have been institutionalized by personnel functions in organizations and by consultants selling packaged 'panaceas' (Gill and Whittle, 1992). Appraisal and goal-setting are contentious processes and are very much in fashion in Britain at present, especially in parts of the public sector. In this context, Townley (1991) rightly contends that performance appraisal represents a return to a more personalized or 'simple' form of control. A current example is the introduction in the public sector of higher education as a component of revised employment contracts.

In a particularly perceptive paper, Hogan (1986) – a former designer of appraisal systems in a local authority – examines the appraisal process from a recipient's point of view. He also notes that the literature on appraisal falls into two groups. There are those proponents of performance appraisal (e.g. Randell *et al.*, 1974) who argue for improving the technical skills of the managers who are likely to do the appraising. There are also those who are critical of appraisal processes in themselves, and who believe they are often neglectful of the complex nature of organizational life. They also consider that they may either not work and result only in piles of useless paper or they will be sabotaged (e.g. McGregor, 1957; Rowe, 1964; Salaman, 1978). A recent survey by the British Institute of Manpower Studies (Bevan and Thompson, 1991, p. 27) 'found no evidence to suggest that improved organisational performance in the private sector is associated with the operation of a formal performance management system. Indeed, poor financial performers were as likely to have performance management as good performers'.

Hogan (1986, p. 317) agrees and focuses particularly on the appraisal interview, which he rightly believes is a crucial part of the process:

the task of obtaining valid information from such an activity should take into account the recipient's perceptions and understanding of the process. In work organisations this can be difficult to accomplish. There are usually power differences between the appraisee and the appraiser which affect what information can be collected and/or declared public . . . such situations can lead to the development of low-trust feelings and resentment either during or after the appraisal event . . . Improvements are likely to come about through a better appreciation of the need to adopt a realistically human model of the superior–subordinate relationship within the specific context of an organisation.

What is being argued for is an approach to designing organizations that is akin to Likert's (1961) system 4, which is based on principles of supportive super-visory relationships, group decision-making in multiple, overlapping group structures, and high-performance goals. These, it is predicted, will result in favourable attitudes towards superiors, high confidence and trust, high re-ciprocal influence, high peer-group loyalty and high peer-performance goals at all levels. On the other hand, Likert's systems 1 and 2 (based on high pressure through tight work standards, personal limitations and tight, imposed budgets and a generally coercive, authoritarian culture) will, it is predicted, give rise to unfavourable attitudes, low levels of co-operation and low-performance goals.

The paradox appears to be that, given the conditions present in system 4, there would probably be little need of any institutionalized performance ap-praisal system, for high performance would emerge naturally from the culture and, particularly, the supportive superior–subordinate relationships. What also seems clear is that authoritarian cultures and externally administered controls will not facilitate attempts to introduce self-controlling organizations; at best they will result only in introducing grudging compliance and low mor-ale – at worst, sabotage.

It will be recalled that earlier in this chapter, and in more detail in Chapter 4, we discussed the requirements necessary for high intrinsic motivation and referred to research evidence that suggests a number of conditions need to be present. First, the tasks undertaken need to provide feedback and have moder-ately difficult, acceptable goals. Commitment-based self-control also seemed most likely to be present in people who desire intrinsic rewards and who are comfortable with participation in decision-making.

As we have seen, motivation theory has made a significant contribution to theories of intrinsic motivation. The literature on self-management has been developed from at least three other main sources. First, it originated from social learning theory and related work (e.g. Bandura, 1969; Mahoney and Thoreson, 1974), which we have already considered. Second, it has its orig-ins in the organization literature, specifically that concerned with self-managed or autonomous work groups or teams (e.g. Luthans and Davies, 1979; Andrasik and Heimberg, 1982; Manz and Sims, 1987). Third, it has been stimulated by recent advances in technology and the consequent struc-tural changes.

Work redesign programmes that focused largely on the individual or the group were introduced in the Sixties, Seventies and Eighties throughout the developed economies of the West and Japan. Trist (1970) and others interested in the impact of technology on organization structure have considered that the shopfloor worker has a new role – primarily as fact finder, interpreter, diag-nostician, judge, adjuster and change agent. Management's role may change in these circumstances to 'more of a process than a role filled by a group of people' (McWhinney and Krone, 1972, p. 7). Trist (1970, p. 28) believes that 'the autonomous work group . . . would appear to be the organisational para-digm which matches . . . the information technology. The advance of technol-ogy itself has reversed the world of Frederick Taylor'. While many organization theorists agree with Trist, writers such as Braverman (1974) do not agree, believing that Taylor's influence is undiminished and that the potential inherent in the new technology has destroyed craftsmanship rather than creating the scope for increased autonomy and enriched jobs.

Nevertheless it is certainly the case that there are many examples of experiments involving autonomous work groups that seem to be employing a highly participative, team approach designed to create a significant degree of decision-making autonomy and behavioural control at the work-group level. The self-managed group apparently results in a shift in focus from individual methods of performing work to group methods on the basis that the group can, more effectively, allocate its resources when and where required than can an aggregate of individuals. As we have suggested, management's role will, in such circumstances, probably change significantly and it seems likely that management as a process might be undertaken spontaneously and informally by a wide variety of individuals at various levels rather than formally and more permanently through the organizational hierarchy. These conditions are to be found in a wider organizational context in matrix organizations or in Mintzberg's terms, 'adhocracies' (Galbraith, 1973; Mintzberg, 1979a).

A number of different strands seem to be coming together. Not surprisingly, the conditions we describe are also predicted for the manufacturing organizations of the future on the basis of research work undertaken in British manufacturing industry into appropriate manufacturing organization for computer-integrated technology (Smith *et al.*, 1991). At the outset of the research it was predicted that future work organizations would display increasing integration of tasks; team-working and role sharing; semi-autonomous work groups; cellular manufacturing; flexible teams, multiple roles and skilling; increasing local discretion; alternative payment systems (e.g. for team output and quality); and supervision as a resource rather than as a controller. Similarly, it was suggested that control was more likely to be exercised by informal mechanisms and to be self-organized in a broad framework rather than by formal rules and procedures. Further, bureaucratic lines of control were likely to be replaced with more flexible control systems and a hierarchical power structure with simultaneous centralization (tight controls) and decentralization (loose controls). Communications in such organizations are, it was suggested, likely to be networked in flat structures with few levels. At the same time, the control of work was predicted to change from formalized standards controlled by appraisal by superiors to various forms of self-assessment. These predictions, while not particularly novel in that they are essentially in outline Burns and Stalker's (1961) findings from the early Sixties that have been elaborated on by others since, were, nevertheless, in large part confirmed by empirical work undertaken during the introduction of computer-integrated technology in British manufacturing industry.

Given these findings, which have been drawn widely from a number of sources, it seems reasonable to predict that the roles of supervision and management and their control functions may change substantially in future in terms of their leadership styles and in the way they control their organizations. Some evidence of this is reported by Manz and Sims (1987), who identified salient leader behaviours in one medium-sized, small-parts manufacturing plant that had been operating for several years under a system of self-managed work teams. The investigation focused on the external leaders of these work groups, the objective being to identify leader behaviours in such situations. The researchers wished to discover, specifically, what behaviours the leaders used (the leaders were called co-ordinators) in the self-managed work groups and how this compared with leadership behaviour elsewhere. They were especially interested to discover the relationship between certain leader behaviours and their effectiveness, and they hypothesized that leaders who encouraged employee self-management would be particularly effective.

The small-parts engineering plant was in the south of the USA and it employed about 320 employees. From the start it had been organized on a self-managed work-team basis, each work group being assigned to a sequence of interdependent, related tasks. Organizationally, the plant was structured into three hierarchical levels. Upper-plant management (known as the support team) took many of the traditional plant-management responsibilities and were responsible, for example, for planning production and dealing with clients. The support team, as its title suggests, attempted to work as a team and played a supportive rather than a directive role.

The work-team co-ordinators formed the middle layer in the organization, and they were the main focus of the study. They acted in a supportive role to the work teams themselves. Most work teams had between eight and twelve members, and each had an elected team leader who, for the most part, performed the same work as other members of the team. Apart from performing routine work, teams met on a regular weekly basis to engage in problem-solving discussions to improve work performance. External co-ordinators did not attend meetings routinely but might be invited often, for example, to help team members deal with a particularly difficult problem.

As already mentioned, the study's focus was on the co-ordinator role, which was external to the teams. This role clearly poses contradictions and ambiguities for those performing such roles in organizations with self-management philosophies. Co-ordinators were observed carrying out supportive roles in relation to problem-solving activities, and training activities to encourage groups to undertake self-evaluation. They did not give direct commands and instructions to the teams; rather, they encouraged teams to question their own activities and to practise team and self-control.

> The underlying theme of leadership practice was to influence the team and team members to be able to do it themselves, rather than for the coordinators to direct control or do it for the team. There was an abundance of deliberate and calculated efforts to foster independence rather than allow the traditional dependence of more traditional work groups.
>
> (Manz and Sims, 1987, p. 114)

In summarizing their findings, Manz and Sims (*ibid.*) contrast them with the work of Schriesheim, House and Kerr (1976) and Lord, Foti and De Vader (1984) – research designed to examine aspects of traditional leader behaviours. Despite differences in the period in which these researches were undertaken, the findings of both studies were similar. Both regarded leaders traditionally, as people who do something to influence others directly on the assumption that the power, initiation and control is entirely with the leaders. In contrast, self-management leader behaviours in the case presented by

Manz and Sims (1987) were designed to encourage self-reinforcement; self-observation, evaluation and control; self-expectation and goal-setting; and rehearsal and self-criticism.

Self-management strategies advocated by, for example, Mahoney and Arnkoff (1978, 1979) and Manz and Sims (1989), provide a number of approaches to self-management derived from their application to clinical contexts. These include the development of self-leadership through modelling; self goal-setting and productive thought patterns; self-reward and reprimand; and cueing strategies, all of which are covered in detail in Manz and Sims (1989) and Manz (1992).

Managing without Managers?

We now examine some of the implications for organizational control that arise from the trend towards self-managed and self-controlling organizations. The chief consequence of this is that most organizations may be over-managed and that this has unforeseen and dysfunctional results. At the informal level we have all experienced the smooth way organizations seem to function when managers are absent, particularly those who manage by controlling their subordinates closely. There may be many people who are designated as managers but who not only perform largely unnecessary functions but who also, by their close controlling styles (which they believe to be the hallmark of the manager), interfere with others' effective performance.

There is a mystique about the nature of management, which is supported by a number of myths that were probably made durable by the assumption that direct human labour needs to be controlled by those not directly involved in it. Without this control, it is assumed, work will not be done. In her review of her research on the management of public bureaucracies in North America, Martin (1983) suggests these management myths are challenged by a number of propositions based on organizational analysis and on which an alternative approach to work organization may be built. The belief that management is supremely important to organizations has dominated the literature. However, it seems that, after an initial training period, most individuals can perform work without close and direct supervision. They need support and information as an enabling rather than a controlling activity.

The myth that managers are concerned primarily with planning and controlling has been exploded by Mintzberg (1973) and others, who have discovered that managers, especially those at senior and middle levels, engage more frequently in routine functions of a short duration than, for example, planning organizational strategy.

In addition, work and organizational design based on self-management concepts seem to be reasonably successful and, as we have seen, this is likely to become more widespread with the growth of advanced technical change and increasingly competitive market pressures. As Martin (1983, p. 128) suggests, 'a reduction in the numbers and functions of superordinates and the creation of self-managing work groups would respond to pressures to reduce costs and at the same time provide an opportunity to improve the working environment and performance of government employees'. We would add that this might not only apply to the public sector in the USA but also, for all the reasons already mentioned, might have a much wider utility.

Conclusion

It has been argued that many of our organizations are over-managed and over-controlled. A case has been made for a reduction in management control, and trends in a number of directions seem to support this. It has been argued that such a reduction in close control will help create self-controlling organizations based on the intrinsically motivated individual. Management leadership and control in such organizations will be based not on control through command and authority but in more supportive behaviours, so encouraging employees to control and lead themselves. Not only are attempts to rely solely on uni-laterally imposed controls likely to be dehumanizing and bureaucratizing but also all this effort as a sure means of control is probably illusory. We therefore predict a reduction in the number of managers in future organizations and a change in the roles of those who remain. Finally, we end on a cautionary note. Such developments would seem to depend on the democratization of society in general and its institutions and, at the present, there would seem to be no cause for a great deal of optimism about this. However, times may change.

Further Reading

Useful books on leadership are Smith and Peterson (1988) and, specifically on charismatic leadership, Bryman (1992). As Smith and Peterson confess, they have largely omitted references to the processes of self-leadership and self-control. We suggest these omissions might be remedied by reference to Manz's work, especially Manz (1986, 1992) and to the special issue of the *Journal of Management Systems* on leading self-managers: individuals and teams, Vol. 3, no. 3, 1991.

A useful critique of charismatic leadership is contained in Pauchant (1991). For psychoanalytic criticisms of leadership concepts in general, see Kets de Vries and Miller (1984), Kranz and Gilmore (1990) and Gemmill and Oakley (1992).

Accounting for management's obsession with control, its consequences and remedies, is well covered in the last chapter of Mintzberg (1989).

7

Power and Management Control

Introduction

As we have shown in previous chapters, administrative controls can be seen as processes through which managers try to regulate members' activities so that their performance will come up to management's expectations. In this way, organizations must be regarded here not as 'neutral technical systems but as ensembles of formalised action to secure domination' (Storey, 1983, p. 123). However, this also implies a potential for conflict, since management is not the only group who will attempt to exert control from a multiplicity of different desires, expectations and vested interests. Because people do not necessarily share the same goals in their involvement with an organization, there will inevitably be some degree of conflict, as different groups pursue different objectives and resist others' attempts to modify that behaviour.

This brings us to power in organizations as different individuals and groups might attempt to exercise any power at their disposal to enable them to pursue their vested interests (see Lee and Lawrence, 1991). So Crozier's (1964) famous dictum that people's behaviour in organizations cannot be understood without some reference to 'power' has all the more force when we focus our attention on the relationship between management control and members' behaviour. As Storey (1983, p. 54) has argued, this is because we cannot consider control without considering the nature of power in organizations: 'when we talk of "being in control" this implies the successful end-result of applying power', while 'controlling suggests that someone is actively engaged in applying power'. So, generally, management control may be seen as involving management's capacity to funnel subordinates' labour into the production process. In an organization, 'power will be exercised to re-assert control' by management (Clegg and Dunkerley, 1980a, p. 481).

Despite its obvious importance, the literature on power seems to suffer from ambiguous definitions and applications deriving from conflicting philosophical

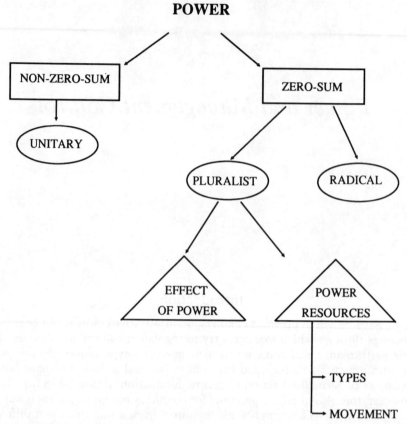

Figure 7.1 The concept of power in organizations

assumptions. This is a difficult situation made worse by the fact that these arguments are often conducted in highly esoteric idioms. The purpose of this chapter, therefore, is to introduce the reader to aspects of this 'most "contested" of concepts' (Clegg, 1989, p. xv) and, it is hoped, enable a better understanding of power and its deployment in work organizations, with particular reference to control. This entails describing, comparing and criticizing the different perspectives that have developed. Before beginning, it is helpful to represent these different strands of thought and their various interrelationships by outlining the patterns discernible in their key assumptions, even though this will lose some of their subtlety and complexity (see Figure 7.1).

Whether exercising power benefits one group at the expense of another is the point of departure for the various approaches to understanding power in organizations.

Non-Zero-Sum

A non-zero-sum approach begins its analysis by assuming that exercising power is something that benefits an organization's whole membership. This is exemplified in Parsons (1951). Parsons treats power as a 'generalized re-source', created by society, for regulating social relations. Power is, therefore, assumed to be of functional importance since it relates to the collective ability to maintain a social system by achieving 'its' common goals. In this way power becomes inextricably linked to 'authority' – the legitimate exercise of com-mand to fulfil collective goals. As Giddens (1968, p. 260) has commented, Parsons' view of power is 'directly derivative of authority: authority is the institutionalised legitimation which underlies power'.

Underlying this functionalist approach is the reification of such concepts as 'goals' and the (related) development of a unitary view of organizations. Elsewhere we have dismissed such a reification as unhelpful in developing an understanding of control in organizations. A unitary view uses reification to consider organizations as being united under the umbrella of 'organizational goals', which 'it' attempts to achieve in a 'team-like' manner (Fox, 1974). Hence organizations are seen as harmonious, consensual phenomena existing for the pursuit of common purposes. There is no inherent conflict of interest between members since all are seen to depend on the revenues flowing from the organization's activities.

Like all successful teams, an organization needs leadership. This is manage-ment's responsibility, who exercise authority (power) in the interests of all since it is they who are the best qualified to decide how these common interests are most effectively pursued. Management are often likened to the nervous system of the body corporate, as meritocratic arbiters of members' interests (see Zeitlin, 1974). They exercise power given to them by being accorded a legitimate custodial right to seek optimal solutions to achieve the organiza-tion's unambiguous goals. All employees owe loyalty to the organization and to its management. Employees are functionally important to enabling the or-ganization's survival. Any conflict is explained in terms of various pathological causes (e.g. ignorance or stupidity) rather than being seen as rational and the natural and inevitable result of differences of interest.

Power is, hence, considered in such a way that it is limited to management – it is management's 'legitimate' authority to guide the organization towards achieving common interests (see Burrell and Morgan, 1979, p. 204). A unitary view of power has obvious ideological benefits for managers and, in this sense, its invocation might be largely self-directed in that it privileges the versions of reality on which management's decisions are based. It is not surprising that such a view has been widely criticized, especially regarding its naïve lack of descriptive accuracy and normative connotations (e.g. Fox, 1974; Hyman, 1975; Palmer, 1983).

The problematic nature of such a view of power is further compounded as it disregards the exercise of power by people pursuing their own sectional inter-ests (see Knights and Willmott, 1985). These sectional interests confront man-agement with resistance when management attempts to exercise power by designing and implementing administrative controls. Thus what is needed is a concept of power that does not relegate such resistance to the realms of wilful irrationality but, on the other hand, sees it as a natural part of organizational life. This is close to the position outlined by Giddens (1968), who emphasizes how Parsons ignored the hierarchical nature of power and the clash of the divisions of interest that characterize modern society. This is not to claim that it is impossible for power to 'rest upon "agreement" to code authority which can be used for collective aims' (*ibid.* p. 264) – a point pursued in this chapter when we consider managerial prerogative.

Zero-Sum

Zero-sum approaches to power are, perhaps, the most helpful means of understanding the relationship of power and control. These approaches are based on the view that power is a zero-sum phenomenon in that it benefits one group at the expense of another. Most zero-sum approaches seem to be based on Weber's (1968, p. 53) view of power, in which power is seen as the 'probability that one actor within a social relationship will be in a position to carry out his own will despite resistance'. Within this general idea it is possible to differentiate between pluralist and radical frames of reference.

Pluralist Approaches to Power

Pluralist approaches see organizations and society in general as consisting of diverse socio-economic groups whose pursuit of sectional interests inevitably creates some conflict (Fox, 1974). Therefore, conflict between management and other organizational stakeholders (e.g. shareholders, labour, etc.) is not abnormal: it is only to be expected. However, these differences (i.e. because of mutual dependency and the subsequent need for mutual survival) are not so great that they cannot be accommodated and harmonized through procedures that allow for the negotiation of compromise.

To pluralists, power is the medium through which conflicts of interest are resolved as different groups and individuals secure and mobilize different power resources in their pursuit of sectional interests. However, as organizations are seen to be composed of a multiplicity of different interest groups (who draw their power from a plurality of different sources), these groups cancel each other out; pluralists assume that there is a balance of power between these conflicting parties. In other words, there is a situation of countervailing power (Kerr *et al.*, 1964; Galbraith, 1969) so that one group can never dominate other groups continuously. This stalemate, in effect, reinforces the need for negotiation and compromise.

The notion of countervailing power has come under considerable attack from writers who have a radical frame of reference (e.g. Bachrach and Baratz, 1962; Lukes, 1974; Brown, 1978; Clegg, 1979). Basically, these writers argue that pluralism fails to recognize the extent and persistence of marked inequalities in the distribution of material and symbolic power. This inequality, according to the radicals, creates a situation in which certain organizational élites have the power to impose their will on employees whose interests are regarded as being inherently antagonistic to (and ultimately irreconcilable with) those of the organizational élites. The pluralists have obviously been concerned to defend their position in the face of such criticisms. It is in this context that we can identify two different but related themes in the research: those who seek to operationalize power by reference to its observable outcomes (or effects); and those who attempt to explain what it is that creates power by concentrating on the nature and distribution of power resources in organizations.

The Effects of Power

One possible way of demonstrating and defending the pluralist stance would be to observe the exercise of power in conflict situations and identify who 'wins'. If, over a period of time, no one group wins constantly, this would suggest that the pluralist thesis is valid. On the other hand, if one group does appear to win constantly, this would suggest that the notion does not hold. Dahl (1957, 1961) studied such outcomes by recording wins and losses in order to see who prevails in conflict. His power-effects approach thus scrutinized power when two parties were in overt, observable conflict. From Weber he developed the view that 'A has power over B to the extent that he can get B to do something that B would not otherwise do' (1957, p. 202). To explain this operational definition of power, Dahl uses the example of the power a policeman (A) has to make car drivers (B) do what they would not otherwise do when the policeman directs traffic. His stress was on looking at observable behaviour in conflict situations with the assumption that a decision will be made that favours a particular party. The winner is, therefore, the more dominant or powerful because he or she has been able to realize their objective in the face of opposition.

Dahl argues that power can only be attributed when its exercise has been observed. His most famous empirical research (1961) concerns the decision-making processes about urban development, public education and political nominations in New Haven. Dahl interprets his findings as emphasizing a pluralistic view of society and its institutions: they illustrate how a diversity of individuals and groups exercise power in different areas and, importantly, how no group élite dominates. (See Newton (1969) for a critique of Dahl's interpretation of his own findings.)

Power Resources

An alternative pluralist approach suggests that power derives from a multiplicity of sources that vary from situation to situation and over time. For the sake of clarity we refer to this as the power-resources approach. It assumes and tries to illustrate that there are different spheres of influence in which different interest groups have different degrees of power, derived from different resources or bases.

Some writers focus on distinguishing different power resources while others concentrate on how their distribution can vary temporally. This disparate group of writers have worked to demonstrate the variety of power resources available to groups as they pursue their vested interests, and also (because the resources are so dispersed and so many, and because their distribution can change within the organization) how resources are not concentrated in particular élites. Thus one can infer that by demonstrating that countervailing power exists in society and its institutions the often-hidden agenda of such an approach is to counter radical critiques.

Many of these writers tend to create 'lists' in a similar way to Etzioni (1961). Many also approach their subject from a management point of view by distinguishing the power resources available to them in the pursuit of their objectives. Etzioni uses a typology based on different structures of control, in which those who control organizations use power resources to ensure other members' conformity. A threefold classification is used to arrive at an effective 'fit' between organizational goals and the power resources used to gain control:

1. Prisons use physical and coercive power resources.
2. Utilitarian structures (such as work organizations) use material power resources.
3. Normative structures (such as political parties or religious organizations) use normative (i.e. persuasive power) resources.

Etzioni suggests that most organizations will tend to emphasize one type of resource but that any organization will use all three to varying degrees in attempting to control members' behaviour.

French and Raven (1959) similarly start from the concept of power bases located in organizational resources, but they look specifically at those resources used by supervisors to influence hierarchical subordinates' behaviour. Their fivefold classification depends on the responses of those at the receiving end of the exercise of power:

1. Rewards are defined as cash, promotions, recognition and job satisfaction where the recipient values the chosen method and believes he or she will benefit and that the reward will be available.
2. Coercive resources are the capacity to enforce discipline that rests on the fear of psychological or material punishment.
3. Referent power is considered available where the supervisor is liked by the subordinates and who identify with him or her. This is similar to the power exercised by a charismatic leader.
4. Expert power is exercised by those believed to have specialized knowledge or technical skill others feel obliged to accept. They defer to what is taken to be superior knowledge.
5. Legitimate power is where subordinates defer to the leader's right to exert influence over them by virtue of the leader's formal authority.

French and Raven (*ibid.*) consider that all five bases can occur in a work organization – in fact, all could be 'possessed' by one individual. Apart from their treatment of legitimate power, their taxonomy correlates closely with Etzioni's – coercive, remunerative and normative (i.e. referent and expert) power resources. To Etzioni, however, legitimate power is not the discrete category French and Raven claim. It is a variable quality each of his three power resources might have. Coercive power or expert power might be used legitimately or otherwise. Further, legitimacy is not some absolute quality. It is related to the values and beliefs projected onto events by those observing the exercise of power.

Other researchers (e.g. Mechanic, 1962; Crozier, 1964; Pettigrew, 1973; Wilson, 1982) focus on the power of 'lower participants' – power that derives from their control over information and/or uncertainty. Pettigrew (1973) and

Wilson (1982), in their studies of organizational decision-making, demonstrate how a person's control over information is important to subordinates in that it allows them to influence organizational events to their personal advantage. Earlier work by Crozier (1964) studied maintenance engineers' behaviour in a French tobacco factory. This demonstrated how the engineers had more power than their colleagues who operated the factory's machinery. This was because they controlled and tried to continue to control the only source of uncertainty for management in an otherwise highly routinized production process – their ability to rectify breakdowns in a mechanized plant. Similarly, Mechanic (1962), when studying the behaviour of hospital orderlies, found that these 'lower participants' had taken over aspects of the administration and had thus succeeded in acquiring the skills, knowledge and information needed by their hierarchical superiors. They then used this power to improve their organizational status and conditions of service.

An overview of some of the power resources employees might exercise is provided by Batstone *et al.* (1978). Basically they identify four sources of power:

1. The extent to which employees have skills that cannot be replaced easily.
2. The extent to which they occupy a position in the production process that is crucial to that process.
3. The ease with which they can disrupt that production process.
4. The extent to which they can create or cope with uncertainty in the production process.

However, this is by no means a complete picture. Although these power resources may be important in countervailing management's power, perhaps the main source of power comes from the ability and willingness of 'lower participants' to engage in collective action in defence or furtherance of their perceived vested interests. A precursor to this may well be the development of a 'collective conscience' (see Marchington and Armstrong, 1983). However, people can and do engage in strikes or works to rule that exploit the dependency management has on their co-operation and labour power.

Of those writers who analyse how the distribution of power resources can vary temporally, Hickson *et al.* (1971) and Marchington (1979) are perhaps the most significant. Hickson *et al.* (1971) suggest that the division of labour in organizations can cause power differences to arise among the resulting functional segments, and that these power differences will depend on how critical the segments are in enabling the organization's success and survival. As success and survival are related to other situations faced by an organization – the environment or technology of an organization changes – so will the distribution of power in the organizational segments. Building on and consolidating a number of earlier studies (e.g. Landsberger, 1961; Crozier, 1964) Hickson *et al.* (1971) developed their strategic contingencies theory of power. This theory suggests that the power of an organizational segment or department depends on the following:

1. Its ability to cope with uncertainty.
2. Its centrality.
3. Its workflow immediacy.
4. Its substitutability.

The capacity to cope with uncertainty, which is important to organizational functioning, is a source of considerable power. The division of labour results in some departments or groups coping with ambiguous and unpredictable situations. Through being able to cope they make other segments dependent on them, and they thus are more influential and powerful.

Centrality refers to how the workflows of an organizational segment are interlinked to the activities of other segments. Hickson *et al.* split this variable into two elements: workflow pervasiveness and workflow immediacy. Workflow pervasiveness is the degree to which an organizational segment's activities connect with those of other segments – i.e. its strategic position in the organization of work. A number of writers have drawn attention to the power that flows from the strategic position of groups in the production process (Sayles, 1965; Kuhn, 1961; Pettigrew, 1973; Purcell *et al.*, 1978). Pettigrew (1973) and Purcell *et al.* (1978) studied the increasingly powerful strategic positions in organizations of computer specialists.

Workflow immediacy is the extent and speed to which the cessation of a segment's activities would disrupt the rest of the organization and thereby impede the organization's outputs. For example, flow-line production processes in chemical or automobile plants are prone to disruption by the activities of small but strategic groups. Similarly, work stoppages have greater immediacy when they occur at times of greatest demand.

Substitutability is whether or not a segment's activities are readily substitutable by other parts of the organization. In other words, the dependency of other parts of an organization on the activities of a particular segment would be reduced if there were alternative providers of those activities. Hence, the power of any part of an organization is reduced if its activities are readily substitutable.

Hickson *et al.* (1971) conclude that there is an imbalance in the interdependencies between organizational segments – an imbalance that confers greater or lesser amounts of power. The more central a segment is, the more uncertainty it can cope with and the less substitutable it is, then the more power it will have. However, as the activities, technologies and environment of an organization change, so will the division of labour and therefore the amount of power a segment might have at its disposal.

Hickson *et al.* produce a powerful argument about the ways in which an organization's division of labour creates variations in intra-organizational power. However, they are much too deterministic in their approach. Members might be unaware of the power available to them in the pursuit of their interests: there may be a gap between the 'possession' of power and the exercise of that power. Hickson *et al.* appear to assume, deterministically, that members have perfect knowledge and act on that knowledge. These problems are compounded by their implicit unitary view of relationships in organizational segments. They appear to assume that within a segment there is consensus over interests and goals. This fails to recognize the impact of internal hierarchical relationships on members' behaviour in an organizational segment. It is in the context of these problems that Marchington's contribution (1979, 1982) might be understood.

Marchington suggests that the four variables put forward by Hickson *et al.*

may be regrouped into two main factors. He combines workflow pervasiveness and immediacy into what he calls 'disruption' – the ability to halt production. Substitutability and coping with uncertainty are combined into 'replaceability' – the long-term ability to increase indispensability. Although Marchington then goes on to apply this model specifically to an analysis of work-group power, what is most important in his work is its attempt to resolve the problems already noted in Hickson *et al.*'s work. Marchington avoids their determinism by recognizing the potential gap between structural power-resource possession (i.e. capacity) and the subsequent exercise of that power (i.e. realization). Capacity and realization are mediated by the consciousness of individual actors and their cohesiveness as a group. Thus he draws attention to the importance of ideology and culture on power relations.

However, even if a group is aware of its power it may be unwilling to use it. This seems to be the case with, for example, nurses in the National Health Service, who are concerned not to harm patients. Power testing is reached when the work group has to choose the appropriate moment to take action, press home its claim and choose an appropriate method of winning it. Finally, if action is taken, the group needs to ensure that the outcome is favourable in order for it to provide a basis for future action or just the threat of action – threat may be just as effective (as in the case of powerful trade unions) as the action itself. As Marchington (1982, p. 104) says,

> it is the interaction of the two – the largely structurally influenced facets of power capacity and the largely behavioural or attitudinal aspects of group solidarity and willingness to act through power realisation – that a group is able to test its potential for influence over management and hopefully [for it] reaffirm or strengthen its perception of its relative power.

We can summarize Marchington's work as the model illustrated in Figure 7.2.

Marchington, by referring to Purcell (1979), considered how management might in turn attempt to countervail and undermine manifestations of such employee power. He outlines three types of activity:

1. Reducing dependency on a particular group by, for example, stock-piling in the automobile and coal industries to avoid vulnerability at times of heavy demand.

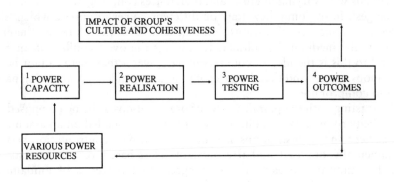

Figure 7.2   Marchington's model of group power

2. Inhibiting the development of solidarity and beliefs in the legitimacy of industrial action by using personal letters in times of conflict.
3. Ensuring that, if power is tested, the outcome is to weaken rather than affirm the group's perception of its power.

Unfortunately, because of the exploratory nature of his approach, Marchington fails to develop his important insights about employee power fully. For a fuller treatment, we have to turn to writers who are more clearly in the 'radical' camp. Before doing so it is, however, worth pointing out that Marchington shares with Hickson *et al.* one major limitation – a limitation that has been the concern of 'radical' writers. This is the tendency to relate power capacity to structural position in an organization through the development of, and changes to, the division of labour. Clegg points out (1975, p. 49) that such an understanding of power is rather like attempting to understand a game of chess by thinking that

> the pieces gain their power through their current position, rather than gaining their current position through their power to make moves according to the rules of the game. In short, the power which a piece has is defined totally in terms of its relationship. This definition entirely neglects the progress of the game in terms of its history and rules.

Thus Clegg implies that strategic position may well be an expression of power in itself. It is therefore important to consider the power needed by groups to achieve their structural positions and to consider members' differential ability to structure and control situations by setting the 'rules of the game'.

In order to consider Clegg's argument, as well as to consider a more explicit analysis of the role of culture and ideology, we turn to those writers broadly classified as 'radical'.

Radical Approaches to Power

A pluralist approach to power in work organizations is, as we have shown, based on an understanding that organizations are made up of different interest groups who vie with one another as they pursue their self-interests. Pfeffer and Salancik (1978, p. 26) describe organizations as 'settings in which groups and individuals with varying interests and preferences come together and engage in exchanges'. In so doing they draw on different power resources, which 'shift' under the influences of various contingencies. For the pluralist, therefore, power is the medium that ultimately resolves the overt conflict of interests. Central to this is the idea of countervailing power – that there cannot be one continuous winner and that, because of mutual dependency, conflicting parties have to compromise.

Contrasting with the pluralist view of organizations as being composed of a multiplicity of interests, a radical view of power is founded on an assumption that society and its institutions are characterized by a confrontation between fundamentally opposed and irreconcilable class-based vested interests. Although a radical approach to power agrees that power is of fundamental importance to understanding human behaviour in organizations, it also argues that power is unequally distributed – in other words, that the material and symbolic power of owners and their surrogates (i.e. management) far out-weighs that of labour. Thus it is not surprising that a radical view of pluralism has concentrated on labour's countervailing power.

While the radical school of thought derives from many theoretical sources, the most important ideas largely come from attacks on Dahl's (1961) concern to analyse the exercise of power in observable decision-making situations – situations that involve overt conflict (i.e. where A gets B to do something he or she would otherwise not do). Bachrach and Baratz (1962) draw attention to a subtle and less visible activity where power is exercised to prevent decisions being taken over potential issues in which there would be a conflict of interests. They argue that power has two faces. The first face more or less corresponds to that put forward by Dahl, but Bachrach and Baratz (1970, p. 7) argue that power is also exercised when

> A devotes his energies to creating or reinforcing social and political values and institutional practices that limit the scope of the political process to public consideration of only those issues which are comparatively innocuous to A. To the extent that A succeeds in doing this B is prevented for all practical purposes from bringing to the fore any issues that might in their resolution be seriously detrimental to A's set of preferences.

To Bachrach and Baratz, management would usually be in a much stronger position to exercise power based on an agenda setting as they are strategically better placed than employees and their representatives. Bachrach and Baratz apparently expose a serious limitation in certain pluralist themes – by noting how grievances expressed outside the decision-making arena fail to be trans-lated into demands within it, they draw attention to situations where 'the dominant values, the accepted rules of the game, the existing power relations among groups, and the instruments of force singly, or in combination, effec-tively prevent certain grievances from developing into full-fledged issues which call for decisions' (Bachrach and Baratz, 1963, p. 641). Such a 'non-decision making situation' (*ibid.*) therefore involves what Schattschneider (1960) had priorly called 'the mobilization of bias' in that it refers to how power is exercised by the conscious creation of areas of non-decisions – areas that remain hidden or become submerged in an organizational setting and, thereby, constitute that which is not open to negotiation.

We are all aware of examples of this in organizations where individual's or group's action exerts control by supporting the non-decision-making process: decision-making where there is cause for grievance is avoided precisely because it would have an adverse effect on the individual's or group's interests (for example, by excluding items from the agenda of formal meetings). A similar situation occurs where critical organizational decisions are made informally by élites, who then arrange for them to be rubber-stamped in formal committees. This behaviour may give rise to further conflict when those who are excluded from the decision-making realize it. This is frequently the case in the workings of joint consultative committees that, accordingly, may fall into disrepute.

Bachrach and Baratz point out how Ouchi's behavioural controls (1979) can serve to set agendas. We have already shown how output controls (and, by implication, rules, etc.) might be seen as conventions that set a 'gaze': they define and categorize those aspects of organizational reality that are important in evaluating members' job performance. The ensuing socially constructed account often appears to be separate from the human subjective processes, as it appears to be 'objective'. This makes visible only certain aspects of organizational reality out of the myriad possible. As argued in Chapter 4, output controls only illuminate certain conventionally prescribed segments of organizational reality. This excludes other realities, which remain invisible or barely perceptible and thus unavailable for inspection. Discourse and decision-making are therefore narrowed by confining them to particular, conventionally determined issues, which create areas of 'non-decisions' resulting in the 'suppression or thwarting of a latent or manifest challenge to the values or interests of the decision maker' (Bachrach and Baratz, 1970, p. 44) or the controller. By setting the decision-making agenda through the imposition of compulsory visibility on some aspects of reality and thus rendering others invisible, such controls potentially set boundaries for what is negotiable by making only those visibilities understandable to members. In this way they shape members' perception of what is important. The partiality of these perceptions limits subsequent discourse to things that are relatively safe in terms of the interests encoded into the infrastructure of the control systems while, at the same time, preserving an appearance of fact and immutability.

Although in undermining Dahl's approach Bachrach and Baratz have made an important contribution to our understanding of power in organizations, they, also, have been subject to criticism. Their methodology confines its investigation to an examination of overt and thus observable conflict (i.e. the ways in which grievances about which there is conflict are excluded from the decision-making agenda and are, thereby, suppressed). What their methodology therefore tends to ignore is the ways in which, in the first place, bias might be mobilized to forestall the generation of conflict. It is here that Lukes (1974) provides an important contribution.

Lukes (*ibid.*) considers that Bachrach and Baratz do not go far enough. He adds to their study a further aspect, which he calls the 'third dimension of power' (the first being Dahl's and the second Bachrach and Baratz's). His discussion of the first two dimensions of power focuses on the researchers' concern with the exercise of power in conflict situations. Although Lukes admits that this is important, what this concern ignores is insidiously exercising power to forestall generating conflict in the first place. As Lukes (*ibid.* p. 23) put it,

A may exercise power over B by getting him to do what he does not want to do but he also exercises power over him by influencing, shaping or determining his very wants. Indeed is it not the supreme exercise of power to get another or others to have the desires you want them to have – that is to secure their compliance by controlling their thoughts and desires?

Lukes' third dimension of power considers the ways in which potential issues are suppressed by both agenda-setting and 'the socially constructed and culturally patterned behaviour of groups and practices of institutions' (*ibid.* p. 24). This radical approach suggests that shaping preferences, perceptions and cognitions operates so that subordinates 'accept their role in the existing order of things either because they can see or imagine no alternative to it, or because they see it as natural and unchangeable, or because they value it as divinely ordained and beneficial' (*ibid.*). What we have here, Lukes suggests, is a latent conflict where there may be a contradiction between the interests of those exercising power and the 'real interests' of those they exclude. This power is so masked that its beneficiaries may themselves be unaware of their role in its application and perpetuation. Moreover, as we move away from the pluralist one-dimensional approaches to the second and third dimensions, the main beneficiaries are organizational élites, such as shareholders and management.

Marchington (1982) points out that, in Britain recently, there have been examples of employees being persuaded to accept partial redundancies to ensure company survival in economically recessive times or to moderate wage claims to ensure competitiveness with foreign imports. These exhortations may be prudent, realistic and, perhaps, in the interests of at least some employees, but the fact that such statements are, for the most part, readily accepted suggests support for the three-dimensional view. What is also inferred by this view is exercising power by controlling values and opinions so that society is socialized into unquestioning acceptance of the traditional natural order of things. Hence Lukes' perspective on organizational power, articulated in his three-dimensional view, coincides with Marxist analyses of the deeper roots of domination.

Lukes' whole position is important for understanding management control since it draws attention to further aspects of the impact of behavioural controls on members' subjective apprehension of themselves and the organizational situations they engage. It also points out the role of managerial prerogative as a fundamental basis of any attempt at management control.

When we see output controls in terms of Lukes' second dimension, they appear as vehicles for non-decision-making that avoid articulating existing conflict into organizational agendas. However, when we add the third dimension they also appear as a means by which members' cognitions and preferences are shaped so that conflict is forestalled in the first place. This directs attention to 'the ways in which "issues" are actually constructed in particular settings . . . in terms of the rationality of the setting' (Clegg, 1975, p. 27). This leads to a consideration of the 'rationality' transmitted by such controls, which can become influential in the 'culture(s)' which members subjectively refer and defer to in their construction of meaningful action. But this 'structure of domination' (*ibid.* p. 56–66) is dyadic in that it involves the 'self understandings of the powerless as well as the powerful' (Fay, 1987, p. 130). Thus the 'bias of the system can be mobilised and reinforced in ways that are neither consciously chosen nor the intended result of particular individuals' choices' (Lukes, 1974, p. 21). The operation of any administrative control might weave into the participants' consciousnesses concepts of the status quo as, in some sense, rational and inevitable. Particular avenues to making sense of reality are eliminated and participants become entrapped in what Morgan (1986) calls a 'Psychic Prison', which takes as legitimate, rather than threatening, the interests vested in that status quo. As Fay (1975, p. 62–3), in a different but related context, has commented:

their language and their understanding of themselves and their society would consist of concepts which reflected this illusion, but they would know nothing about this because they would have neither the vocabulary nor the perspective to discuss the true relationships; they would think their relationships . . . had to be the way they were, that they were natural and 'given'.

Once members accept, in construction of action, particular modes of rationality which make that action meaningful, they are provided with a rationale for judging what is normal or abnormal, acceptable or unacceptable. In this way hegemonic domination is constituted. For Williams (1960, p. 587), such domination might be construed as 'an order in which a certain way of life and thought is diffused throughout society in all its institutional and private manifestations, informing with all its spirit all taste, morality, customs, relations and political principles, particularly in their intellectual and moral connotations'. By signifying what is normal and routine, hegemony is a subtle and insidious form of power. It is not so much exercised by agents but it operates by influencing members' capacity for action – it pervades life by being unquestioned and unchallenged (see Clegg, 1979, pp. 84–6). Such may be the nature of managerial prerogative, which could well be the cornerstone of management control.

Management Prerogative

The second and, particularly, the third dimensions of power are interwoven with and supportive of the fabric of authority embodied in management's right to manage – managerial prerogative (Storey, 1983, pp. 58–9). As Storey suggests, the boundaries of managerial prerogatives or rights serve to delineate those functional tasks that give management its distinctiveness. It is not, therefore, surprising that such rights are hotly defended. These boundaries are constantly shifting and, at the present, are the subject of much discussion among industrial-relations academics (e.g. Dunn, 1990; Guest, 1991; Keenoy, 1991). It has been pointed out that, since the earliest days of the industrial revolution, owners and managers sought to legitimate what they regarded as their essential managerial function of control. Some form of subordination and domination is essential to ensure the control of employment relationships in modern, complex organizations, and this is secured by ideas and statements known collectively as managerial ideology. McGivering, Mathews and Scott (1969, p. 91), for example, define managerial ideology as 'a set of beliefs which management seeks to propagate in order to inspire acceptance and approval of managerial autonomy by the general public and by specific groups of workers'.

Justification for the maxim 'management must manage' apparently rests on a number of factors: owners or managers have control over their own capital assets; they are supported by the statutory law of company ownership responsibility; and the argument that it is in everyone's economic interest that managers (who are carefully chosen for their expertise) should be left free to manage as they think best.

Management prerogative might be likened to the 'divine right of kings'. Hill (1969) describes how, prior to the Civil War, English monarchs and many of their subjects believed in the divine origin of the king's authority. In 1640 the clergy were ordered to tell their congregations that 'the most high and sacred order of kings is of divine right . . . a supreme power . . . given to this most excellent order by God himself' (*ibid.* p. 86). It was therefore almost inconceivable that people could challenge the king, for that was to challenge divine authority. As Fox (1985, p. 53) has suggested, 'rulers of all kinds in all societies and at all times have been and are much exercised as to how to secure legitimation from their subjects and thereby promote willing compliance with their rules, policies and decisions'.

Golding (1980) invokes such an analogy in his ethnographic analysis of the social interaction between managers and subordinates. He shows how management's right to manage is a taken-for-granted and tacit assumption of those conversing in the organizational setting. But the maintenance of such prerogative depends on it not being overtly recognized or challenged – the sheer status of being a manager was enough to ensure subordinates' compliance to orders. Thus Golding indicates ways in which the prerogative is mystified and justified.

As with royal prerogative (at least until the events leading to the English Civil War), the result is that employees rarely challenge managers' rights to manage and control their activities. One result of this is that

> non-negotiable demands are not generated in the first place. Workers, in the main, accept the configurations of industrial hierarchy, the extreme division of labour, production for profit and not for need, market rationality and material and symbolic inequality. These are, by and large, perceived as 'givens' in the taken-for-granted world order.
>
> (Storey, 1983, p. 59)

Thus it would seem that why management prerogative tends to go unchallenged lies in employees' prior socialization, which promotes a tendency to accept most aspects of the status quo and to narrow down any challenges to 'aggressive economism'. This again particularly points to the dyadic nature of Lukes' third dimension of power. This is precisely the point Storey (1983) seems to make when he provides a brief analysis of Willis's work (1977) (see also Knights and Wilmott, 1985).

Willis's is an ethnographic study based primarily on the conversations of twelve working-class adolescent boys who displayed 'anti-school' attitudes. These self-styled 'lads' rejected the school's values of academic success and career achievement as expressions of fulfilment and individuality. They disparaged the boys who conformed and subscribed to those values as 'the ear'oles'. They deferred to a rebellious, anti-intellectual and macho 'counterculture' characterized by an 'entrenched, general and personalized opposition to authority'. This involved denigrating those who conformed to the school's conventional values by the celebration of having a 'laff', drinking, fighting and womanizing. These activities they saw as giving them an adult status, something denied to the 'ear'oles'. To finance their activities, the 'lads' had part-time jobs, which further symbolized their adulthood. On graduating from this counter-school culture, the 'lads' enthusiastically (and realistically, given their lack of qualifications) sought manual work that matched their assessment of personal worth in terms of masculine physical toughness rather than contemptible mental or white-collar employment.

Willis argues that this counterculture 'fits' with the culture of the workplace and made the 'lads' transition to work relatively painless. Willis thus claims that their counterculture is rooted in the beliefs dominant in their class background – an anti-authority, masculine chauvinism that emphasizes a clear distinction between 'us and them'. To Storey (1983), such prior social conditioning (with its acceptance of the 'cash nexus') is instrumental in forming attitudes towards work and the celebration of manual work over contemptible white-collar work. It serves to ease the boys' passage into the world of work, with its divorce of conception from execution, and to precondition them culturally into accepting their lot and to accept management's right to manage. The 'lads' become trapped and disempowered by their very rebellion.

Although Willis' work has been subject to much criticism (e.g. Hammersley and Atkinson, 1983; Knights and Wilmott, 1985), it does seem to lend support to the view that establishing management control and prerogative relies on the dyadic aspects of power – that aspects of employees' culture may, in effect, forestall the generation of non-negotiable demands in the first place and in a way that is independent of managerial actions and strategies. This leads us to suggest that any management control may perhaps be impossible without first establishing such a prerogative, a prerogative that in some way legitimates the right to control.

Conclusions

Lukes' approach appears to present a thorough-going challenge to the pluralist notion of countervailing power. However, his critics (see Benton, 1981; Clegg, 1989) point out how he develops his argument from Bachrach and Baratz by making a distinction between the culture(s) to which employees defer in making sense of their world(s) and their objectively identifiable 'real' or 'true' interests. In other words, his idea of the third dimension is based on the development of employee cultures, which obscure and subvert their 'real' interests by producing what amounts to a 'false' consciousness. Thus Lukes argues that, to associate the absence of conflict with genuine consensus, is to rule out 'the possibility of false or manipulated consensus by definitional fiat' (1974, p. 24). As conflict has been averted successfully, Lukes argues that we may have a situation of 'latent conflict', which consists of 'a contradiction between the interests of those exercising power and the *real interests* of those they exclude' (*ibid.* pp. 24–5). Lukes bases his argument on an appeal to the existence of interests outside situations in which power is exercised insidiously (Knights and Wilmott, 1985). But how can Lukes know what these interests (that, according to his own analysis, would only be articulated in circumstances free from constraint and domination) might be? Is the only justification for his argument an appeal to privileged knowledge on his own part – something that is surely incompatible with his own analysis?

This notion of 'real interests' is, in Clegg's (1989) view, a serious weakness of Lukes' analysis. Clegg states his objections in the form of a conundrum. Judgements of what are 'real interests' must be made either by subjects or by observers. If the observer, it will be made according to some standard of 'real interests', capriciously or inconsistently. If the subject, it is impossible to isolate an authentic, real articulation of interest, which is made from 'without' power, from an unauthentic, false expression of interest – which is made as a

A/B relations	First dimension	Second dimension	Third dimension
Power of A over B	Prevalence of A over B through A's control of superior bargaining resources	A constructs barriers to the participation of B through non-decision-making and the mobilization of bias	A influences and shapes B's consciousness about the existence of inequalities through the production of myths, information control, ideologies, etc.
Rebellion of B against the benefits held by A relative to B	A defeats B owing to B's lack of resources	B does not participate in the existing political agendas because of real and perceived barriers to entry and owing to anticipation by B that to participate would mean defeat	Susceptibility to myths, legitimation of ideologies; a sense of powerlessness; an uncritical or fragmentary and multiple consciousness about issues on B's part as a result of A's influence, shaping and barriers to entry
Powerlessness of B relative to A	Open conflict between A and B, with each holding competing resources, the conflict occurring over clearly defined issues	Mobilization upon issues and action against barriers	Formulation of issues and strategies

Figure 7.3   Clegg's adaptation of Gaventa's model (from Clegg, 1989, p. 110)

result of power constraints. If subjects cannot know their own minds, how can observers (Clegg, 1989, p. 100)?

Clegg suggests the use of a comparative analysis of distinct approaches to power, such as that developed by Gaventa (1980). Gaventa studied an Appalachian coal-mining community and, while his study corresponds to Lukes' three dimensions, it avoids the notions of 'real interests'. To Clegg, Gaventa's model (Figure 7.3) improves Lukes' original model by not making the focus on interests a constitutive feature.

Gaventa's modification of Lukes seems to resolve many of the problems in his original model by avoiding any reference to interests. By analysing a historical case study, Gaventa provides illustrations of the processes through which the third dimension of power might operate. Clegg (1989) provides a useful summary of Gaventa's work. He lists the three indirect mechanisms of power's third dimension:

> First . . . Bs who lose a lot give up trying to win against A after a while. Apathy or fatalism can become the norm . . . Second . . . where people are not political participants, for whatever reasons, their level of political consciousness will not be developed as it would be if they were participating . . . Third, consciousness may be chronically disorganized.
>
> (*Ibid.* p. 109)

Both Lukes' and Gaventa's formulations suggest that, when we move away from the notion of the one-dimensional level of power, the main beneficiaries of the other two more obscure dimensions are likely to be such power-holders as owners and managers. This is because these hidden 'faces of power' are, to a large degree, supportive of the authority embodied in the managers' strategic position and their right to manage – managerial prerogative. Without first establishing managerial prerogative, any managerial attempt to control employees' organizational behaviour would, perhaps, be doomed to failure.

Further Reading

Lukes (1974) is still key reading for anyone attempting to understand the issues raised in this chapter. His book is brief and very accessible. It covers, critically, the contributions of Dahl and Bachrach and Baratz. However, Lukes is best read in conjunction with either Benton (1981) or Knights and Wilmott (1985) – both of whom provide important critiques. It is then worth comparing these with Gaventa's (1980) reformulation of Lukes' original model.

It is in this context that Clegg's (1989) development of his earlier work (1975, 1979) should be read. Although difficult in parts, Clegg (1989) provides a comprehensive review and analysis, which is a *tour de force*. Central to Clegg's contribution is Lukes' work, which he theoretically and epistemologically contextualizes and criticizes. Out of this he develops his notion of 'circuits of power'.

For an important analysis of management control and prerogative, Storey (1983) is key reading. For comparatively limited but easily understood considerations of power in work organizations, see Pfeffer (1981b) and Mintzberg (1983). A highly entertaining approach to power and politics in organizations, which develops a 'political approach' to understanding organizational behaviour, is provided by Lee and Lawrence (1991).

Finally, Morgan (1986) analyses power by looking at how metaphors lead us to see and understand organizations in distinctive but partial ways. His metaphor 'organizations as political systems' to a great extent correlates with a pluralist approach, while the metaphors 'organizations as instruments of domination' and 'organizations as psychic prisons' can be understood as correlating with and elaborating on a more radical perspective.

8

Conclusion

Introduction

It would seem that the changing economic and political circumstances of the last decade or so have been instrumental in promoting changes in how the management and control of people is approached in work organizations. Many commentators (e.g. Martin, 1988; Sisson, 1989, 1990) have identified key developments that appear to have significant implications for the design and management of British organizations.

First, it has been argued that there have been changes in the manufacturing base of the British economy, which Blackaby (1978) describes as 'deindustrialization'. This, together with the impact of microelectronic technology and the growth of a service sector geared to information processing, has resulted in the emergence of new industries and services in new geographical locations (Leadbeater and Lloyd, 1987). Second, it is believed that British organizations are now confronted by expanding and intensified international competition. This has been caused, apparently, by several factors, which include: the rise of the technologically sophisticated and cost-competitive economies of the Pacific Rim and South East Asia; the movement from 'command' to 'market' economies in former Eastern Europe; the implications of developing wider markets, such as the 'Single European Market' with, ultimately, the elimination of all 'technical, physical and fiscal barriers' in the European Community (Krulis-Randa, 1990, p. 133); and the continued increase in the number of multinational corporations organized and competing upon a global basis.

Third, although Britain is not alone in facing these pressures, the policies of successive Conservative governments (underpinned by 'market principles') have resulted in Britain being much more exposed to the vicissitudes created by these pressures than, say, its European partners. Sisson (1989, 1990) points to other aspects of government policy that could have had a significant impact on the management of work organizations. For example, in contrast to the Keynesian demand-management policies of successive post-war governments, recent Conservative governments have operated and implemented vigorous monetarist economic principles that are associated with the 'new right'. Not only has this resulted in abandoning 'full' employment as a policy objective but it has also created a new legitimacy for both entrepreneurialism and aggressive individualism. It has also been the impetus behind legislation to constrain and undermine the collective powers of employees and their representatives, as well as to reduce drastically the nature and scope of employment protection available to individuals under the legislation of the 1970s (Beaumont, 1987; Mac-Innes, 1987).

An important effect of such policies, together with higher levels of unemployment and structural shifts in the patterns of employment away from manufacturing to service industry, has been a sharp decline in trade-union membership and influence during the last decade. This seems to have had a profound effect on how employment relationships are managed (Legge, 1988).

Even though there may be countervailing pressures that limit the scope and pace of any such transitions in the management of employment relationships (Storey and Sisson, 1990), it could be claimed that the developments mentioned above constitute 'destabilising disturbances' (Martin, 1988, p. 216). These developments appear to have implications for the management of work organizations as managers face up to finding ways of coping with the uncertainties that, in part, derive 'from a need for a continuous rapid adjustment to a market environment that seems to have become permanently more turbulent than in the past' (*ibid*. p. 265).

The Implications

At a general theoretical, conceptual and prescriptive level, though subject to the vagaries stemming from managements' 'strategic choice' (Child, 1972), an analysis of the above development using contingency theory might suggest that there are specific organizational arrangements that would be more 'effective' at coping with the uncertainties created by such political, social, economic and technological exigencies (Lawrence, 1981; Donaldson, 1985). Contingency theory would propose that, given those changes, organizations may well move towards more organic forms of organization in order to be more capable of coping with and adapting to the current levels of accelerated change and uncertainty. Although the idioms are rather different, this basic point is evident in the recent, interrelated but rather divorced debates in both organizational sociology and organization theory about post-modernism, organizational flexibility and human resources management (HRM).

Clegg (1990) calls the current levels of accelerated change 'the postmodern condition' (see also Fox, 1990). 'Post-modernity' originally developed as an architectural concept that, among other things, referred to randomness, anarchy and fragmentation, in contrast to the monolithic architectural structures of modernism (Ryan, 1988). This suggests that society and its institutions are moving from a modern to a post-modern epoch, characterized by a search for new organizational methods of coping with an increasingly turbulent and uncertain world. In his discussion of 'postmodern consumption', Clegg (1990, p. 18) argues that in contrast to the 'modernist world of consumption', post-modernism is based on an 'increasing proliferation of differentiated items of consumption . . . Yet the basis of this degree of differentiated consumption is a relative de-differentiation in production'. This, he claims, has significant implications for post-modern forms of organization, which 'might be centred on a concern with flexible specialisation' (*ibid.*).

At the risk of over-simplification, we can gather from this debate that 'modernist' organizational forms were or are characterized by highly specialized or differentiated divisions of labour controlled through various 'bureaucratic' mechanisms, which either attempted to pre-programme organizational tasks and/or establish control through the measurement of outputs. As Gergen (1992, p. 211) succinctly puts it, modernism entails the 'absorption of the machine metaphor'. In contrast, 'post-bureaucratic' or 'post-modernist' organizational forms are or will be comparatively non-hierarchical, with an informal division of labour, and characterized by a 'strategy of increasing the flexibility of social structures and making them amenable to new forms of indirect and internalised control, including cultural and ideological control' (Heydebrand, 1989, p. 345).

Underlying such an assertion must be the view that, because of the prevalence of instability and uncertainty, it is increasingly more difficult for the management of many organizations to establish some degree of control by either pre-programming members' tasks or measuring the outputs of their task performance meaningfully. Therefore administrative controls based on those procedures are no longer possible or appropriate in an increasing number of organizations. Hendry *et al.* (1988) – from their analysis of twenty case studies – say that there is some evidence to suggest that many enterprises have initiated organizational developments in response to the perceived pressures deriving from, for example, heightened competition, to improve their financial viability and gain competitive advantage.

In a similar way, Horwitz (1990, pp. 13–14) argues that economic and political crises have led organizational decision-makers to consider greater flexibility in the management of human, financial and material resources and costs. This has been associated with shifts towards organizational decentralization and, in some cases, the development of ostensibly more enlightened and participative forms of management control as a defence against such intensified domestic and international competition (Edwards, 1987), as well as uncertainty resulting from dynamic product markets.

So it is not surprising that, as Parker (1992) has suggested, management writers are already beginning to produce books that are discourses to help managers manage organizations in a post-modern epoch – a concern invoked by such titles as *Thriving on Chaos* (Peters, 1987) or *The Age of Unreason* (Handy, 1989). It is here that it might be possible to try to understand the significance of what many commentators have called 'HRM' in contrast to 'personnel management', and how the 'flexibility debate' has a bearing on these developments.

Although the term HRM has been in use in the USA for over thirty years (Lawrence, 1985), its recent appearance as a subject for theory and research seems to be tied intimately to the populist (and sometimes almost evangelical) management literature published in the 1980s – as exemplified by the work of Peters and Waterman (1982), Peters (1987) and Deal and Kennedy (1982). This 'new-wave management' literature (Wood, 1989) can be seen to derive either from a concern to analyse and replicate what are assumed to be the adoptable aspects of Japanese organizations' apparent competitive edge (e.g. Pascale and Athos, 1982) or from an attempt to seek out indigenous (mainly to North America) 'excellent' management practices (e.g. Peters and Waterman, 1982). Regardless of the source of inspiration, the effect has been to cultivate a fixation with culture and charismatic leadership as the determinants of entrepreneurial success (see Blunt, 1990).

In this it is possible to see the development of further managerial panaceas to what Hyman (1987, p. 41) considers a perpetual problem for managers, in that 'labour control involves both the direction, surveillance and discipline of subordinates whose enthusiastic commitment to corporate objectives cannot be taken for granted; and the mobilisation of the discretion, initiative and diligence which coercive supervision, far from guaranteeing, is likely to destroy'. The term 'new wave' is rather inappropriate since there is nothing particularly 'new' about this approach. The only novelty seems to be that 'new wave' implies a dismissal of bureaucratic forms of control in an anti-hierarchical manner, with repeated exhortations to maintain high performance by stimulating innovation in a proactive, entrepreneurial fashion (Wood, 1989). As we have argued earlier, 'new-wave management' can be traced to Mayo's Durkheimian interpretation of the Hawthorne studies and the subsequent popularization of 'human relations' (Silver, 1987). Although drawing attention to the potential role of emotions and sentiments in regulating employees' organizational behaviour, this created a need to 'repair social solidarity' by instilling in employees a 'sense of corporate consciousness' (Clegg and Dunkerley, 1980a, p. 122). This Durkheimian derivation is thus illustrated by the 'new wave' view that, if the appropriate values and attitudes are internalized, a common sense of purpose or 'moral involvement' (activated through emotion and sentiment) develops, which makes the constant surveillance of employees as a form of control redundant (Mitchell, 1985).

Kanter (1989, p. 280) argues that the need to move away from bureaucratic modes of control towards forms of control that instil personal commitment arises because such rules and procedures 'stifle initiative and creativity' in an atmosphere that is 'emotionally repressive'. Presumably in dynamic and unpredictable situations it is this very initiative and creativity that is essential. However, one might question cynically a key assumption that underlies such 'new wave' prescriptions. How can control through cultural homogenization, supposedly achievable through the manipulation of employees' emotions and sentiments, possibly facilitate employees' exercise of creativity and initiative when such qualities may require their repeated deviance from that culture? Such behaviour would probably be intolerable to the organizational guardians of the 'strong cultures' prescribed by 'new wave' writers (Coopey and Hartley, 1991, pp. 26–8).

Despite the socio-economic context described above, and especially given the current ideological climate, it would seem unlikely that the notion of 'self-management', as described in Chapter 6, will gain much ground. This is not to say that post-modern organizational forms (arising in alternative political and ideological situations) will not be based on 'self-management'. As Clegg (1990, p. 235) so forcefully argues, 'no necessity attaches to the future of organisational diversities'.

However, given the socio-economic circumstances described above, and the prevailing ideological climate, Guest (1990) argues that the last decade has been a good period for HRM in the UK as it seemed to offer an attractive alternative to the rather jaded image of conventional personnel management (PM). However, what is rather strange is that what is understood as HRM as opposed to PM remains somewhat ambiguous. This is mirrored by the practitioners: Guest (1987, p. 506) notes that former personnel departments have become HRM departments without any evident change in role. Although Paauwe (1991) attempts to envisage the contingencies that might shape HRM practice, when attempts have been made to distinguish the main differences between HRM and PM this has rarely been done by reference to a contingency model that locates their relative appropriateness to the exigencies created by different contextual variables. Instead, in line with the universalism of the 'new wave' management literature referred to above, many commentators appear to assert the inherent superiority of HRM over PM, even though the criteria by which this alleged superiority has been discerned remain vague. For example, the claim that HRM is an 'empirical model . . . based on an analysis of the policies . . . pursued by successful companies' (Guest, 1987, p. 42) seems to agree with the approach and claims made by Peters and Waterman (1982). However, what are particularly useful are the attempts made by several writers to investigate the most significant differences between HRM and PM.

Legge (1989) begins her examination of the differences between the 'normative models' of PM and HRM by reviewing the existing literature. She observes that, in contrast to the unitary frame of reference adopted in North America, Britain tends to adopt a pluralistic perspective. However, certain things are held in common. PM involves facilitating the achievement of organizational goals, as defined by senior management, since it is about 'selecting, developing and directing employees in such a way that they achieve satisfaction and "give of their best" at work' (*ibid.* p. 22).

From this it is apparent that control is at the heart of PM but, as Guest (1987, 1991) argues, this is a particular approach to control, which is very different from that embraced by HRM. Guest argues that PM is primarily associated with external and instrumental 'compliance-based' systems of control, which are largely dependent on collectively negotiated systems of extrinsic reward to ensure efficiency and cost minimization in a centralized, mechanistic, organization structure. In contrast to what might be termed 'direct control' (Friedman, 1977), HRM seems to aim at 'responsible autonomy' through administrative controls that either specify tasks through the generation of rules or output-based controls. Output-based controls are idealized as the development of self-regulated 'members', who have internalized management-derived cultural norms and who thereby proceed to exercise self-control in a manner that accords with managerial aims and objectives (see Burawoy, 1979; 1985). Both Horwitz (1990) and Guest (1987, 1991) argue that, in contrast to PM,

HRM is typically allied to internalized forms of 'commitment-based' self-control in order to support the development of a more flexible and adaptive workforce. This should ensure the highest performance from members in a decentralized and organic organization structure.

Streeck (1987, p. 281) defines flexibility as organizations ' 'general capacity to reorganize in close response to fluctuations in their environment'. Whitaker (1992) differentiates between 'investment-led' flexibility, which entails the use of new manufacturing technologies, and 'labour-led' flexibility, in which the emphasis is on the variable use of labour. Streeck argues that 'labour-led' flexibility is pursued in both internal and external labour markets. External flexibility, or what Atkinson (1984) has called numerical flexibility, relates to the ease with which the numbers of workers employed can be varied to meet fluctuations in demand. Internal or functional (*ibid.*) flexibility refers primarily to labour-process restructuring and to the ease with which employees' tasks can be adapted to fluctuations in demand. Thus functional-internal flexibility emphasizes the development of a multi-skilled and itinerant (in terms of the ability to move between tasks) workforce. A flexible firm will avoid an orthodox hierarchical structure by dividing the workforce into 'peripheral' numerically flexible workgroups organized round a numerically stable 'core' of employees (*ibid.*). The 'core' will have greater job security, provided they are willing to and capable of learning new skills according to organizational requirements, as they undertake the organization's key, firm specific, activities.

Empirical evidence about any British trend towards a permanent 'flexibility offensive' (Atkinson and Gregory, 1986, p. 15) is, to put it mildly, confusing. Some researchers (Nichols, 1986; Prowse, 1990) have identified a British trend in the form of a differentiation between 'core' and 'peripheral' employees. Although there is some evidence to suggest that there have been changes in working practices, such as multi-skilling and a reduction in demarcation (Daniel, 1987), both MacInnes (1988) and Storey (1989) have argued that there is conflicting evidence about how widespread the flexible firm is in practice, and whether or not British management is actually seeking to introduce a core and peripheral workforce as a conscious strategy.

Pollert (1991) claims that flexibility implies there has been a split from the past. Rigid mass production was unable to cope with 'new market uncertainty'. However, she argues that there is no valid basis for suggesting the development of organizational flexibility based on a functionally flexible core employee, who is committed to the employer, and a non-permanent numerically flexible periphery. She argues that the growth in unemployment and non-permanent work may simply be a result of structural changes in the economy rather than a search for organizational flexibility (*ibid.* p. 11). It is, therefore, open to dispute whether or not there is a trend towards developing organizational flexibility in the face of increasing uncertainty and, if there is a trend, how far this is a product of intentional and concerted managerial strategies or whether it has arisen in a piecemeal, unco-ordinated and fragmented manner – a logical incrementalism arising from the need to keep the show on the road (Purcell and Sissons, 1983; Thurley and Wood, 1983).

Whether or not this trend exists, one might predict that if a differentiation into core and periphery did occur it would probably be accompanied by a differentiation in control. Nichols (1986) found that core employees were subject to 'ideological' controls in a similar way to what Guest called commitment-based controls – controls that seemed to be considered unnecessary for peripheral employees. The future might thus bring about a situation where a relatively privileged and functionally flexible 'core' of employees are subject to HRM and its dependence on administrative controls, which attempt to influence the value premises of their organization behaviour. Such controls could, presumably, be based on 'social technologies' derived either from human relations (as with 'new wave' management) and/or neo-human-relations techniques that could entail a degree of job enrichment that would possibly be necessary to engender functional flexibility – both backed up by selective recruitment of conformist personnel (Maguire , 1986).

A numerically flexible periphery of relatively underprivileged workers would be subject to the direct control of various bureaucratic mechanisms typical of PM. The imagery invoked by Clegg (1990, p. 234) to describe this possible future scenario is one of a series of exclusive enclaves of privileged employees who have, or are willing and able to develop, the necessary skills, and who have been seduced by the organizational benefits on offer. They are surrounded by a marginalized and under-privileged majority: 'Postmodernity would be a series of privileged enclaves stockaded within the bleak vistas of modernity' (*ibid.*). In other words, organic cores with mechanistic peripheries.

As a mode of management control over human resources, the mainstay of HRM (commitment-based control) has been linked to the development of post-modern organizational forms. Discernible in HRM is a 'new wave' emphasis on management's role as creator, custodian and manipulator of their organization's culture to establish control by influencing the value premises of members' decision-making processes. Referring to this aim to homogenize cultures, Fox (1990, pp. 204–5) observes that management thinking and action has begun to attempt to tackle cultural change deliberately in organizations, in that it is now seen as legitimate 'to meddle with the company's culture and each other's and employees' values and competencies'. To Fox, the result has been the commodification of culture. This has spawned a growing labour market in 'culture and knowledge workers of many kinds'. For example, much HRM literature refers to the need to secure employees' identification with and sense of commitment to the firm, as well as their 'behavioural commitment' (Guest, 1989, p. 42) to the everyday implementation of corporate strategy.

The links this has with the Durkheimian lineage of the 'new wave' desire to develop 'strong cultures' and 'turned-on workforces' (at least among 'core' employees) who enhance the 'pursuit of excellence' by increasing their sense of common purpose or social solidarity and so motivate members to maximize their contribution, are only too evident. Again this brings into play Guest's (1987) claim that there is something new and distinctive about HRM. It shares a 'new wave' lineage that may be traced back to human relations, Mayo and ultimately to Durkheim. Moreover, it has been rightly pointed out that the organization development movements of the Sixties and Seventies, which sought to integrate strategy, mission and culture change into a high-trust organization using such technologies as team development, are also close to HRM (Iles and Johnston, 1989). What we are perhaps witnessing or perhaps will witness is a major shift to an internal point of control for some, but not all, employees. This may have been brought about by changes in political, economic and technological environments, but such changes should not be accorded the status of a paradigm shift or revolution.

In a similar way, some HRM literature may, at first sight, appear to be couched in ostensibly humanistic values. However, the primary purpose of such rhetoric may be to legitimate an approach to managing people based on an 'intensification in the control of work and increased commodification of labour under the disguise of reconstructing employee responsibility, autonomy and commitment' (Keenoy, 1990, p. 379). So, while much of PM is entrenched in pluralism, HRM appears to be concerned to replace this acknowledged diversity of organizational interest groups (with their attendant and often conflicting cultures) with a unitary organization (or at least a unitary 'core') based on a socially engineered monolithic culture.

Most HRM literature follows the 'new wave' vogue of cultural homogenization as the foundation of control based on a restructuring of members' attitudes towards 'mutuality' (Walton, 1985). Therefore, what stands out is the notion that human beings should be treated as a valued asset that, if appropriately managed, will be a source of competitive advantage (Legge, 1989). A significant element in such managerial practice is an emphasis on culture management to develop members' commitment and to foster their self-discipline and ability to exercise the initiative necessary for promoting flexibility 'in the interests of the adaptive organisation's pursuit of excellence' (*ibid.* p. 25).

It is possible to conjecture that the emergence of HRM, and the flexibility debate in general, could well be associated with the evolution of certain possible post-modern forms of organization, as well as the plethora of particular ideas about how to manage complex organizations (which entail a degree of repackaging of what is essentially human-relation ideology, and which, in practice, could also include neo-human-relations techniques entailing job (re)designs commensurate with developing functional flexibility). As with 'new-wave management', the debate around HRM can be seen as demonstrating a search for methods of managing and controlling human behaviour at work – methods that will cope with the exigencies of a post-modern world and that make surveillance and control through bureaucracy inappropriate for particular groups of employees. Considering the future evolution of post-modern organizational forms, Heydebrand (1989, p. 327) considers that they will thus possess a 'division of labour [that] is informal and flexible and [a] postbureaucratic control structure even though prebureaucratic elements such as clanlike personalism, informalism, and corporate culture may be used to integrate an otherwise loosely coupled, centrifugal system'.

In conclusion it is worth bearing in mind Whitley's (1992) view (demonstrated by his comparative analysis of different forms of economic organization and business practice in various countries) that organizations are 'social constructs' dependent on dominant conventions and beliefs, which vary between social contexts. The result for Whitley is that these different business recipes, logics of action or rules of the game imply 'that there are a variety of forms of business organisation which are effective and that no single economic logic can be regarded as uniquely "rational" ' (*ibid.* p. 139). To Whitley, a key variable that influences the form organizations take and will take in the future is 'how controllers of major economic resources conceive and evaluate realities and possibilities' (*ibid.*). Whether or not the future of management control in work organizations is of the order described above by Heydebrand and whether or not such a form of control will be limited to a relatively privileged core of employees, while the peripheral, under-privileged majority remain subject to modernist or bureaucratic modes of control, or whether self-management becomes the future order, or whether new and unforeseen forms of organization might develop, ultimately – only time will tell.

Further Reading

Storey (1989) contains a highly instructive selection of readings that covers much of the recent debates about HRM and PM. Both Whitaker (1992) and Pollert (1991) provide excellent overviews and evaluations of the debates around changing forms of work organization, with a more specific focus on flexibility. These debates can be related to Clegg's (1990) work, in which he explores (through the use of a variety of international examples) the concepts of 'modernity' and 'post-modernity'.

Finally, both Gergen (1992) and Parker (1992) discuss and review the epistemological basis of post-modernist thought. Parker is particularly helpful in the way in which he distinguishes between the implications of 'post-modernist' epistemology for writing about organizations and for writings that are concerned with providing prescriptions intended to help organizations cope with the exigencies of a 'post-modern' epoch.

References

Abrams, P. (ed.) (1978) *Work, Urbanism and Inequality*, Weidenfeld & Nicolson, London.

ACAS (1977) *Code of Practice 2: Disclosure of Information to Trade Unions for Collective Bargaining Purposes*, HMSO, London.

Ackroyd, S. and Crowdy, P. A. (1990) Can culture be managed? *Personnel Review*, Vol. 19, no. 5, pp. 3–13.

Adams, J. S. (1965) Inequity in social exchange, in L. Berkowitz (ed.) *Advances in Experimental Social Psychology*, Academic Press, New York, NY.

Alderfer, C. P. (1972) *Existence, Relatedness, and Growth: Human Needs in Organizational Settings*, Free Press, New York, NY.

Allaire, Y. and Firsirotu, M. (1984) Theories of organisational culture, *Organisational Studies*, Vol. 5, no. 3, pp. 193–226.

Amigoni, F. (1978) Management planning and control systems, *Journal of Business Finance and Accounting*, Autumn, pp. 279–91.

Andrasik, F. and Heimberg, J. S. (1982) Self-management procedures, in L. W. Frederikson (ed.) *Handbook of Organizational Behavior Management*, Wiley, New York, NY.

Ansari, S. L. (1977) An integrated approach to control system design, *Accounting, Organisations and Society*, Vol. 2, no. 2, pp. 101–12.

Anthony, P. D. (1977) *The Ideology of Work*, Tavistock, London.

Anthony, P. D. (1990) The paradox of the management of culture or 'he who leads is lost', *Personnel Review*, Vol. 19, no. 4, pp. 3–8.

Anthony, R. N., Dearden, J. and Vancil, R. F. (1965) *Management Control Systems*, Irwin, Homewood, Ill.

Anthony, R. N. and Dearden, J. (1976) *Management Control Systems*, Irwin, Homewood, Ill.

Argyris, C. (1954) *The Impact of Budgets on People*, Controllership Foundation, New York.

Argyris, C. (1957) *Personality and Organization*, Harper & Row, New York, NY.

Argyris, C. (1962) *Interpersonal Competence and Organizational Effectiveness*, Irwin, Homewood, Ill.

Argyris, C. (1964) *Integrating the Individual and the Organisation*, Wiley, Chichester.

Argyris, C. (1977) Organisational learning and management information systems, *Accounting, Organisations and Society*, Vol. 2, no. 2, pp. 113–23.

Argyris, C. and Schon, D. A. (1974) *Theory in Practice: Increasing Professional Effectiveness*, Jossey-Bass, San Francisco, Calif.

Argyris, C. and Schon, D. A. (1978) *Organizational Learning*, Addison-Wesley, Reading, Mass.

Arendt, H. (1959) *The Human Condition*, Doubleday, New York, NY.

Armstrong, M. (1988) *A Handbook of Human Resource Management*, Kogan Page, London.

Asch, S. E. (1951) Effects of group pressures upon the modification and distortion of judgements, in M. Guetzkow (ed.) *Groups, Leadership, and Men*, Carnegie Press, Pittsburgh, Pa.

Ashworth, P. and Johnson, P. D. (1991) The meaning of participation (unpublished working paper), Sheffield City Polytechnic.

Atkinson, J. (1984) Manpower strategies for flexible organisations, *Personnel Management*, Vol. 16, no. 8, pp. 28–31.

Atkinson, J. and Gregory, D. (1986) A flexible future, *Marxism Today*, April, pp. 12–17.

Bachrach, P. and Baratz, M. S. (1962) Two faces of power, *American Political Science Review*, Vol. 56, pp. 947–52.

Bachrach, P. and Baratz, M. S. (1963) Decisions and nondecisions, *American Political Science Review*, Vol. 57, pp. 641–51.

Bachrach, P. and Baratz, M. S. (1970) *Power and Poverty: Theory and Practice*, Oxford University Press.

Bachrach, S. B. and Lawler, J. L. (1980) *Power and Politics in Organizations*, Jossey-Bass, San Francisco, Calif.

Badham, R. and Matthews, J. (1989) The new production systems debate, *Labour and Industry*, Vol. 2, no. 2, pp. 194–246.

Bandura, A. (1969) *Principles of Behavior Modification*, Holt, Rinehart & Winston, New York, NY.

Baritz, L. (1965) *Servants of Power*, Wesleyan University Press, Middletown, Mass.

Barley, S. (1984) The professional, the semi-professional, and the machine: the social ramifications of computer based imaging in radiology (unpublished PhD dissertation, MIT), Sloan School of Management.

Bartell, T. (1976) The human relations ideology: an analysis of the social origins of a belief system, *Human Relations*, Vol. 29, no. 8, pp. 737–49.

Bass, B.M. (1985) *Leadership and Performance beyond Expectations*, Free Press, New York, NY.

Bate, P. (1990) Using the culture concept in an organisation development setting, *Journal of Applied Behavioural Science*, Vol. 26, no. 1, pp. 83–106.

Batstone, E. *et al.* (1978) *The Social Organisation of Strikes*, Blackwell, Oxford.

Beaumont, P. (1987) *The Decline of Trade Union Organisation*, Croom Helm, London.

Becker, H. S. and Geer, B. (1960) Latent culture, *Administrative Science Quarterly*, Vol. 5, pp. 303–13.

Becker, S. and Green, D. (1962) Budgeting and employee behaviour, *The Journal of Business*, Vol. 35, no. 4, pp. 392–402.

Bennis, W. G. (1959) Leadership theory and administrative behaviour, *Administrative Science Quarterly*, Vol. 22, pp. 259–301.

Bennis, W. G. (1966) *Changing Organizations*, McGraw-Hill, New York, NY.

Bennis, W. G. and Schein, E. H. (1965) *Personal and Organizational Change through Group Methods*, Wiley, New York, NY.

Bennis, W. and Nanus, B. (1985) *Leaders: Strategies for Taking Charge*, Harper & Row, New York, NY.

Benton, T. (1981) 'Objective' interests and the sociology of power, *Sociology*, Vol. 15, no. 2, pp. 161–84.

Berger, P. L. and Luckmann, T. (1967) *The Social Construction of Reality*, Penguin Books, Harmondsworth.

Berlew, D. E. and Hall, D. T. (1965) The socialization of managers: effects of expectations upon performance, *American Sociological Review*, Vol. 21, pp. 341–7.

Bevan, S. and Thompson, M. (1991) Performance management at the crossroads, *Personnel Management*, November.

Beyer, J. M. and Trice, H. M. (1987) How an organisation's rites reveal its culture, *Organisational Dynamics*, Spring, pp. 5–24.

Beynon, H. (1973) *Working for Ford*, Penguin Books, Harmondsworth.

Beynon, H. (1977) *Living with Capitalism*, Routledge & Kegan Paul, London.

Bion, W. R. (1959) *Experiences in Groups*, Tavistock, London.

Blackaby, F. T. (1978) *De–industrialisation*, Heinemann, London.

Blake, R. R. and Mouton, J. S. (1964) *The Managerial Grid*, Gulf, Houston, Tex.

Blau, P. M. and Schoenherr, P. A. (1971) *The Structure of Organizations*, Basic Books, New York, NY.

Blau, P. M. and Scott, W. R. (1962) *Formal Organizations*, Chandler, San Francisco, Calif.

Blauner, R. (1964) *Alienation and Freedom*, Chicago University Press, Chicago, Ill.

Blumer, H. (1969) *Symbolic Interactionism: Perspective and Method*, Prentice-Hall, Englewood Cliffs, NJ.

Blunt, P. (1990) Recent developments in human resource management: the good, the bad and the ugly, *International Journal of Human Resource Management*, Vol. 1, no. 1, pp. 45–59.

Boland, R. J. jr (1987) Discussion of 'accounting and the governable person', *Accounting, Organisations and Society*, Vol. 12, no. 3, pp. 267–72.

Brannen, P., Batstone, E., Fatchett, D. and White, P. (1976) *The Worker Directors – A Sociology of Participation*, Hutchinson, London.

Braverman, H. (1974) *Labor and Monopoly Capital: The Degradation of Work in the Twentieth Century*, Monthly Review Press, New York, NY.

Brim, O. G. (1968) Adult socialization, in J. Clausen (ed.) *Socialization and Society*, Little Brown & Co, Boston, Mass.

Brown, R. (1965) *Social Psychology*, Collier-Macmillan, London.

Brown, R. K. (1978) Work, in P. Abrams, (ed.) *op. cit.*

Brownell, P. (1981) Participation in budgeting, locus of control and organisational effectiveness, *Accounting Review*, Vol. 56, pp. 844–60.

Brownell, P. (1982) Participation in the budgeting process: when it works and when it doesn't, *Journal of Accounting Literature*, Vol. 1, no. 2, pp. 124–53.

Brownell, P. and McInnes, M. (1986) Budgetary participation, motivation, and managerial performance, *The Accounting Review*, pp. 587–600.

Bryman, A. (1992) *Charisma and Leadership in Organisations*, Sage, London.

Buchanan, D. A. and Huczynski, A. A. (1985) *Organisation Behaviour*, Prentice-Hall, London.

Burawoy, M. (1979) *Manufacturing Consent: Changes in the Labor Process under Monopoly Capitalism*, Chicago University Press, Chicago, Ill.

Burawoy, M. (1985) *The Politics of Production*, Verso, London.

Burchell, S. *et al.* (1980) The role of accounting in organisations and society, *Accounting, Organisations and Society*, Vol. 5, no. 1, pp. 5–27.

Burnham, J. (1941) *The Managerial Revolution*, Day, New York, NY.

Burns, J. M. (1978) *Leadership*, Harper & Row, New York, NY.

Burns, T. (1955) The reference of conduct in small groups: cliques and cabals in occupational milieux, *Human Relations*, Vol. 8, pp. 467–86.

Burns, T. and Stalker, G. M. (1961) *The Management of Innovation*, Tavistock, London.

Burrell, G. (1987) No accounting for sexuality, *Accounting, Organisations and Society*, Vol. 12, no. 1, pp. 89–101.

Burrell, G. (1988) Modernism, post modernism and organisational analysis 2, *Organisation Studies*, Vol. 9, no. 2, pp. 221–335.

Burrell, G. and Morgan, G. (1979) *Sociological Paradigms and Organisational Analysis*, Heinemann Educational, London.

Butler, G. V. (1986) *Organisation and Management: Theory and Practice*, Prentice-Hall, London.

Calder, B. J. and Staw, B. M. (1975) Self-perception of intrinsic and extrinsic motivation, *Journal of Personality and Social Psychology*, Vol. 31, pp. 509–605.

Campbell, J. P. and Pritchard, R. D. (1976) Motivation theory in industrial and organizational psychology, in M. D. Dunnette, (ed.) *Handbook for Industrial and Organizational Psychology*, Rand McNally, Chicago.

Camman, C. (1976) Effects of the use of control systems, *Accounting, Organisations and Society*, Vol. 1, no. 4, pp. 301–13.

Carlisle, H. M. (1974) A contingency approach to decentralisation, *Advanced Management Journal*, July, pp. 9–19.

Carlson, S. (1951) *Executive Behaviour: A Study of the Work Load and the Working Methods of Managing Directors*, Strombergs, Stockholm.

Cartwright, D. and Zander, A. (eds.) (1953) *Group Dynamics: Research and Theory*, Harper & Row, New York, NY.

Chandler, A. D. (1977) *The Visible Hand: The Managerial Revolution in American Business*, Harvard University Press, Cambridge, Mass.

Chenhall, R. H. (1986) Authoritarianism and participative budgeting: a dyadic analysis, *The Accounting Review*, pp. 263–72.

Chenhall, R. H. and Brownell, P. (1988) The effect of participative budgeting on job satisfaction and performance: role ambiguity as an intervening variable, *Accounting, Organisations and Society*, Vol. 13, no. 3, pp. 225–33.

Child, J. (1969) *British Management Thought*, Allen & Unwin, London.

Child, J. (1972) Organisation structure, environment and performance: the role of strategic choice, *Sociology*, Vol. 6, pp. 1–22.

Child, J. (1975) Managerial and organisational factors associated with company performance – part II, a contingency analysis, *Journal of Management Studies*, Vol. XII, pp. 12–27.

Child, J. (1984) *Organisations: A Guide to Problems and Practice* (2nd edn), Paul Chapman, London.

Child, J. (1987) Organisation design for advanced manufacturing technology, in T. Wall *et al.* (eds.) *The Human Side of Advanced Manufacturing Technology*, Wiley, Chichester.

Chinoy, E. (1955) *Automobile Workers and the American Dream*, Doubleday, New York, NY.

Chua, W. F., Lowe, E. A. and Puxty, A. G. (1989) *Critical Perspectives in Management Control*, Macmillan, London.

Cicourel, A. (1958) The front and backpage of organizational leadership: a case study, *Pacific Sociological Review*, Vol. 1, pp. 54–8.

Clark, B. R. (1972) The organisational saga in higher education, *Administrative Science Quarterly*, Vol. 17, no. 2, pp. 178–84.

Clegg, S. R. (1975) *Power, Rule and Domination: A Critical and Empirical Understanding of Power in Sociological Theory and Organisational Life*, Routledge & Kegan Paul, London.

Clegg, S. R. (1979) *The Theory of Power and Organisation*, Routledge & Kegan Paul, London.

Clegg, S. R. (1989) *Frameworks of Power*, Sage, London.

Clegg, S. R. (1990) *Modern Organisations: Organisation Studies in the Postmodern World*, Sage, London.

Clegg, S. and Dunkerley, D. (1980a) *Organisation, Class and Control*, Routledge & Kegan Paul, London.

Clegg, S. R. and Dunkerley, D. (eds.) (1980b) *Critical Issues in Organisations*, Routledge & Kegan Paul, London.

Coch, L. and French, J. R. P. (1948) On overcoming resistance to change, *Human Relations*, Vol. 1, no. 4, pp. 512–32.

Collins, F. (1978) The interaction of budget characteristics and personality variables with budgetary response attitudes, *The Accounting Review*, pp. 324–35.

Collins, F. (1982) Management accounting systems and control: a role perspective, *Accounting, Organisations and Society*, Vol. 7, no. 2, pp. 102–22.

Commission on Industrial Relations (1972) *Disclosure of Information*, Report no. 31, CBI, London.

Conger, J. A. and Kanungo, R. N. (1988) *Charismatic Leadership: The Elusive Factor in Organizational Effectiveness*, Jossey-Bass, San Francisco, Calif.

Cooke, S. and Slack, N. (1985) *Making Management Decisions*, Prentice-Hall, Hemel Hempstead.

Cooley, M. (1980) *Architect or Bee?*, Langley Technical Services, Slough.

Coopey, J. and Hartley, J. (1991) Reconsidering the case for organisational commitment, *Human Resource Management Journal*, Vol. 1, no. 3, pp. 18–32.

Coriat, B. (1980) The restructuring of the assembly line: a new economy of time and control, *Capital and Class*, Vol. 11, pp. 34–43.

Covaleski, M. A. and Dirsmith, M. W. (1988) The use of budgetary symbols in the political arena: an historically informed field study, *Accounting, Organisations and Society*, Vol. 13, no. 1, pp. 1–24.

Craft, J. A. (1981) Information disclosure and the role of the accountant in collective bargaining, *Accounting, Organisations and Society*, Vol. 6, no. 1, pp. 97–107.

Crenson, M. A. (1971) *The Un-Politics of Air Pollution: A Study of Non-Decisionmaking in the Cities*, Johns Hopkins University Press, Baltimore, Md.

Crozier, M. (1964) *The Bureaucratic Phenomenon*, University of Chicago Press, Chicago, Ill.

Curran, J. and Stanworth, M. J. K. (1981) A new look at job satisfaction in the small firm, *Human Relations*, Vol. 34, no. 5, pp. 343–66.

Dahl, R. A. (1957) The concept of power, *Behavioural Science*, Vol. 2, pp. 209–15.

Dahl, R. A. (1961) *Who Governs? Democracy and Power in an American City*, Yale University Press, New Haven, Con.

Dalton, G. W. (1971) Motivation and control in organizations, in G. W. Dalton and P. R. Lawrence (eds.), op. cit.

Dalton, G. W. and Lawrence, P. R. (eds.) (1971) *Motivation and Control in Organizations*, Irwin, Homewood, Ill.

Dalton, M. (1959) *Men Who Manage*, Wiley, New York, NY.

Daniel, W. W. (1969) Industrial behaviour and orientation to work – a critique, *Journal of Management Studies*, Vol. 6, pp. 366–75.

Daniel, W. W. (1987) *Workplace Industrial Relations and Technical Change*, Pinter Publishers, London.

Davis, L. E. and Taylor, J. C. (1978) *Design of Jobs*, Goodyear, Santa Monica, Calif.

Davis, M. and Lawrence, R. (eds.) (1977) *Matrix*, Addison-Wesley, Reading, Mass.

Deal, T. E. and Kennedy, A. A. (1982) *Corporate Cultures: The Rites and Rituals of Corporate Life*, Addison-Wesley, Reading, Mass.

Deci, E. L. (1971) The effects of externally mediated rewards on intrinsic motivation, *Journal of Personality and Social Psychology*, Vol. 18, pp. 105–15.

Deci, E. L. (1975) *Intrinsic Motivation*, Plenum Press, London.

Deci, E. L., Nezlek, R. and Sheinman, L. (1981) Characteristics of the rewarder and intrinsic motivation of the rewardee, *Journal of Personality and Social Psychology*, Vol. 40, pp. 1–10.

Dermer, J. (1988) Control and Organisational Order, *Accounting Organisations and Society*, Vol. 13, no. 1, pp. 25–36.

Dermer, J. D. and Lucas, R. G. (1986) The illusion of managerial control, *Accounting, Organisations and Society*, Vol. 11, no. 6, pp. 471–82.

Donaldson, L. (1985) *In Defence of Organisation Theory: A Response to Critics*, Cambridge University Press.

Dore, R. P. (1973) *British Factory, Japanese Factory*, Allen & Unwin, London.

Douglas, J. D. (1971) *American Social Order*, Free Press, New York, NY.

Douglas, J. D. (1976) *Investigative Social Research: Individual and Team Field Research*, Sage, London.

Duncan, R. (1972) Characteristics of organisational environments and perceived uncertainty, *Administrative Science Quarterly*, Vol. 17, pp. 3–27.

Dunn, S. (1990) Root metaphor in the old and new industrial relations, *British Journal of Industrial Relations*, Vol. 28, no. 1, pp. 1–31.

Durkheim, E. (1960) *The Division of Labor in Society*, Free Press, New York, NY.

Dyer, W. G. jr (1984) Tracking cultural evolution in organisations: an historical approach (working paper, MIT), Sloan School of Management.

Edwards, P. K. (1987) *Managing the Factory*, Blackwell, Oxford.

Edwards, R. (1979) *Contested Terrain: The Transformation of the Workplace in the Twentieth Century*, Basic Books, New York, NY.

Eisenhardt, K. M. (1985) Control, organisational and economic approaches, *Management Science*, Vol. 31, pp. 134–49.

Eldridge, J. E. T. and Crombie, A. D. (1974) *A Sociology of Organisations*, Allen & Unwin, London.

Emmanuel, C. and Otley, D. T. (1985) *Accounting for Management Control*, Van Nostrand Reinhold, Wokingham.

Erez, M. and Kanfer, F. H. (1983) The role of goal acceptance in goal setting and task performance, *Academy of Management Review*, Vol. 8, no. 3, pp. 454–63.

Etzioni, A. (1961) *A Comparative Analysis of Complex Organizations: On Power, Involvement and their Correlates*, Free Press, New York, NY.

Euske, K. J. (1984) *Management Control: Planning, Control, Measurement and Evaluation*, Addison-Wesley, Reading, Mass.

Evans, P. B. (1975) Multiple hierarchies and organisational control, *Administrative Science Quarterly*, Vol. 20, pp. 250–9.

Faunce, W. (1968) *Problems of an Industrial Society*, McGraw-Hill, New York, NY.

Fay, B. (1975) *Social Theory and Political Practice*, Allen & Unwin, London.

Fay, B. (1987) *Critical Social Science*, Polity Press, Cambridge.

Fayol, H. (1914) *General and Industrial Management* (trans. 1949), Pitman, London.

Feldman, D. C. and Arnold, H. J. (1986) *Organisational Behaviour*, McGraw-Hill, New York.

Festinger, L. A. and Carlsmith, J. M. (1959) Cognitive consequences of forced compliance, *Journal of Abnormal and Social Psychology*, Vol. 58, pp. 203–10.

Fiedler, F. E. (1967) *A Contingency Theory of Leadership Effectiveness*, McGraw-Hill, New York, NY.

Fineman, S. (1983) Work meanings, non-work, and the taken for granted, *Journal of Management Studies*, Vol. 20, no. 4, pp. 143–57.

Flamholtz, E. G., Das, T. K. and Tsui, A. S. (1985) Toward an integrative framework of organisation control, *Accounting, Organisations and Society*, Vol. 10, no. 1, pp. 35–50.

Foley, B. and Maunders, K. (1973) Accounting information, employees and collective bargaining, *Journal of Business Finance and Accounting*, Vol. 1, no. 1, pp. 107–27.

Foley, B. and Maunders, K. (1977) *Accounting Information Disclosure and Collective Bargaining*, Macmillan, London.

Foley, B. and Maunders, K. (1984) Information disclosure and the role of the accountant in collective bargaining – some comments, *Accounting, Organisations and Society*, Vol. 9, no. 2, pp. 99–106.

Follet, M. P. (1924) *Creative Experience*, Longmans & Green, New York, NY.

Foucault, M. (1979) *Discipline and Punish: The Birth of the Prison*, Penguin Books, Harmondsworth.

Foucault, M. (1981) *The History of Sexuality*, Penguin Books, Harmondsworth.

Fox, A. (1974) *Beyond Contract, Work, Power and Trust Relations*, Faber & Faber, London.

Fox, A. (1985) *Man Mismanagement*, Hutchinson, London.

Fox, S. (1990) Strategic HRM: postmodern conditioning for the corporate culture, *Management Education and Development*, Vol. 21, Pt 3, pp. 192–206.

French, J. R. P. and Raven, B. H. (1959) The social bases of power, in D. Cartwright (ed.) *Studies in Social Power*, Ann Arbor, University of Michigan Press, East Lansing, Mich.

French, W. L. and Bell, C. H. (1973) *Organization Development: behavioural science interventions for Organization improvement*, Prentice-Hall, Englewood Cliffs.

French, W. L., Bell, C. H. and Zawacki, R. A. (1983) *Organization Development: Theory, Practice and Research*, Business Publications Inc., New York.

Fridenson, P. (1978) *Corporate Policy, Rationalisation and the Labour Force: French Experiences in International Comparison, 1900–1929*, Nuffield Paper, London.

Friedman, A. L. (1977) *Industry and Labour*, Macmillan, London.

Frost, P. J., Moore, L. F., Louis, M. R., Lundberg, C. C. and Martin, J. (1985) *Organizational Culture*, Sage, Beverly Hills, Calif.

Frost, P. J., Moore, L. F., Louis, M. R., Lundberg, C. C. and Martin, J. (1991) *Reframing Organizational Culture*, Sage, Beverly Hills, Calif.

Galbraith, J. K. (1969) *The New Industrial State*, Penguin Books, Harmondsworth.

Galbraith, J. (1973) *Designing Complex Organizations*, Addison-Wesley, Reading, Mass.

Galbraith, J. and Cummings, L. L. (1967) An empirical investigation of the motivational determinants of past performance; incentive effects between instrumentality, valence, motivations, and ability, *Organisation Behaviour and Human Performance*, Vol. 8, pp. 237–57.

Gallie, D. (1978) *In Search of the New Working Class*, Cambridge University Press.

Gartman, D. (1979) Origins of the assembly line and capitalist control of work at Ford, in A. Zimbalist (ed.) *Case Studies on the Labor Process*, Monthly Review Press, New York, NY.

Gaventa, J. P. (1980) *Power and Powerlessness: Quiescence and Rebellion in an Appalachian Valley*, University of Illinois Press, Urbana-Champaign, Ill.

Gemmill, G. and Oakley, J. (1992) Leadership: an alienating social myth, *Human Relations*, Vol. 45, no. 2, pp. 113–29.

Georgeopoulos, B. S. *et al.* (1957) A path-goal approach to productivity, *Journal of Applied Psychology*, Vol. 41, pp. 345–53.

Gergen, K. J. (1992) Organisation theory in the postmodern era, in M. Reed and M. Hughes (eds.), *op. cit.*

Giddens, A. (1968) 'Power' in the recent writings of Talcott Parsons, *Sociology*, Vol. 3, no. 2, pp. 257–72.

Gill, J. (1985) *Factors Affecting the Survival and Growth of the Smaller Company*, Gower Studies in Small Business, Aldershot.

Gill, J. and Farrar, S. (1992) Leadership as developing subordinate self-control and managing without managers (Occasional Paper No. 6), Sheffield Business School, Sheffield City Polytechnic.

Gill, J. and Frame, P. G. (1990) Managing financial stringency in the public sector, *Public Administration*, Vol. 68, Winter, pp. 517–37.

Gill, J. and Johnson, P. (1991) *Research Methods for Managers*, Paul Chapman Publishing, London.

Gill, J. and Pratt, J. (1986) *Responses to Financial Constraint of Institutions of Higher Education in the Public Sector*, DES, London.

Gill, J. and Whittle, S. (1993) Management by panacea: accounting for transience, *Journal of Management Studies*, November (in press).

Golding, D. (1980) Establishing blissful clarity in organizational life: managers, *Sociological Review*, Vol. 28, no. 4, pp. 763–83.

Goldsmith, W. and Clutterbuck, D. (1984) *The Winning Streak*, Weidenfeld & Nicolson, London.

Goldthorpe, J. *et al.* (1968) *The Affluent Worker: Industrial Attitudes and Behaviour*, Cambridge University Press.

Goodrich, C. (1975) *The Frontier of Control*, Pluto Press, London.

Gouldner, A. (1954) *Patterns of Industrial Bureaucracy*, Free Press, New York, NY.

Gouldner, A. W. (1959) Organizational analysis, in R. K. Merton (ed.) *Sociology Today*, Basic Books, New York, NY.

Graen, G. B. (1969) Instrumentality theory of work motivation: some experimental results and suggested modifications, *Journal of Applied Psychology*, Vol. 16, pp. 345–53.

Gregory, K. L. (1983) Native-view paradigms: multiple cultures and culture conflicts in organisations, *Administrative Science Quarterly*, Vol. 28, pp. 359–76.

Grint, K. (1991) *The Sociology of Work: An Introduction*, Polity Press, Cambridge.

Guest, D. E. (1987) Human resource management and industrial relations, *Journal of Management Studies*, Vol. 25, no. 4, pp. 503–21.

Guest, D. E. (1989) Human Resource Management: its implications for trade unions, in J. Storey (ed.)

Guest, D. E. (1990) Human resource management and the American dream, *British Journal of Industrial Relations*, Vol. 29, no. 2, pp. 377–97.

Guest, D. E. (1991) Personnel management: the end of orthodoxy, *British Journal of Industrial Relations*, Vol. 29, no. 2, pp. 149–75.

Gulick, L. H. (1937) Notes on the theory of organization, in L. H. Gulick and L. Urwick (eds.) *Papers on the Science of Administration*, Columbia University, New York, NY.

Hackman, J. R. and Lawler, E. E. (1971) Employee reactions to job characteristics, *Journal of Applied Psychology Monograph*.

Hall, T. and Nougain, K. E. (1968) An examination of Maslow's hierarchy of needs in an organisational setting, *Organisation and Human Performance*, Vol. 3, pp. 12–35.

Hammersley, P. and Atkinson, P. (1983) *Ethnography: Principles in Practice*, Tavistock, London.

Handy, C. B. (1982) *Understanding Organisations* (2nd edn), Penguin Books, Harmondsworth.

Handy, C. B. (1985) *Understanding Organisations* (3rd edn), Penguin Books, Harmondsworth.

Handy, C. B. (1989) *The Age of Unreason*, Business Books, London.

Haraszti, M. (1977) *A Worker in a Workers' State*, Penguin Books, Harmondsworth.

Harrell, A. and Stahl, M. J. (1986) Additive information processing and the relationship between expectancy of success and motivational force, *Academy of Management Journal*, Vol. 29, pp. 424–33.

Harrison, R. G. (1984) Reasserting the radical potential of OD, *Personnel Review*, Vol. 13, no. 2, pp. 12–18.

Hedberg, B. and Jonsson, S. (1978) Designing semi-confusing information systems for organisations in changing environments, *Accounting, Organisations and Society*, Vol. 3, no. 1, pp. 47–64.

Hedberg, B., Nystrom, P.C. and Starbuck, W. H. (1976) Camping on seesaws: prescriptions for a self-designing organisation, *Administrative Science Quarterly*, Vol. 21, no. 1, pp. 41–65.

Heider, F. (1958) *The Psychology of Interpersonal Relations*, Wiley, New York, NY.

Heilmann, M. E., Hornstein, H. A., Cage, J. H. and Herschlag, J. K. (1984) Reactions to prescribed leader behaviour as a function of role perspective: the case of the Vroom-Yetton model, *Journal of Applied Psychology*, Vol. 69, pp. 50–60.

Hellreigel, D. and Slocum, J. W. (1978) *Management: Contingency Approaches*, Wiley, New York, NY.

Hendry, C. *et al.* (1988) Changing patterns of Human Resource Management, *Personnel Management*, Vol. 19, no. 2, pp. 37–41.

Hendry, C. and Pettigrew, A. (1990) Human resource management: an agenda for the 1990s, *International Journal of Human Resource Management*, Vol. 1, no. 1, pp. 17–43.

Henry, S. (1981) Disciplining deviance at work: the changing technology of industrial social control (working paper, mimeo), Centre for Occupational and Community Research, Middlesex Polytechnic.

Herzberg, F., Mausner, B. and Snyderman, B. (1959) *The Motivation to Work*, Wiley, New York, NY.

Heydebrand, W. (1989) New organisational forms, *Work and Occupations*, Vol. 16, no. 3, pp. 323–57.

Hickson, D. J., Hinings, C. R., Lee, C. A., Schneck, R. E. and Pennings, J. M. (1971) A strategic contingencies theory of intraorganisational power, *Administrative Science Quarterly*, Vol. 16, pp. 216–29.

Hill, C. (1969) *The Century of Revolution*, Sphere, London.

Hines, R. D. (1988) Financial accounting: in communicating reality, we construct reality, *Accounting, Organisations and Society*, Vol. 13, no. 3, pp. 251–61.

Hinings, C. R., Hickson, D. J., Pennings, J. M. and Schneck, R. E. (1974) Structural conditions of intraorganisational power, *Administrative Science Quarterly*, Vol. 19, pp. 22–44.

Hinton, B. L. and Reitz, H. J. (1971) *Groups and Organization: Integrated Readings in the Analysis of Social Behavior*, Wadsworth, Belmont, Calif.

Hirsch, P. M. and Andrews, J. A. Y. (1983) Ambushes, shootouts and knights of the round table: the language of corporate take-overs, in L. R. Pondy *et al.* (eds.) *Organizational Symbolism*, JAI Press, Greenwich, Conn.

Hobbes, T. (1964) in F. B. Randal (ed.) *Leviathan*, Washington Square Press, New York, NY.

Hobsbawm, E. J. (1964) *Labouring Men*, Weidenfeld & Nicolson, London.

Hofstede, G. H. (1968) *The Game of Budget Control*, Tavistock, London.

Hofstede, G. (1978) The poverty of management control philosophy, *Academy of Management Review*, pp. 450–61.

Hogan, D. J. (1986) A question of appraisal?, *Management Education and Development*, Vol. 17, Pt. 4, pp. 315–23.

Hollway, W. (1991) *Work Psychology and Organisation Behaviour: Managing the Individual at Work*, Sage, London.

Homans, G. C. (1950) *The Human Group*, Harcourt Brace Jovanovich, New York, NY.

Hopper, T. M. and Berry, A. J. (1984) Organisation design and management control, in A. Lowe and L. J. Machin (eds.), *op. cit.*

Hopwood, A. (1974) *Accounting and Human Behaviour*, Prentice-Hall, London.

Horwitz, M. (1990) HRM – an ideological perspective, *Personnel Review*, Vol. 19, no. 2, pp. 11–15.

Hoskin, K. W. and Macve, R. H. (1988) The genesis of accountability: the West Point connection, *Accounting, Organisations and Society*, Vol. 13, no. 1, pp. 37–78.

House, R. J. (1971) A path-goal theory of leader effectiveness, *Administrative Science Quarterly*, Vol. 16, pp. 321–8.

House, R. J. (1977) A 1976 theory of charismatic leadership, in J. G. Hunt and L. L. Larson (eds.) *Leadership: The Cutting Edge*, Southern Illinois University Press, Carbondale, Ill.

House, R. H. (1984) Power in organizations: a social psychological perspective (unpublished paper), Faculty of Management, University of Toronto.

House, R. J., Spangler, W. D. and Woycke, J. (1990) Personality and charisma in the US presidency, a psychological theory of leadership effectiveness, in *Academy of Management*, Best Paper Proceedings, Academy of Management, Chicago, Ill.

Humble, J. (1970) *Management by Objectives*, McGraw-Hill, London.

Hunt, J. (1979) *Managing People at Work*, Pan Books, London.

Hunt, J. G. (1991) *Leadership: A New Synthesis*, Sage, London.

Hyman, R. (1972) *Strikes*, Fontana, London.

Hyman, R. (1975) *Strikes*, Fontana, London.

Hyman, R. (1987) Strategy or structure? Capital, labour and control, *Work, Employment and Society*, Vol. 1, no. 1.

Iles, P. A. and Johnston, T. (1989) Searching for excellence in second-hand clothes? A note, *Personnel Review*, Vol. 18, no. 6, pp. 32–5.

Jackson-Cox, J. *et al.* (1984) The disclosure of information to trade unions: the relevance of the ACAS code of practice on disclosure, *Accounting, Organisations and Society*, Vol. 9, nos. 3–4, pp. 253–73.

Jago, A. G. (1982) Leadership: perspectives in theory and research, *Management Science*, Vol. 28, no. 3, pp. 315–36.

Jaques, E. (1955) Social systems as a defence against persecutory and depressive anxiety, in M. Klein, P. Heimann and R. Money-Kyrle (eds.) *New Directions in Psychoanalysis*, Tavistock, London.

Jaques, E. (1967) *Equitable Payment*, Penguin, Harmondsworth.

Jones, E. E. *et al.* (eds.) (1972) *Attribution: Perceiving the Causes of Behavior*, General Learning Press, New York.

Kamata, S. (1984) *Japan in the Passing Lane*, Allen & Unwin, London.

Kanter, R. M. (1968) Commitment and social organization: a study of commitment in Utopian communities, *American Sociological Review*, Vol. 33, no. 4, pp. 499–517.

Kanter, R. M. (1989) *When Giants Learn to Dance: Mastering the Challenges of Strategy, Management and Careers in the 1990s*, Unwin Hyman, London.

Kast, F. E. and Rosenzweig, J. E. (1979) *Organisation and Management* (2nd edn), McGraw-Hill, Maidenhead.

Katz, D. (1967) The motivational basis of organisation behaviour, in W. A. Hill *et al.* (eds.) *Readings in Organisation Theory*, Allyn & Bacon, London.

Katz, D. and Kahn, R. L. (1978) *The Social Psychology of Organizations* (2nd edn), Wiley, New York, NY.

Keenoy, T. (1990) HRM: a case of the wolf in sheep's clothing?, *Personnel Review*, Vol. 19, no. 2, pp. 3–9.

Keenoy, R. (1991) The roots of metaphor in the old and new industrial relations, *British Journal of Industrial Relations*, Vol. 29, no. 2, pp. 313–28.

Kelly, H. H. (1972) Causal schemata and the attribution process, in E. E. Jones *et al.* (eds.), *op. cit.*

Kelly, J. (1985) Management's redesign of work: labour process, labour markets and product markets, in D. Knights *et al.* (eds.) *Job Redesign*, Gower, Aldershot.

Kelman, H. (1961) The processes of opinion change, *Public Opinion*, Vol. 25, pp. 57–78.

Kenis, I. (1979) Effect of budgetary goal characteristics on managerial attitudes and performance, *The Accounting Review*, Vol. 54, no. 4, p. 707–21.

Kernan, M. C. and Lord, R. G. (1990) Effects of valencies, expectancies and goal-performance discrepancies in single and multiple goal environments, *Journal of Applied Psychology*, Vol. 75, pp. 194–203.

Kerr, C., Dunlop, J. T., Harbison, F. and Myers, C. A. (1964) *Industrialisation and Industrial Man* (2nd edn), Oxford University Press.

Kerr, S. (1975) On the folly of rewarding A, while expecting B, *Academy of Management Journal*, Vol. 18, no. 4, pp. 769–83.

Kets de Vries, M. F. R. (1990) The organisational fool: balancing a leader's hubris, *Human Relations*, Vol. 43, no. 8, pp. 751–70.

Kets de Vries, M. F. and Miller, D. (1984) *The Neurotic Organization: Diagnosing and Changing Counterproductive Styles of Management*, Jossey-Bass, San Francisco, Calif.

Kimberly, J. R., Miles, R. H. and associates (1980) *The Organizational Life Cycle*, Jossey-Bass, San Francisco.

Kingdon, D. R. (1973) *Matrix Organisation*, Tavistock, London.

Klatt, L. A. *et al.* (1978) *Human Resources Management: A Behavioral Systems Approach*, Irwin, Homewood, Ill.

Klein, H. J. (1989) An integrated control theory model of motivation, *Academy of Management Review*, Vol. 14, no. 2, pp. 150–72.

Kluckholn, F. R. and Strodtbeck, F. L. (1961) *Variations in Value Orientations*, Harper & Row, New York, NY.

Knight, K. (ed.) (1977) *Matrix Management*, Gower, London.

Knights, D. and Wilmott, H. (1985) Power and identity in theory and practice, *Sociological Review*, Vol. 33, no. 1, pp. 22–46.

Kochan, T. A., Katz, H. C. and Mower, N. R. (1984) *Worker Participation and American Unions*, W. E. Upjohn Institute for Employment Research, Kalamazoo, Mich.

Kolb, D. A., Rubin, I. M. and Osland, J. S. (1990) *The Organisational Behaviour Reader*, Prentice-Hall, London.

Koontz, H. and O'Donnell, C. (1972) *Principles of Management*, McGraw-Hill, New York.

Kotter, J. P. (1982) *The General Managers*, Free Press/Collier Macmillan, London.

Kotter, J. P. (1988) *The Leadership Factor*, Free Press, New York, NY.

Krantz, J. and Gilmore, T. N. (1990) The splitting of leadership and management as a social defense, *Human Relations*, Vol. 43, no. 2, pp. 183–204.

Krulis-Randa, J. (1990) Strategic human resource management (SHRM) in Europe, *International Journal of Human Resource Management*, Vol. 1, no. 2, pp. 131–9.

Kuhn, J. (1961) *Bargaining in Grievance Settlement*, Columbia University Press, New York, NY.

Kumar, K. (1984) The social culture of work: work, employment and unemployment as ways of life, in K. Thompson (ed.), *op. cit.*

Landsberger, H. A. (1961) Parson's 'Theory of Organizations', in M. Black (ed.) *The Social Theories of Talcott Parsons*, Prentice-Hall, Englewood Cliffs, NJ.

Langer, E. J. (1981) Rethinking the role of thought in social interaction, in J. H. Harvey *et al.* (eds.) *New Directions in Attribution Research*, Lawrence Erlbaum Associates, New York, NY.

Lasch, D. (1979) *The Culture of Narcissism. American Life in the Age of Diminishing Expectations*, Warner Books, New York, NY.

Latham, G. P. and Locke, E. A. (1979) Goal setting – a motivational technique that works, *Organisational Dynamics*, Autumn, pp. 68–80.

Latham, G. P. and Yukl, G. A. (1975) Review of research on the application of goal setting in organisations, *Academy of Management Journal*, December, pp. 824–5.

Latham, G. *et al.* (1978) Importance of participative goal setting and anticipated rewards on goal difficulty and job performance, *Journal of Applied Psychology*, pp. 163–71.

Lawler, E. E. (1971) *Pay and Organizational Effectiveness: A Psychological View*, McGraw-Hill, New York, NY.

Lawler, E. E. (1973) *Motivation and Work Performance*, Brooke/Cole, Monterey, Calif.

Lawler, E. E. and Rhode, J. R. (1976) *Information and Control in Organisations*, Goodyear, London.

Lawrence, P. (1981) The Harvard organization and environment research program, in A. H. van de Ven and W. F. Joyce (eds) *Perspectives on Organization Design and Behavior*, Harper & Row, New York, NY.

Lawrence, P. R. and Lorsch, J. W. (1967) *Organization and Environment: Managing Differentiation and Integration*, Harvard University Press, Boston, Mass.

Lawrence, P. R. (1985) The history of HRM in American industry, in R. E. Walton and P. R. Lawrence (eds.).

Leadbeater, C. and Lloyd, J. (1987) *In Search of Work*, Penguin, Harmondsworth.

Lee, R. and Lawrence, P. (1991) *Politics at Work*, Stanley Thornes, Cheltenham.

Legge, K. (1988) Personnel management in recession and recovery: a comparative analysis of what the surveys say, *Personnel Review*, Vol. 17, no. 2, pp. 2–70.

Legge, K. (1989) HRM: a critical analysis, in J. Storey (ed.), *op. cit.*

Lenin, V. I. (1968) The immediate tasks of the Soviet government, in *Selected Works*, Progress Publishers, New York, NY.

Lewin, K. (1951) *Field Theory and Social Science*, Harper & Row, New York, NY.

Lewin, K. R., Lippitt, R. and White, R. K. (1939) Patterns of aggressive behaviour in experimentally created social climates, *Journal of Social Psychology*, Vol. 10, pp. 271–99.

Lewis, R. and Stewart, R. (1958) *The Boss*, Phoenix, London.

Lifton, R. J. (1956) 'Thought reform' of westerners in Chinese communist prisons, *Psychiatry*, Vol. 19, pp. 173–95.

Likert, R. (1961) *New Patterns of Management*, McGraw-Hill, New York, NY.

Likert, R. (1967) *The Human Organization*, McGraw-Hill, New York, NY.

Littler, C. R. (1982) *The Development of the Labour Process in Capitalist Societies*, Heinemann, London.

Littler, C. R. and Salaman, G. (1982) Bravermania and beyond: recent theories of the labour process, *Sociology*, Vol. 16, no. 2, pp. 251–69.

Locke, E. A. and Bryan, J. F. (1967) *Goals and Intentions as Determinants of Performance Level. Task Choice and Attitudes*, American Institute for Research, Washington DC.

Long, P. (1986) *Performance Appraisal Revisited*, Institute of Personnel Management, London.

Lord, R. G., Foti, R. J. and De Vader, C. L. (1984) A test of leadership categorisation theory: internal structure, information processing, and leadership perceptions, *Organisational Behaviour and Human Performance*, Vol. 34, pp. 343–78.

Lorsch, J. W. (1970) Introduction to the structural design of organizations, in G. W. Dalton *et al.* (eds.) *Organization Structure and Design*, Irwin, Homewood, Ill.

Lorsch, J. W. and Morse, J. (1974) *Organizations and their Members: A Contingency Approach*, Harper & Row, New York, NY.

Louis, M. R. (1980a) Surprise and sense making; what newcomers experience in entering unfamiliar organisational settings, *Administrative Science Quarterly*, Vol. 25, pp. 226–51.

Louis, M. R. (1980b) Organizations as culture-bearing milieux, in L. R. Pondy *et al.* (eds.) *Organizational Symbolism*, JAI Press, Greenwich, Conn.

Louis, M. R. (1985) An investigator's guide to workplace culture, in P. J. Frost *et al.* (1985), *op. cit.*

Lowe, E. A. and Machin, L. J. (1984) *New Perspectives in Management Control*, Macmillan, London.

Lowe, E. A. and Puxty, A. G. (1989) The problems of a paradigm: a critique of the prevailing orthodoxy in management control, in W. F. Chua, E. A. Lowe and A. G. Puxty (eds.), *op. cit.*

Lukes, S. (1974) *Power: A Radical View*, Macmillan, London.

Lukes, S. (1978) Alienation and anomie, in P. Laslett and W. G. Runciman (eds.) *Philosophy, Politics and Society*, Blackwell, Oxford.

Lupton, T. (1963) *On the Shopfloor*, Pergamon, Oxford.

Lupton, T. (1971) *Management and the Social Sciences*, Penguin Books, Harmondsworth.

Lussato, B. (1972) *A Critical Introduction to Organisation Theory*, Macmillan, London.

Luthans, F. (1981) *Organisation Behaviour* (3rd edn), McGraw-Hill, Maidenhead.

Luthans, F. and Davies, T. (1979) Behavioural self-management (BSM): the missing link in managerial effectiveness, *Organisational Dynamics*, Vol. 8, pp. 42–60.

McClelland, D. C. (1961) *The Achieving Society*, Van Nostrand, Princeton, NJ.

McGivering, I. C., Mathews, C. G. J. and Scott, W. H. (1969) *Management in Britain*, Liverpool University Press.

McGregor, D. (1957) An uneasy look at performance appraisal, *Harvard Business Review*, Vol. 35, no. 3, pp. 89–94.

McGregor, D. (1960) *The Human Side of Enterprise*, Harper & Row, New York, NY.

MacInnes, J. (1987) *Thatcherism at Work*, Open University Press, Milton Keynes.

MacInnes, J. (1988) The question of flexibility, *Personnel Review*, Vol. 17, no. 3, pp. 12–15.

McWhinney, W. and Krone, C. (1972) *Open Systems Planning* (unpublished manuscript available from Enthusion, Venice, Calif.).

Maguire, M. (1986) Recruitment as a means of control, in K. Purcell *et al.* (eds.) *The Changing Experience of Employment, Restructuring and Recession*, Macmillan, London.

Mahoney, M. J. and Arnkoff, D. B. (1978) Cognitive and self-control therapies, in S. L. Garfield and A. E. Borgin (eds.) *Handbook of Psychotherapy and Therapy Change*, Wiley, New York, NY.

Mahoney, M. J. and Arnkoff, D. B. (1979) Self-management theory, research and application, in J. P. Brady and D. Pomerleau (eds.) *Behavioral Medicine: Theory and Practice*, Williams & Wilkins, Baltimore, Md.

Mahoney, M. J. and Thoreson, C. E. (eds.) (1974) *Self-Control: Power to the Person*, Brooks/Cole, Monterey, Calif.

Mann, R. D. (1959) A review of the relationship between personality and performance in small groups, *Psychological Bulletin*, Vol. 56, pp. 241–70.

Mant, A. (1976) *The Rise and Fall of the British Manager*, Macmillan, London.

Manz, C. C. (1986) Self-leadership: towards an expanded theory of self-influence processes in organisations, *Academy of Management Review*, Vol. 11, no. 3, pp. 585–600.

Manz, C. C. (1991) Leading employees to be self-managing and beyond: towards the establishment of self-leadership in organizations, *Journal of Management Systems*, Vol. 3, no. 3, pp. 15–24.

Manz, C. C. (1992) *Mastering Self-Leadership: Empowering Yourself for Personal Excellence*, Prentice-Hall, Englewood Cliffs, NJ.

Manz, C. C. and Sims, H. P. (1987) Leading workers to lead themselves: the external leadership of self-managing work teams, *Administrative Science Quarterly*, Vol. 32, pp. 106–28.

Manz, C. C. and Sims, H. P. (1989) *SuperLeadership: Leading Others to Lead Themselves*, Prentice-Hall, Berkeley, Calif.

March, J. G. and Simon, A. H. (1958) *Organisations*, Wiley, New York.

Marchington, M. (1979) The issue of union power, *Employee Relations*, Vol. 1, no. 4, pp. 3–7.

Marchington, M. (1982) *Managing Industrial Relations*, McGraw-Hill, London.

Marchington, M. and Armstrong, P. (1983) Shop steward organisation and joint consultation, *Personnel Review*, Vol. 12, no. 1, pp. 24–31.

Martin, J. and Meyerson, D. (1988) Organisational cultures and the denial, channeling and acknowledgment of ambiguity in L. R. Pondy, R. J. Boland and H. Thomas (eds.) *Managing Ambiguity and Change*, Wiley, New York.

Martin, J., Sitkin, S. B. and Boehm, M. (1985) Founders and the elusiveness of a cultural legacy, in P. J. Frost *et al.* (eds.) *op. cit.*

Martin, R. (1988) Industrial capitalism in transition: the contemporary reorganisation of the British space economy, in D. Massey and J. Allen (eds.) *Uneven Redevelopment: Cities and Regions in Transition*, Hodder & Stoughton, Sevenoaks.

Martin, S. (1983) *Managing without Managers*, Sage Library of Social Research, Beverly Hills, Calif. Vol. 147.

Marx, K. (1973) *Economic and Philosophical Manuscripts of 1844*, Lawrence & Wishart, London.

Maslow, A. (1943) A theory of human motivation, *Psychological Review*, Vol. I, pp. 370–96.

Maslow, A. (1954) *Motivation and Personality*, Harper & Row, New York, NY.

Mathias, P. (1969) *The First Industrial Nation: An Economic History of Britain 1700–1914*, Methuen, London.

Mathias, P. (1972) (ed.) *Science and Society*, Cambridge University Press.

Mayo, G. E. (1940) *The Human Problems of an Industrial Civilization*, Harvard Business School, Boston, Mass.

Mayo, G. E. (1949) *The Social Problems of an Industrial Civilisation*, Routledge & Kegan Paul, London.

Mead, G. H. (1934) *Mind, Self and Society*, Chicago University Press, Chicago, Ill.

Meakin, D. (1976) *Man and Work: Literature and Culture in Industrial Society*, Methuen, London.

Mechanic, D. (1962) Sources of power of lower participants in complex organisations, *Administrative Science Quarterly*, Vol. 7, no. 4, pp. 349–64.

Meek, V. L. (1988) Organisation culture: origins and weaknesses, *Organisation Studies*, Vol. 9, no. 4, pp. 453–73.

Melossi, D. (1979) Institutions of social control and the capitalist organisations of work, in B. Fine *et al.* (eds.) *Capitalism and the Rule of Law*, Hutchinson, London.

Merchant, K. A. (1981) The design of the corporate budgeting system: influences on managerial behaviour and performance, *The Accounting Review*, pp. 813–29.

Merchant, K. A. (1984) Influences on departmental budgeting: an empirical examination of a contingency model, *Accounting, Organisations and Society*, Vol. 9, no. 3–4, pp. 291–307.

Merchant, K. A. (1985) Budgeting and the propensity to create budgetary slack, *Accounting, Organisations and Society*, Vol. 10, no. 2, pp. 201–10.

Merton, R. K. (1957) *Social Theory and Social Structure*, Glencoe, New York, NY.

Meyerson, D. E. and Martin, J. (1987) Cultural change: an integration of three different approaches, *Journal of Management Studies*, Vol. 24, no. 4, pp. 623–47.

Milgram, S. (1963) Behavioural study of obedience, *Journal of Abnormal Social Psychology*, Vol. 67, pp. 371–8.

Milgram, S. (1974) *Obedience to Authority*, Tavistock, London.

Miller, D., Kets de Vries, M. F. R. and Toulouse, J. M. (1982) Top executive locus of control and its relationship to strategy-making, structure, and environment, *Academy of Management Journal*, Vol. 85, no. 2, pp. 237–53.

Miller, L. E. and Grush, J. E. (1988) Improving predictions in expectancy theory research: effects of personality, expectancies and norms, *Academy of Management Journal*, Vol. 31, pp. 107–22.

Miller, P. and O'Leary, T. (1987) Accounting and the construction of the governable person, *Accounting, Organisations and Society*, Vol. 12, no. 3, pp. 255–66.

Mills, C. W. (1959) *The Sociological Imagination*, Oxford University Press.

Mills, P. K. (1983) Self-management: its control and relationship to other organisational properties, *Academy of Management Review*, Vol. 8, no. 3, pp. 445–53.

Mintzberg, H. (1973) *The Nature of Managerial Work*, Harper & Row, New York.

Mintzberg, H. (1979a) *The Structuring of Organizations*, Prentice-Hall, Englewood Cliffs, NJ.

Mintzberg, H. (1979b) An emerging strategy of 'direct' research, *Administrative Science Quarterly*, Vol. 24, pp. 582–9.

Mintzberg, H. (1983) *Power in and around Organizations*, Prentice-Hall, Englewood Cliffs, NJ.

Mintzberg, H. (1989) *Mintzberg on Management*, Free Press, New York, NY.

Mitchell, T. (1985) In search of excellence versus the hundred best companies to work for in America: a question of values and perspective, *Academy of Management Review*, Vol. 10, no. 2, pp. 350–5.

Mitchell, T. R. and Wood, R. E. (1980) Supervisors' responses to subordinate poor performance: a test of an attributional model, *Organisation Behaviour and Human Performance*, pp. 123–38.

Mooney, J. D. and Reiley, A. C. (1939) *The Principles of Organization*, Harper & Row, New York, NY.

Morgan, G. (1982) Cybernetics and organisation theory: epistemology or critique?, *Human Relations*, Vol. 35, no. 7, pp. 521–37.

Morgan, G. (1986) *Images of Organisation*, Sage, London.

Mowday, R. T. (1991) Equity theory predictions of behaviour in organisations, in R. M. Steers and L. W. Porter (eds.), *op. cit.*

Nadler, D. A. (1991) Motivation: a diagnostic approach, in D. A. Kolb *et al.* (eds.) *The Organization Behavior Reader* (5th edn), Prentice-Hall, Englewood Cliffs, NJ.

Nadler, D. A. and Lawler, E. E. (1991) Motivation: a diagnostic approach, in D. A. Kolb, I. M. Rubin and J. S. Osland (eds.), *op. cit.*

National Training Laboratories (1953) *Explorations in Human Relations Training*, Washington DC.

Newcomb, T. M. (1966) Attitude development as a function of reference groups: the Bennington study, in E. E. Maccoby *et al.* (eds.) *Readings in Social Psychology*, Tavistock, London.

Newton, K. (1969) A critique of the pluralist model, *Acta Socilogica*, Vol. 12, pp. 209–43.

Nichols, T. (1986) *The British Worker Question*, Routledge & Kegan Paul, London.

Nichols, T. and Beynon, H. (1977) *Living with Capitalism*, Routledge, London.

Nove, A. (1977) *The Soviet Economic System*, Allen & Unwin, London.

Nyland, C. (1987) Scientific planning and management, *Capital and Class*, no. 33, pp. 55–83.

Offe, C. (1976) *Industry and Inequality*, Edward Arnold, London.

Ogbonna, E. and Wilson, B. (1990) Corporate strategy and corporate culture: the view from the checkout, *Personnel Review*, Vol. 19, no. 4, pp. 9–15.

Ogden, S. G. and Bougen, P. (1985) A radical perspective on the disclosure of accounting information to trade unions, *Accounting, Organisations and Society*, Vol. 10, no. 2, pp. 211–24.

Onsi, M. (1973) Factor analysis of behavioural variables affecting budgetary slack, *Accounting Review*, pp. 535–48.

O'Reilly, C. (1989) Corporations, culture and commitment: motivation and social control in organizations, *California Management Review*, Summer, pp. 9–25.

Otley, D. T. (1977) The behavioural aspects of budgeting, *Accountants Digest*, no. 49, pp. 14–25.

Otley, D. T. and Berry, J. (1979) Risk distribution in the budgetary process, *Accounting and Business Research*, Vol. 9, pp. 325–37.

Otley, D. T. and Berry, A. J. (1980) Control, organisation and accounting, *Accounting, Organisations and Society*, Vol. 5, no. 2, pp. 231–44.

Ouchi, W. G. (1977) The relationship between organisational structure and organisational control, *Administrative Science Quarterly*, Vol. 22, pp. 95–112.

Ouchi, W. G. (1978) The transmission of control through organisational hierarchy, *Academy of Management Journal*, Vol. 12, no. 2, pp. 173–92.

Ouchi, W. G. (1979) A conceptual framework for the design of organisational control mechanisms, *Management Science*, Vol. 25, pp. 833–48.

Ouchi, W. G. (1980) Markets, bureaucracies and clans, *Administrative Science Quarterly*, Vol. 25, pp. 129–41.

Ouchi, W. G. (1981) *Theory Z: How American Business can Meet the Japanese Challenge*, Addison-Wesley, Reading, Mass.

Ouchi, W. G. and Price, R. L. (1978) Hierarchies, clans and theory Z: a new perspective on organisational development, *Organisational Dynamics*, Vol. 7, pp. 25–44.

Paauwe, J. (1991) Limitations to freedom: is there a choice for human resource management?, *British Journal of Management*, Vol. 2, pp. 103–19.

Palmer, G. (1983) *British Industrial Relations*, Allen & Unwin, London.

Palmer, J. R. (1977) *The Use of Accounting in Labor Negotiations*, National Association of Accountants, New York, NY.

Parker, M. (1992) Post-modern organisations or post-modern organisation theory?, *Organisation Studies*, Vol. 13, no. 1, pp. 1–17.

Parker, S. R. (1972) *The Future of Work and Leisure*, Paladin, London.

Parsons, T. (1951) *The Social System*, Free Press, New York, NY.

Parsons, T. (1963) On the concept of political power, *Proceedings of the American Philosophical Society*, Vol. 107, pp. 232–62.

Pascale, R. (1985) The paradox of 'corporate culture': reconciling ourselves to socialization, *California Management Review*, Vol. XXXVII, no. 2, Winter, pp. 26–41.

Pascale, R. T. and Athos, A. G. (1982) *The Art of Japanese Management*, Penguin Books, Harmondsworth.

Pauchant, T. C. (1991) Transferential leadership. Towards a more complex understanding of charisma in organisations, *Organisation Studies*, Vol. 12, no. 4, pp. 507–27.

Perrow, C. A. (1967) A framework for the comparative analysis of organizations, *American Sociological Review*, Vol. 32, pp. 194–208.

Peters, T. (1987) *Thriving on Chaos*, Harper & Row, New York, NY.

Peters, T. and Waterman, R. H. (1982) *In Search of Excellence: Lessons from America's Best Run Companies*, Harper & Row, New York, NY.

Pettigrew, A. (1973) *The Politics of Organisational Decision-Making*, Tavistock, London.

Pettigrew, A. (1985) *The Awakening Giant: Continuity and Change in ICI*, Blackwell, Oxford.

Pfeffer, J. (1981a) Management as symbolic action: the creation and maintenance of organizational paradigms, in L. Cummings and B. Staw (eds.) *Research in Organizational Behavior*, Vol. 3, JAI Press, Greenwich, Conn.

Pfeffer, J. (1981b) *Power in Organizations*, Pitman, Boston, Mass.

Pfeffer, J. and Salancik, G. R. (1978) *The External Control of Organizations: A Resource Dependent Perspective*, Harper & Row, New York, NY.

Pinder, C. C. (1991) Valence–instrumentality–expectancy theory, in R. M. Steers and L. W. Porter (eds.), *op. cit.*

Piore, M. J. (1986) Perspectives on labour market flexibility, *Industrial Relations*, Vol. 25, no. 2, pp. 146–66.

Piore, M. J. and Sable, C. F. (1984) *The Second Industrial Divide*, Basic Books, New York, NY.

Plant, R. and Ryan, M. (1988) Managing your corporate culture, *Training and Development Journal*, September, pp. 61–5.

Pollard, S. (1965) *The Genesis of Modern Management*, Penguin Books, Harmondsworth.

Pollert, A. (1991) *Farewell to Flexibility*, Blackwell, Oxford.

Pope, P. F. and Peel, D. A. (1981a) A fresh look at employee disclosure policy, *The Accountant's Magazine*, November, pp. 376–80.

Pope, P. F. and Peel, D. A. (1981b) Information disclosure to employees and rational expectations, *Journal of Business Finance and Accounting*, Vol. 8, no. 1, pp. 139–46.

Porter, L. W. and Lawler, E. E. (1968) *Managerial Attitudes and Performance*, Dorsey Press, Homewood, Ill.

Poulantzas, N. (1972) The problems of the capitalist state, in R. Blackburn (ed.) *Ideology in Social Science*, Fontana, London.

Prowse, P. (1990) Assessing the flexible firm, *Personnel Review*, Vol. 19, no. 6, pp. 13–17.

Pugh, D. S. *et al.* (1968) Dimensions of organisation structure, *Administrative Science Quarterly*, Vol. 13, pp. 65–91.

Pugh, D. S., Hickson, D. J. and Hinings, C. R. (1969) An empirical taxonomy of work organisations, *Administrative Science Quarterly*, Vol. 14, pp. 115–26.

Purcell, J., Dagleish, J., Harrison, I., Lonsdale, I., McConachy, I. and Robertson, A. (1978) Power from technology: computer staff and industrial relations, *Personnel Review*, Vol. 7, no. 1, pp. 30–9.

Purcell, J. and Sissons, K. (1983) A strategy for management control in industrial relations, in J. Purcell and R. Smith (eds.) *The Control of Work*, Macmillan, London.

Puxty, A. G. (1989) The problems of a paradigm: a critique of the prevailing orthodoxy in management control, in W. F. Chua, A. Lowe and A. G. Puxty (eds.), *op. cit.*

Raelin, J. A. (1985) *The Clash of Cultures: Managers and Professionals*, Harvard Business School, Cambridge, Mass.

Randell, G. *et al.* (1984) *Staff Appraisal*, Institute of Personnel Management, London.

Rattansi, P.M. (1972) The social interpretation of science in the seventeenth century, in P. Mathias (ed.), *op. cit.*

Ray, C. A. (1986) Corporate culture: the last frontier of control?, *Journal of Management Studies*, Vol. 23, no. 3, pp. 287–97.

Reed, B. D. and Palmer, B. W. (1972) *An Introduction to Organisational Behaviour*, Grubb Institute of Behavioural Studies, London.

Reed, M. and Hughes, M. (eds.) (1992) *Rethinking Organisation: New Directions in Organisation Theory and Analysis*, Sage, London.

Reid, S. (1978) *Computers and De-Skilling*, Nuffield Paper, London.

Roberts, J. (1989) Authority or domination: alternative possibilities for the practice of control, in W. F. Chua, E. A. Lowe and A. G. Puxty (eds.), *op. cit.*

Roberts, J. and Scapens, R. (1985) Accounting systems and systems of accountability – understanding accounting practices in their organisational contexts, *Accounting, Organisations and Society*, Vol. 10, no. 4, pp. 443–56.

Roethlisberger, F. J. and Dickson, W. J. (1939) *Management and the Worker*, Harvard University Press, Cambridge, Mass.

Rogers, C. R. (1942) *Counselling and Psychotherapy: New Concepts in Practice*, Houghton Mifflin, Boston, Mass.

Rogers, C. R. (1951) *Client-centred therapy*, Houghton Mifflin, Boston, Mass.

Rogers, C. R. (1980) *A Way of Being*, Houghton Mifflin, Boston, Mass.

Ronen, J. and Livingstone, J. L. (1975) An expectancy theory approach to the motivational impact of budgets, *The Accounting Review*, pp. 671–85.

Rose, A. (1962) (ed.) *Human Behaviour and Social Processes: An Interactionist Approach*, Routledge & Kegan Paul, London.

Rose, M. (1975) *Industrial Behaviour: Theoretical Developments Since Taylor*, Penguin Books, Harmondsworth.

Rose, R. (1985) *Re-Working the Work Ethic*, Batsford, London.

Rosenbrock, H. (1982) *Technical Policies and Options*, EEC 'FAST' Conference, London.

Rosenbrock, H. (1988) Engineers and the work that people do, in R. Finnegan *et al.* (eds.) *Information Technology: Social Issues*, Hodder & Stoughton, Sevenoaks.

Rousseau, J–J. (1983) *On the Social Contract and Discourses*, Hackett Publishing, Indianapolis, Ind.

Rowe, A. (1964) An appraisal of appraisals, *Journal of Management Studies*, Vol. 1, pp. 1–25.

Roy, D. (1952) Quota restriction and goldbricking in a machine shop, *American Journal of Sociology*, Vol. 57, pp. 427–42.

Roy, D. (1960) Banana time: job satisfaction and informal interaction, *Human Organisation*, Vol. 18, no. 2, pp. 156–68.

Ryan, M. (1988) Postmodern politics, *Theory, Culture and Society*, Vol. 5, no. 2–3, pp. 559–76.

Sackmann, S. A. (1991) *Cultural Knowledge in Organisations: Exploring the Collective Mind*, Sage, Newbury Park, Calif.

Salaman, G. (1978) Management development and organisation theory, *Journal of European Industrial Training*, Vol. 2, no. 7, pp. 7–11.

Salaman, G. (1979) *Work Organisation: Resistance and Control*, Longman, London.

Sayle, M. (1982) The yellow peril and the red haired devils, *Harper's*, November, pp. 23–35.

Sayles, L. (1965) *The Behaviour of Industrial Work Groups*, Wiley, New York.

Sayles, L. R. (1979) *Leadership – What Effective Managers Really Do and How They Do It*, McGraw-Hill, Maidenhead.

Schall, M. (1983) A communication-rules approach to organisational culture, *Administrative Science Quarterly*, Vol. 28, pp. 557–81.

Schattschneider, E. E. (1960) *The Semi-Sovereign People: A Realist's View of Democracy in America*, Holt, Rinehart & Winston, New York, NY.

Schein, E. H. (1956) The Chinese indoctrination programme for prisoners of war, *Psychiatry*, Vol. 19, pp. 149–72.

Schein, E. H. (1965) *Organizational Psychology*, Prentice-Hall, Englewood Cliffs, NJ.

Schein, E. H. (1984a) Organisational socialisation and the profession of management, in D. A. Kolb, I. M. Rubin and J. M. McIntyre (eds.) *Organisational Psychology: Readings on Human Behaviour in Organisations*, Prentice-Hall, Englewood Cliffs, NJ.

Schein, E. H. (1984b) Coming to a new awareness of organisation culture, *Sloan Management Review*, Winter, pp. 3–16.

Schein, E. H. (1985) *Organizational Culture and Leadership: A Dynamic View*, Jossey-Bass, San Francisco.

Schiff, M. and Lewin, A. Y. (1970) The impact of people on budgets, *Accounting Review*, pp. 259–68.

Schriesheim, C. A., House, R. J. and Kerr, S. (1976) Leader initiating structure: a reconciliation of discrepant research results and some empirical tests, *Organisational Behaviour and Human Performance*, Vol. 15, pp. 297–321.

Schriesheim, C. A. and von Glinow, M. A. (1977) The path-goal theory of leadership: a theoretical and empirical analysis, *Academy of Management Journal*, Vol. 20, pp. 398–405.

Seeman, M. (1959) On the meaning of alienation, *American Sociological Review*, Vol. XXIV, pp. 783–91.

Selznick, P. (1953) *TVA and the Grass Roots*, University of California Press, Berkeley, Calif.

Shibutani, T. (1962) Reference groups and social control, in A. Rose (ed.), *op. cit.*

Shotter, J. (1975) *Images of Man in Psychological Research*, Methuen, London.

Siehl, C. (1985) After the founder: an opportunity to manage culture, in P. J. Frost *et al.* (eds.), *op. cit.*

Silver, J. (1987) The ideology of excellence: management and neo-conservatism, *Studies in Political Economy*, Vol. 24, Autumn, pp. 105–29.

Silverman, D. (1970) *The Theory of Organisations*, Heinemann Educational, London.

Simon, H. A. (1957) *Administrative Behaviour* (2nd edn), Macmillan, London.

Simon, H. A. (1977) *The New Science of Management Decision*, Prentice-Hall, Englewood Cliffs, NJ.

Simons, R. (1991) Strategic orientation and top management attention to control systems, *Strategic Management Journal*, Vol. 12, pp. 49–62.

Sims, H. P. (1992) *The New Leadership Paradigm: Social Learning and Cognition in Organisations*, Sage, Beverly Hills.

Sisson, K. (1989) (ed.) *Personnel Management in Britain*, Blackwell, Oxford.

Sisson, K. (1990) Introducing the *Human Resource Management Journal*, *Human Resource Management Journal*, Vol. 1, no. 1, pp. 1–11.

Smart, B. (1985) *Michel Foucault*, Tavistock, London.

Smircich, L. (1983) Concepts of culture and organisation analysis, *Administrative Science Quarterly*, Vol. 28, pp. 339–58.

Smircich, L. (1985) Is the concept of culture a paradigm for understanding organizations and ourselves?, in P. J. Frost *et al.* (eds.), *op. cit.*

Smith, A. (1937) *Inquiry into the Nature and Causes of the Wealth of Nations*, Modern Library, New York, NY.

Smith, C. (1989) Flexible specialisation, automation and mass production, *Work, Employment and Society*, Vol. 3, no. 2, pp. 203–20.

Smith, J. S., Tranfield, D. R., Ley, D. C., Bessant, J. R. and Levy, P. (1990) Changing organisation design and practices for computer integrated technologies, *Proceedings of the Operations Management Association Conference on Manufacturing Strategy: Theory and Practice*, London, 26–7 June, pp. 862–73.

Smith, J. S., Tranfield, D. R., Ley, D. C., Bessant, J. R. and Levy, P. (1991) Manufacturing organisation for computer integrated technology, volume 1 (unpublished final report to the Joint Committee of the Science and Engineering Research Council and the Economic and Social Research Council), London.

Smith, K. (1992) Culture and ethics: confusing bedfellows (unpublished working paper), Sheffield Business School, Sheffield Hallam University.

Smith, P. B. and Peterson, M. F. (1988) *Leadership, Organisations and Culture*, Sage, London.

Sofer, C. (1973) *Organisations in Theory and Practice*, Heinemann, London.

Spinelli, E. (1989) *The Interpreted World*, Sage, London.

Stanworth, M. K. J. (1977) The meaning of work, in R. L. Boot, A. G. Cowling and M. K. J. Stanworth (eds.) *Behavioural Sciences for Managers*, Edward Arnold, London.

Staw, B. M. (1976) *Intrinsic and Extrinsic Motivation*, General Learning Press, Morristown, NJ.

Steers, R. M. and Porter, L. W. (eds.) (1991) *Motivation and Work Behaviour* (5th edn), McGraw-Hill, Maidenhead.

Stewart, A. and Stewart, V. (1981) *Tomorrow's Managers Today*, Institute of Personnel Management, London.

Stewart, R. (1967) *Managers and their Jobs*, Pan/Macmillan, London.

Stewart, R. (1976) *Contrasts in Management*, McGraw-Hill, Maidenhead.

Stogdill, R. M. (1948) Personal factors associated with leadership: a survey of the literature, *Journal of Psychology*, Vol. 25, pp. 35–71.

Stogdill, R. M. (1974) *Handbook of Leadership*, Free Press, New York, NY.

Stogdill, R. M. and Coons, A. E. (eds.) (1957) *Leader Behavior: Its Description and Measurement*, Bureau of Business Research, Ohio State University, Columbus, Ohio.

Stopford, J. M. and Wells, L. T. (1972) *Managing the Multinational Enterprise*, Longman, London.

Storey, J. (1983) *Managerial Prerogative and the Questions of Control*, Routledge & Kegan Paul, London.

Storey, J. (ed.) (1989) *New Perspectives on Human Resources Management*, Routledge, London.

Storey, J. and Sisson, K. (1990) Limits to transformation: human resource management in a British context, *Industrial Relations Journal*, Vol. 21, no. 1, pp. 60–5.

Straw, B. M. (1977) Motivation in organizations: toward a synthesis and redirection, in B. M. Straw and G. R. Salancik (eds.), *New Directions in Organization Behavior*, St. Clair Press, Chicago, Ill.

Streeck, W. (1987) The uncertainties of management in the management of uncertainty: employers, labour relations and industrial adjustment in the 1980s, *Work, Employment and Society*, Vol. 1, pp. 281–308.

Swinth, R. L. (1974) *Organization Systems for Management*, Grid, Columbus, Ohio.

Tannenbaum, A. S. (1968) *Control in Organizations*, McGraw-Hill, New York, NY.

Taylor, F. W. (1947) *Scientific Management*, Harper & Row, New York, NY.

Taylor, L. and Walton, P. (1971) Industrial sabotage: motives and meanings, in S. Cohen (ed.) *Images of Deviance*, Penguin Books, Harmondsworth.

Thomas, A. P. (1984) Self-control, in A. Lowe and J. L. T. Machin (eds.), *op. cit.*

Thompson, G. (1987) Inflation accounting in a theory of calculation, *Accounting, Organisations and Society*, Vol. 12, no. 5, pp. 523–43.

Thompson, J. D. (1967) *Organisations in Action*, McGraw-Hill, Maidenhead.

Thompson, K. (ed.) (1984) *Work, Employment and Unemployment: Perspectives on Work and Society*, Open University Press, Buckingham.

Thompson, P. and McHugh, D. (1990) *Work Organisations: A Critical Introduction*, Macmillan, London.

Thurley, K. and Wood, S. (1983) *Industrial Relations and Management Strategy*, Cambridge University Press.

Tichy, N. M. (1983) *Managing Strategic Change*, Wiley, New York.

Tichy, N. M. and Devanna, M. A. (1986) *The Transformational Leader*, Wiley, New York, NY.

Tiles, M. (1987), A science of Mars or of Venus?, *Philosophy*, Vol. 62, no. 241, pp. 293–306.

Tinker, A. M. (1985) *Paper Prophets: A Social Critique of Accounting*, Holt, Rinehart & Winston, London.

Torrington, D. and Hall, L. (1987) *Personnel Management, a New Approach*, Prentice-Hall, London.

Townley, B. (1989) Selection and appraisal: reconstituting 'social relations'?, in J. Storey (ed.).

Trapp, R. (1992) Prisoners of corporate culture, *The Independent*, 1 August.

Traub, R. (1978) Lenin and Taylor: the fate of 'scientific management' in the early Soviet Union, *Telos*, Vol. 37, pp. 82–92.

Trist, E. (1970) A socio-technical critique of scientific management (paper presented at the Edinburgh conference on the Impact of Science and Technology), May.

Tuckman, B. W. (1965) Developmental sequence in small groups, *Psychological Bulletin*, Vol. 63, pp. 384–99.

Turner, B. A. (1972) *Exploring the Organisational Sub-Culture*, Macmillan, London.

Turner, S. P. (1983) Studying organizations through Levi-Strauss's structuralism, in G. Morgan (ed.) *Beyond Method: Social Research Strategies*, Sage, Beverly Hills, Calif.

Turquet, P. M. (1973) Leadership: the individual and the group, in G. S. Gibbard, J. J. Hartman and R. D. Mann (eds.) *Analysis of Groups: Contributions to Theory, Research and Practice*, Jossey-Bass, San Francisco, Calif.

Tyson, S. (1987) Management of the personnel function, *Journal of Management Studies*, Vol. 24, no. 5, pp. 523–47.

Urwick, L. (1943) *Elements of Administration*, Pitman, London.

Van Maanen, J. (1976) Breaking in: socialization to work, in R. Dubin (ed.) *Handbook of Work, Organization and Society*, Rand McNally, Chicago, Ill.

Van Maanen, J. and Barley, S. R. (1985) Cultural organization: fragments of a theory, in P. J. Frost *et al.* (eds.), *op. cit.*

Von Bertalanffy, L. (1967) General systems theory, in N. J. Dermath and R. A. Peterson (eds.) *Systems Change and Conflict*, Free Press, New York, NY.

Vroom, V. H. (1964) *Work and Motivation*, Wiley, New York, NY.

Vroom, V. H. and Yetton, P. W. (1973) *Leadership and Decision-Making*, University of Pittsburgh Press, Pittsburgh, Pa.

Walton, R. E. (1985) From control to commitment in the workplace, *Harvard Business Review*, Vol. 63, pp. 76–84.

Walton, R. E. and Lawrence, P. R. (eds.) (1985) *HRM: Trends and Challenges*, Harvard Business Press, Boston, Mass.

Walton, R. E. and McKersie, R. B. (1965) *A Behavioural Theory of Labour Negotiations*, McGraw-Hill, Maidenhead.

Weber, M. (1947) *The Theory of Social and Economic Organization*, Free Press, Glencoe, Ill. (first published 1924).

Weber, M. (1976) *The Protestant Ethic and the Spirit of Capitalism*, Allen & Unwin, London.

Weber, M. (1968) *Economy and Society*, Bedminster Press, New York.

Weiner, B. *et al.* (1971) *Perceiving the Causes of Success and Failure*, General Learning Press, Morristown, NJ.

Whitaker, A. (1992) The transformation of work: post-Fordism revisited, in M. Reed and M. Hughes (eds.), *op. cit.*

White, M. and Trevor, M. (1983) *Under Japanese Management: The Experience of British Workers*, Heinemann, London.

Whitley, R. D. (1992) The social construction of organisations and markets: the comparative analysis of business recipes, in M. Reed and M. Hughes (eds.), *op. cit.*

Wildavsky, A. (1978) Policy analyses is what information systems are not, *Accounting, Organisations and Society*, Vol. 3, no. 1, pp. 77–88.

Wilkins, A. (1983) Organizational stories which control the organization, in L. R. Pondy *et al.* (eds.) *Organizational Symbolism*, JAI Press, Greenwich, Conn.

Williams, G. (1960) The concept of 'egomania' in the thought of Antonio Gramsci: some notes on interpretation, *Journal of the History of Ideas*, Vol. 21, no. 4, pp. 586–99.

Williams, J. J. (1981) Zero-base budgeting: prospects for developing a semi-confusing budgeting information system, *Accounting, Organisations and Society*, Vol. 6, no. 2, pp. 153–65.

Willis, P. (1977) *Learning to Labour: How Working Class Kids Get Working Class Jobs*, Saxon House, London.

Wilson, D. C. (1982) Electricity and resistance: a case study of innovation and politics, *Organisation Studies*, Vol. 3, no. 2, pp. 119–40.

Wood, S. (1986) The cooperative labour strategy in the US auto industry, *Economic and Industrial Democracy*, Vol. 7, no. 4, pp. 415–48.

Wood, S. (1989) New wave management? *Work, Employment and Society*, Vol. 3, no. 3, pp. 379–402.

Woodward, J. (1965) *Industrial Organisation, Theory and Practice*, Oxford University Press, London.

Wren, D. A. (1980) Scientific management in the USSR, with particular reference to the contribution of Walter N. Polakov, *Academy of Management Review*, Vol. 5, no. 1, pp. 1–11.

Wright, E. O. *et al.* (1982) The American class structure, *American Sociological Review*, Vol. 47, pp. 709–26.

Zaleznik, A. (1977) Managers and leaders: are they different?, *Harvard Business Review*, Vol. 55, no. 5, pp. 67–8.

Zaleznik, A. (1989) *The Managerial Mystique*, Harper Collins, New York, NY.

Zaleznik, A. *et al.* (1958) *The Motivation, Productivity and Satisfaction of Workers*, Harvard University Press, Boston, Mass.

Zaleznik, A. and Kets de Vries, M. F. (1975) *Power and the Corporate Mind*, Houghton Mifflin, Boston.

Zeitlin, J. (1983) Social theory and the history of work, *Social History*, Vol. 8, pp. 365–74.

Zeitlin, M. (1974) Corporate ownership and control: the large corporations and capitalist class, *American Journal of Sociology*, Vol. 79, pp. 1073–119.

Zeldeck, S. (1977) An information processing model and approach to the study of motivation, *Organisation Behaviour and Human Performance*, Vol. 18, pp. 47–77.

Index of Authors

Index of Subjects